THE GROWING BUSINESS HANDBOOK

BARCLAYS
OPEN FOR BUSINESS
Unpaid invoices getting you down? We'll take the weight.
Expanding a business can be a balancing act. On the one hand, you need to pay your suppliers. On the other, you have to wait f
your customers to pay up. Our range of specialised services can play a pivotal role. For example, Sales Financing provides you wi
cash as soon as you raise your sales invoices, cutting your wait to 24 hours. For details, contact Barclays Bank PLC free on 0800 4184

THE

GROWING BUSINESS HANDBOOK

Second Edition

Strategies for Planning, Funding and Managing Business Growth

Consultant Editors:
Richard Willsher and
Adam Jolly

KOGAN PAGE

in association with

CBI

The Confederation of British Industry

and

KPMG

Publisher's note

Every possible effort has been made to ensure that the information contained in this handbook is accurate at the time of going to press, and the publishers cannot accept responsibility for any errors or omissions, however caused. All liability for loss, disappointment, negligence or other damage caused by the reliance on the information contained in this handbook, or in the event of bankruptcy or liquidation or cessation of trade of any company, individual or firm mentioned, is hereby excluded.

Published in 1998

Kogan Page Ltd
120 Pentonville Road
London N1 9JN
kpinfo@kogan-page.co.uk

British Library Cataloguing in Publication Data
A CIP record for this book is available from the British Library
ISBN 0 7494 2890 2

Typeset by Saxon Graphics Ltd, Derby
Printed and bound in Great Britain by Bell and Bain Limited

CBI

A Renaissance for Britain?

Maureen Scholefield, Managing Director of Cullen Scholefield reviews one approach to senior management development.

The Government's recent white paper, the Learning Age - a renaissance for a new Britain, sets out plans to create a framework of lifelong learning opportunities and self-improvement to raise the nation's skills and competitiveness. The University for Industry will use leading edge technology to make learning available at work, in learning centres and at home. Its purpose is to connect people and business and update the skills of individuals. Individual Learning Accounts will help people and business and update the skills of individuals. Individual Learning Accounts will help people save and take ownership of their learning. The Government is determined to maximise the use of potential European funding, for example Objective 4, in support of these initiatives.

Transforming learning at work is seen primarily as the responsibility of employers and employees. The Government will consolidate the position of Investors in People as the main measure of employers' development of their staff. More help will be given to small businesses looking to invest in staff development. TECs will focus on this area and the Government will also strengthen the links between adoption of Investors in People and Government business support.

The Government will also work with the planned Management and Enterprise National Training Organisation to:

- encourage professionals to develop management skills alongside specialist expertise;
- encourage managers in smaller firms to develop new skills needed to help their organisations grow;
- develop the University for Industry's support for managers, including those within small firms;
- improve the links between vocational qualifications and academic and study in management; and
- explore the value of a new management code, incorporating ethical and environmental responsibilities as well as a commitment to learning.

The emphasis on the development of management skills is crucial to the success of the package overall. We have all witnessed how the underperformance of managers is only too clearly mirrored in the performance of their teams. The experience of Cullen Scholefield is that a significant measurable relationship exists between skilled-up, focussed management and profitable business performance.

The systematic training of all staff to underpin change, improve the skills of personnel staff, trainers, managers and operational staff can only be justified if a correlation can be identified between the training and increased bottom line benefits to the organisation. Evaluation criteria and working a finacial case for training are essential aspects of any strategic plan; qualitative and quantitative measures should be in place at the start of any initiative. These measures may include budget target indicators; levels of service, levels of absence, customer/employee satisfaction. Senior managers need to identify the most appropriate measures for their organisation and develop a plan to gather evidence of the expected cost benefits.

When Cullen Scholefield commenced work with one client, recruitment and retention were problematic and an independent management survey showed a lack of inter-departmental communication. Only 27% of staff 'knew what was going on', managers were ignorant of staff opinions. Few employees felt that they were 'given recognition for extra effort', a meagre 29% felt 'highly motivated', only 50% of customers considered themselves valued. Twelve months later recorded profiles now top the group average on almost every count. More than 90% of the staff are proud to be working in the company, they 'enjoy working there' and feel 'loyalty'. Staff turnover is minimal, communications are excellent between departments with 96% of employees 'well understanding each others' pressures'. Focus groups, questionnaires and the management survey show customer satisfaction greatly improved.

Effecting rapid change has required organisations, some more willingly then others, to become learning organisations. It has also required the formation of new teams, some cross-functional, propelling first line workers into supervisory/team leader roles sometimes more quickly than appropriate development can be put in place. Senior managers need a strategic plan to manage the shift in culture they are striving to achieve. A key focus of that plan must be human resource development.

It is possible to employ a flexible and pragmatic approach to management development which gears training to the achievement of particular business goals and links those goals to personal objectives. It requires

- managers and supervisors to be given the authority and opportunity to meet these objectives as part of their responsibilities;
- development training to be organised through practical projects;
- managers and supervisors to be given the support and knowledge required to meet the project objectives as and when needed; and
- managers and supervisors to be encouraged to discuss their projects with their managers and be supported in the achievement of project objectives.

Where possible, support networks should be established to help team development: internal and external support should made available on an 'as and when required' basis and combined with a rapid response capability. Development training is most effectively organised through practical projects such as developing a competence-based appraisal system or implementing a quality improvement and cost reduction process or reviewing and revising health and safety procedures and training.

Involving appropriate senior managers along with the Personnel and Training Managers in the development of the projects briefs is crucial. Their involvement gains their commitment to the overall process and should ensure that a project has clear ties to strategic objectives as it embeds current policies and procedures. Commitment from the top is required to put in place and resource a well-defined development programme if the purpose is to ensure that the skills levels of employees match the needs of the organisation in meeting its business goals.

There were doubts that people at the right level would be interested in achieving a vocational qualification when the NVQ level 5 in Training and Development was launched; even whether it was practical to specify a series of work-based competencies which would be generically appropriate for training and development strategists. Typically professionals in the human resource function would be degree or equivalent qualified. Though the long-sought "parity of esteem" between vocational and academic routes has yet to be achieved, the vocational route has some clear advantages. The knowledge requirements people have to demonstrate are equal to any high-level academic qualification yet they can take their everyday work experiences and map them against the NVQ structure. Pursuit of Training and Development NVQ Level 5 enables a senior person to act as a role model; it is an excellent way of demonstrating continuing professional development; and provides senior staff with a chance to reflect on what they're doing and why they're doing it!

Jackie Foulkes, Ford's Training Manager for its South East plants, started studying with Cullen Scholefield for her Level 5 in November 1997 having already completed the academic route to IPD qualification.

"When you go down the academic channel, it is well structured and you are going into something which is very different - the research element certainly made me more externally focussed. But the value of the NVQ route is in proving competence - that you can actually put into practice what you know... If the message we are giving out is that we should be a learning organisation, managers and supervisors should be in the forefront."

Other National Vocational Qualifications (NVQs) can be used to provide an external measure of the performance of all managers and supervisors working on a project. The application of basic management skills in the project provides evidence for the Management Charter Initiative (MCI) level 3. Middle managers can be used to support and develop line managers. This activity providing them with evidence towards MCI level 4 and the opportunity to generate evidence to qualify as assessors. Senior managers' involvement provides them with evidence towards MCI level 5. Thus the project work is checked against the MCI evidence requirements and the provision of additional evidence can be planned if required. There is lasting benefit from having capable employees providing consultancy through their projects to resolve internal issues.

An integral part of such a strategy should be to train managers as assessors. Because the opportunities to generate evidence come from the managers' normal duties, training is hands-on not theoretical, Managers are not required to be away from their duties for long periods.

This is an economical approach to management development because the process of developing skills builds trust and communication between the teams, their peers and managers whilst providing the main ingredients necessary for the establishment of a new organisational culture. It is organisations with this new culture which will be the source of 'a renaissance for a new Britain'.

Training Towards the Millennium

Aileen Clark
Divisonal Managing Director
Hawksmere, In-Company

A recent survey showed that UK companies spend 8.0 BN a year on training. With this level of spending set to continue into the millennium, increasingly companies are trying to find reliable ways of measuring the effectiveness of training. Although systems and processes for doing this do exist, any experienced trainer will tell you it is a very imprecise science! The difficulty lies in determining the true level of prior knowledge or ability of the potential student. Whilst it may be relatively easy to find out how much a person knows about aspects of commercial law- say, Conditions of Contract - it is much more difficult to establish how good a manager is at, say, helping his or her team stay motivated or at offering individual mentoring to staff.

The training professional unable to produce reliable data on specific competency levels of potential students before training, cannot hope to measure outcome. How then can a company be sure its training budget is giving value for money?

Training is delivered mainly in four ways

- on the job
- in the formal courses delivered by the company's training personnel with perhaps input from experienced company members
- in-company tailored courses delivered by external providers
- sending individuals to public courses and seminars

In most well run companies today training is taken seriously. Gone are the days when people were moved 'sideways' into the training function when they were nearing retirement. Today's trainers are dedicated professionals who can deliver a range of training to acceptable standards, set up and monitor induction programmes, on-the-job training and coaching for staff. When it comes to choosing and using outside providers the good in-house professional will obviously want to be satisfied that the chosen external trainer will perform to the required standard. How then do you as a company trainer set about assessing the quality of a potential provider?

Here are a few guidelines

- Ask colleagues in other companies to recommend suppliers they have successfully used. This can be very valuable, with the proviso that your company is unique and any trainer would have to be well 'matched' to you.
- Approache a well established company and ask them if they have undertaken similar training for other organisations. They should be happy to let you contact their clients for references.
- Invite suppliers to have an initial chat with you about your possible requirements - this will give you the opportunity to judge their suitability to deliver the proposed training. It will also give the provider the chance to get to know you and your company. Good external providers choose their clients carefully. They know that for successful training they need to be 'in tune' with the in-house professional.
- This may sound like a long tedious path down which we are asking a busy over-stretched training department to tread. Whilst it can initially be a bit time consuming, with some planning you only need go

through the process once. These suggestions may help:-

- identify training requirements for the next six to twelve months
- look for a provider who can cover at least a few of the related topics you need. This is likely to be a major training company.

For example Hawksmere, a leading UK training company, runs public seminars and undertakes in-company programmes in the following subject areas:-

Management Development
Finance
Project Management
Commercial and Contract Management
Marketing
PR and Media
Insurance
Personnel and Employment Law

This is probably the widest range of topics offered by a UK company. Each year Hawksmere runs 450 public seminars of one and two days duration. In addition it runs a series of residential programmes, including the long established senior manager programme, Developing the High Performance Manager. About 80% of attendees at this programme are from companies who have been sending staff to it since it started ten years ago. This is an example of how companies, having found a provider they are happy with, carry on using the programme with confidence.

Hawksmere's core programmes covering management development, personnel, health and safety, project and contract management, commercial awareness, marketing, public relations and media, insurance and legal topics all run several times each year. They are used on a regular basis by client companies and Hawksmere constantly reviews feedback from delegates as part of its continuous performance improvement policy.

In choosing the training provider the final scrutiny has to be the quality, ability and experience of the tutor put forward to undertake any training assignment. Beware the trainer who claims competence in too wide a range of topics.

Hawksmere has over 1500 speakers who contribute to both their public seminars and in-company tailored training. All are specialist professionals with a successful track record in their field. Having such a portfolio of experts allows Hawksmere to provide tutors whose background and experience match well with that of the client company. This is vital if the Tutor is to have a clear grasp of the business issues facing the client.

Hawkmere's experienced team of client advisors provide expert guidance and advice to clients about the public seminars and their suitability for individuals within the organisation. The In-Company service works closely with companies in developing tailored and focused training. In short a one-stop shop.

For today's busy professional training departments having a one-step external provider is ideal. For Hawksmere clients this means they effectively increase their own capacity by using Hawksmere in one year to provide say, team building, project management, finance, marketing, commercial awareness and media training in-company for the same organisation. The company is very likely to also have sent a number of people to specialist seminars. Through Hawksmere's publishing company Thorogood, their clients also have access to the very newest thinking on all aspects of management development in its Masters on Management Series and other related titles, and can choose from a wide range of reports, special briefings and videos. This then is the training provider for the millennium.

Contents

Preface

This is the second year we have produced *The Growing Business Handbook* in association with the Confederation of British Industry and supported by our sponsor KPMG.

We aim to build on the success of last year's book without losing the essence of it, which is that this is a book about growing businesses for and by people involved with them.

Again, thanks to all of our contributors. They have all taken time out to share their views and give advice wrought out of their experience with growing businesses.

There is no doubt that the climate for business growth in late 1998/early 1999 is in many ways tougher than it was this time last year. High interest rates, the strength of sterling, turmoil in emerging markets, economic and monetary union and increased competition; all of these factors bring new challenges.

Hopefully, the articles in this book will provide support, advice and inspiration. Nobody said expanding a business was easy, but if you can do it in the teeth of a recession, how robust and resilient that business will be.

Lastly, the same plea as last year. If you have any thoughts as to areas of interest which we might have omitted or subjects that we should cover in the future, please let us know.

RichardWillsher@dial.pipex.com

Part I

Strategies for Growth

1.1 The High-tech Challenge

Paul Duncanson
Gresham Bell

Yesterday is not ours to recover but tomorrow is ours to win or lose.
(Lyndon B. Johnson)

That's the philosophy employed at Gresham Bell, a small but fast-growing consultancy based in the City of London. The focus is on delivering business opportunity and building marketplace advantage for forward-thinking companies. This is achieved by employing the most unique of human talents – creative thought, backed up by the sharpest IT development you'll find anywhere. The creation of wealth for clients is the key measure Gresham Bell considers for success.

What has this meant in tangible terms?

One of the characteristics of Gresham Bell's entrepreneurial approach to business consultancy is its success with large blue-chip companies – such as Glaxo Wellcome, BT, and Ernst & Young.

Here are a few examples of how Gresham Bell has married entrepreneurial thought with innovative technology to solve problems, create opportunities and – ultimately – generate client wealth.

One of the key determinants to success within the highly competitive car market is the ability to react quickly and accurately to changes in the marketplace and the product specifications on offer. One of the leading global car manufacturers relies on this information to construct key pricing and product specifications, on a daily basis.

However, one of the barriers to being able to use this research competitively was the time taken to collate and translate the raw data into usable, company-formatted information.

This company had been trying to solve the problem for several years – to get ahead of the game and use the data to provide real competitive advantage.

Gresham Bell approached the challenge using strategic techniques gained from other data management projects for blue-chip companies. The key challenge was to create a reliable, robust and largely stand-alone system for use across time zones, integration with a very large wide area network (WAN) and browser-interface technology. A further challenge was to make the data feed independent of individual suppliers and to allow the company to combine the strengths of different suppliers in different markets.

Previously, the whole process had taken 18 to 24 hours to get to a point where usable information was available to pricing strategists and sales/marketing managers. Now, using systems that Gresham Bell has developed, such transfers will take half an hour, anytime, anywhere.

This has key implications all year, but especially at times like major motor shows when the flow of new specification information is large and rapid. Most importantly, for the first time this technology allows pricing strategists to do just that – to determine strategy, the inputting and formatting now automatically handled.

It is estimated that this car manufacturer can reap $1 million extra profit for every 24 hours by which it can improve its speed in implementing price changes in the marketplace.

Further value comes through pricing strategists and production and marketing teams sitting down together with the latest, online information to determine the winning price/specification combinations to be enacted straight away.

This success has led to a related but discrete project around car registration data management.

This service currently attempts to marry car ownership/purchase with registered users demographically, geographically and by dealership. The objective of this information is to allow car manufacturers to assess how their sales strategies are performing at dealer level.

This has proved very effective and has become a valuable source of information in developed markets. Now the research company wants to be able to offer it in emerging markets.

Gresham Bell has been commissioned to address the challenge of how to feed the system with data reliably, from any data source, regularly and without physical support in emerging markets.

This work will enable small teams in growing markets to develop a clear understanding of their marketplace as it matures and to focus directly on the needs of local clients. The technology will be able to develop further and remain flexible to handle widely differing market needs and structures.

When Glaxo made its £9.1 billion takeover bid for Wellcome, it could not afford to miscalculate. But when the offer was made, how did Glaxo senior management know that Wellcome would add that much to their business?

The decision to go ahead with the offer was based on a large number of factors. One advantage that the Glaxo decision makers had was access to accurate supporting information. This was made available by a new Glaxo management information initiative, the 'Information Library' project. The library is designed to provide accurate decision-support information to the business very rapidly.

'Information technology was at the heart of the evaluation process,' says Nigel Duke, managing director of Gresham Bell. 'Without the ability to handle information effectively, it would have been difficult to work out the true value of Wellcome.'

To evaluate Wellcome's manufacturing plants and work out how they would enhance Glaxo production, Glaxo management needed to collate a huge amount of textual information that was scattered across the world. Speed was crucial and the information had to be compiled in less than six weeks.

The data was in various forms and had to be captured from 52 different sites in 16 countries across the world. Some information was actual, some anecdotal and much was in people's heads.

'Gresham Bell was employed to carry out this project because of our flexibility, excellent technical skills and very positive attitude. We have been working with this from the start of the Information Library project and have expertise in implementing decision-support systems that really do add value to a large business such as Glaxo Wellcome,' continues Duke.

A system to capture all critical information on sites around the globe, and which used the Information Library architecture, was rapidly developed by Gresham Bell. Each site was given the system and asked to complete a data-gathering exercise immediately.

In less than the six-week deadline, a blueprint of all 52 sites was created. Data was included ranging from size of plant and number of staff, to products manufactured and state of plant repair. Using information such as this, the Glaxo decision makers proceeded with the Wellcome bid.

These examples show how it is possible for a small, fast-growing company to work effectively and successfully with large multinational conglomerates, providing crucial expertise and focus to deliver sustainable business benefit.

1.2

Yorkshire Pantry goes Worldwide on the Web

John Partridge
Secretary, Yorkshire Pantry

In 1996 the Yorkshire Pantry – the Association of Food and Drink Producers in North Yorkshire – became the first regional food network to recognise the importance of the Internet, and established its own Website. This gave instant access to over 30 million potential worldwide customers for its membership, which now totals over 100 companies from the region's food industry.

The Yorkshire Pantry Website was created with the help of North Yorkshire County Council's Economic Development Unit, which provides administrative support for the Yorkshire Pantry and also monitors the Website enquiries on behalf of its members. North Yorkshire boasts a burgeoning food industry and the site was set up to promote this sector under the banner: 'Good Food from Yorkshire'.

The Yorkshire Pantry Website was established to enable member businesses to receive enquiries from retailers, caterers, hotel chains and consumers, throughout the world, without the expense of setting up their own Web pages.

Although still in the early stages of development, the Internet is proving to be an excellent tool for sourcing export opportunities. We have had queries from as far afield as Australia, Japan and Hong Kong.

Many Yorkshire Pantry members have been encouraged to set up their own Websites, the majority of which are linked to the Yorkshire Pantry site.

Jane Bleiker of Bleiker's Smoke House Ltd comments, 'We attended an Internet seminar organised by the Yorkshire Pantry and were encouraged to set up our own site. We received a grant from North Yorkshire County Council and assistance from Business Link North Yorkshire, who also helped to fund the project.

'Since joining the Internet our enquiries have been mostly from the USA, which has led us to investigate ways of sending our smoked salmon using the shortest possible route. However, the Yorkshire Pantry has recently put us in touch with companies from Russia and Belgium who had approached them via the Yorkshire Pantry Internet pages.'

Masham-based Black Sheep Brewery has found that its Website has been successful in sourcing new export markets. The brewery, which currently exports bottled beers to Boston, USA, has generated several retail enquiries, via the Website, from sales agents and distributors across the whole of the USA and also Scandinavia. The company has also received enquiries from individuals throughout the world, from Alaska to Zambia.

As Pat Green, sales manager at the Black Sheep Brewery, explains, 'At the moment, the Internet creates interest in our beers and then orders are made following the normal procedures. However, we are currently updating our Website so that in a few months we will be able to trade and make visa transactions via the Net. Certainly, the Internet offers a vast potential which we have not yet exploited.'

Wensleydale Dairy Products has found that the Internet has proved to be a huge boost to its mail-order service; 40 per cent of enquiries generated by the company's Internet pages come from abroad, especially the USA, but also Finland, the Netherlands and Cyprus, for example.

Alice Amsden, director of Wensleydale Dairy Products, comments, 'Currently, most of the enquiries generated by the Internet are from individuals. However, we are looking into creating links with a wider variety of pages in order to stimulate retail and business interest.'

The Internet is clearly an invaluable tool for those entering the export market. It has certainly opened a number of avenues for Yorkshire Pantry members. As the technology develops, it looks set to give more small and medium-sized businesses the opportunity to widen their horizons.

1.3
Adapting to the Euro

Richard L Brucciani
Chairman, Pal International Ltd

Pal International Ltd is an independent manufacturing company based in the East Midlands. With headquarters in our Leicester factory, a second production plant in Malta and offices or sales staff based in France, Germany and Singapore, we employ 155 people, one-third of whom are based overseas.

Turnover is £13 million in chefs' hats, barrier hygiene headwear and chemical wiping products, chiefly targeted at the food, pharmaceutical and healthcare industries, with 60 per cent going overseas.

Exporting started at Pal many years ago when we developed speciality machines to automate processes in headwear manufacture and this resulted in excess capacity that could not be sold in the UK market. Sales across Europe have grown and we now have distributors stocking our products in every European country.

These exports are now a key part of Pal's business and we have settled into a comfortable regime of processing orders from our overseas customers. Each country has its own price list. Some customers are invoiced in sterling, although most are invoiced in their local currency with varying terms related to varying national customs.

The strength of sterling has been a problem of late but has been tackled on a country-by-country basis in our efforts to maintain market share and maximise potential return. However, life at Pal is about to change, as it will for many other businesses, with the dawn of Economic and Monetary Union (EMU) and the creation of 'euroland', a place where the euro lives and where the way we do business will become very different. Changes will affect many, many businesses, regardless of whether or not they are exporters and of whether or not the UK joins EMU.

Our challenge is to turn the threats of euroland into opportunities. To do this, reviews are being undertaken at Pal to prepare for the introduction of the euro. These are divided between financial, administrative and, most importantly, commercial issues.

Financial

Our first task in Pal has been to look at pricing. Different currencies in different countries have disguised the growth of variations in prices across Europe. In 1999, Pal will need to publish price lists in euros that will give total transparency to our pricing. Moreover, customers will have little sympathy for our reasons for any variations and will seek to buy at the lowest euro price.

We are taking urgent action to coordinate our pricing and avoid our margins being undermined through this new euro exposure.

We need to understand how the introduction of the euro will affect our banking arrangements. At present we operate a number of different currency accounts; in future, most of these might be rolled into a single euro account, saving considerable transaction costs.

We must consider whether there are advantages of using a euroland bank rather than a UK bank. Will there be opportunities to borrow more cheaply in euros?

Administrative

Pal, like many businesses, is dependent on an effective computer system. All IT facilities need to be checked to see if there are any software changes required to cope with euro activities.

Checks need to be made on any cross-border contracts that we have that may be affected by currencies.

Employing staff in euroland will have an implication for Pal's payroll procedures that needs to be investigated.

There will be the opportunity to record and account for taxation in euros; we have to decide a policy on this.

Commercial

Perhaps the most important impact of EMU will be on the commercial environment in which Pal operates. Euroland will accelerate the creation of a true single market, and establishing an effective strategy for prospering in this market will be crucial.

Price transparency, economies of scale, ease of communication, more than 300 million consumers – this all adds up to a marketplace in which the strong will get stronger and the weak will disappear.

Companies that can beat the competition and gain market share in euroland will have the strength to cross the Channel and challenge local UK businesses, in many cases aided by developments in electronic commerce.

Pal is already improving links with customers who operate on a pan-European basis, in the belief that these are the customers who will benefit and grow through EMU.

Opportunities for strategic alliances to grasp greater market share may be an additional way forward for Pal. This is especially important for a medium-sized company such as ours, as we believe that those businesses that move quickest in establishing a wide, coordinated presence in euroland will be the eventual winners.

So, we see Economic and Monetary Union as essentially a political initiative about which the British may feel very lukewarm. Running a company, however, does not allow us the luxury of being spectators while our competitors across Europe are busily preparing to win market share that could be ours.

For Pal International Ltd the emergence of euroland may offer the most profitable opportunity for growth that we have seen for years – I hope you will help us keep it secret!

1.4

Risk Management for Growing Businesses

Stuart Pettet
Independent Insurance

Any business with ambitions to grow profitably needs solid foundations. The obvious cornerstones might be listed as talented management, skilled staff, sound finances, good products and effective sales and distribution; these are factors that can make a positive contribution to the development of an organisation. But awareness must also be shown of possible negative influences and events. In other words, businesses must be conscious of the risks they face and they must ensure that these risks are properly managed.

Risk management, then, is fundamental to healthy growth. It is a process that identifies potential dangers, threats, accidents and catastrophes and formulates plans on how best to prevent them, reduce the likelihood of their taking place or cope with their effects should they occur. Planning of this nature is essentially about using common sense, but it is frequently not given the priority it deserves. This is perhaps because there is no immediate, quantifiable financial benefit; indeed, managing risk can initially cost money and absorb resources and can therefore sometimes be viewed with suspicion and hostility.

However, if a company is pursuing sustainable growth, it will necessarily adopt a long-term perspective – and effective risk management is likely to yield greater financial efficiency and improved overall performance in the long run.

A good example of this is expenditure on insurance. An insurance policy is itself a form of risk management: it provides for financial compensation

P&H
HAUL

should any of a number of 'perils' strike the business. But if steps can be taken to eliminate or contain these perils, then the cost of the insurance will reflect the reduced likelihood of a claim being made.

This also illustrates the benign 'double-whammy' that flows from managing risk effectively; as well as saving money on insurance premiums, it removes or reduces costly disruption and interruption. The business therefore has more time to get on with doing what it does best.

So how does a company set about implementing a professional risk-management strategy? As suggested above, the first step is to identify the risks faced. These are many and varied; some will be general, while others will be specific to the particular enterprise, industry or location. The best way to identify them is to spend a few minutes jotting suggestions on a blank sheet of paper, then to tour the premises, sit down again and add to the list.

Once a few colleagues have completed their own efforts, such a lengthy catalogue of dangers will have been compiled that the contributors may fear for their lives if they step outside their offices and will wonder how the operation manages to survive at all. But it is important to remember that any viable business will already have a number of risk-management measures in place. For example, a security system is a basic element of risk management; simply locking the doors at night is a recognition of the risk of theft.

The development of a more sophisticated approach to risk management is simply a case of amplifying and extending the common-sense principles that have enabled the organisation to reach its present state.

What ideas might the original brainstorming session produce? That sheet of paper could contain the following:

- fire;
- theft;
- storm/weather damage;
- flooding;
- vandalism;
- pollution;
- accidents and injuries;
- mechanical breakdown;
- electrical supply disruption;
- faulty/dangerous product liabilities;
- employee and public liabilities;
- problems with suppliers;
- dishonest employees;
- industrial espionage;
- past insurance claims.

As can be seen, risk management is concerned with much more than straightforward physical risks such as fire and flood. It is about identifying any possible threat to the smooth and efficient running of the business as a whole and plotting a course through the difficulties.

An obvious risk such as fire can be anticipated through careful handling of flammable materials, provision of adequate fire-fighting equipment and, perhaps, installation of a sprinkler system. Arrangements can also be made for the swift and safe evacuation of staff. Vandals and thieves can be deterred by fencing, patrols, alarms and other security measures, with special arrangements being made for valuable or sensitive material.

Difficulties in obtaining components, materials and necessary services form a problem of a different order, however. If a key supplier was, for whatever reason, unable to deliver, what course of action would be taken? How long would existing stock last? Are there alternative sources of supply? Are these of the same quality and price? If there is a power failure, is a back-up system available?

These and other questions, when applied to the above list, will result in another sheet of paper containing the basis of a risk-management programme, with problems becoming evident and possible solutions beginning to manifest themselves:

- *Fire* – Check fire-fighting equipment and systems; make sure dangerous materials are properly managed. Do we have fire-proof storage for vital documents? Is smoking allowed and, if so, do we have designated areas? Do we have adequate housekeeping routines, both inside and outside the building, to ensure rubbish is cleared away and fire risks are monitored? Check there is proper access for fire engines; liaise with the Fire Brigade for possible safety briefings.
- *Theft* – Is theft a problem in this area? And are the thieves professionals or casuals looking for ready cash and valuables? Is the building secure? Are there enough safes for our most valuable items and documents? Are computers and other items security marked?
- *Storm/weather damage* – Is the building sound? Do we take appropriate measures when we know bad weather is on the way? Are we aware of the extra risks we run during icy weather.
- *Flooding* – Is any part of the site or premises vulnerable to flooding from a local water course? If so, can we move vulnerable stock or equipment elsewhere, either permanently or when a flood warning is issued?
- *Vandalism* – Another security issue; if vandalism is a major, persistent problem, is there anything to be gained from acting in concert with other local businesses and the police to mount surveillance?
- *Pollution* – Are we a potential polluter or are we at risk from someone else's pollution? Are we aware of the environmental legislation concerning this area? Do we have a clean-up plan if the worst happens? Have we checked to see whether there is existing pollution at our site? Do we have the right sort of insurance to pay for clean-up work?

- *Accidents and injuries* – Do we have operating conditions and do staff know how to work safely? Do we have the right procedures in place if an accident should occur? Do we have an adequate sick-bay and trained staff? Do we monitor equipment to ensure user safety and do we insist on safety precautions being taken?
- *Mechanical breakdown* – Do we know what we would do if the production line was forced to halt? How do we best limit downtime? Do our schedules allow for adequate maintenance and repair work?
- *Electrical supply disruption* – Do we have a back-up supply if there is a mains supply failure?
- *Faulty/dangerous products* – Do we have a product recall plan? What quality-control measures are in place? Is the quality of bought-in components checked?
- *Employee and public liabilities* – Are we aware of our full responsibilities according to law and to good practice and have we taken whatever steps are required? Do we work at others' premises or do we have visitors to our own? Are we aware of how this affects our potential liabilities?
- *Problems with suppliers* – Have we sourced alternative suppliers and made plans to keep our customers happy if we find ourselves short of vital components?
- *Dishonest employees* – Are we at risk from pilferage? How can the problem be managed sensitively without souring employee relations?
- *Industrial espionage* – Do we look after our good ideas well enough?
- *What problems have we experienced in the past* and what have we learned from our experience? Have we monitored past insurance claims and taken action to ensure they do not recur?

It can be seen from this expanded list that risk management is all about asking the right questions; the answers themselves are more often than not simple common sense. One way to ensure that the questions are asked and the answers followed through is to appoint a senior manager as the person who is ultimately responsible for risk management. This position should carry the seniority and resources to allow initiatives to be implemented, monitored and controlled.

What is more, middle management must be empowered to ensure that risk-management initiatives which originate in the boardroom are actually implemented on the factory floor. Too often, the best intentions of senior management fail to have any genuine impact, because the message is diluted or even lost as it filters through the company hierarchy.

While risk elimination is the ultimate goal of risk-management, it is important to acknowledge that, in the real world, problems will occur. A vital element of any risk-management programme will therefore be a plan for coping with the consequences of a disaster, large or small. Shorthand for this discipline is disaster recovery planning.

Disaster recovery planning

No matter how much time, effort and resources are devoted to making sure things don't go wrong, there will never be an absolutely risk-free working environment. Even if internal routines are superbly organised to minimise the likelihood of problems, there is always the danger of unforeseen, external occurrences affecting the business.

Wherever the danger springs from, the result is the same: interruptions to normal routines, additional costs incurred, strains on customer relationships and, in all too many cases, the eventual liquidation of the business. Every organisation should therefore have a disaster recovery plan in place. This will be a series of well-thought-out, well-rehearsed contingency measures designed to restore normal operations as quickly as possible.

A number of software programs have been developed to help businesses draw up their own disaster recovery plan. Independent Insurance, for example, has a *The Power to Face Disaster* programme, which helps management focus on the various risks, internal and external, faced by the company. Many of these will be familiar, but others will come into consideration for the first time. It is clearly preferable to find out about them in this context than to suffer their full effect and have no route to recovery in place.

Such programmes also guide management through the processes that will aid rapid recovery. For example, it is obviously better to know about alternative facilities and sources of supply before they are needed in an emergency. Equally, decisions taken in the cool of normal routine will be better judged than those made in adversity.

As well as recovering speedily and completely from a disaster, it is important that steps are taken to ensure that the problem does not arise again. In other words, mistakes may be inevitable, but it is vital to learn from these mistakes to minimise the likelihood of repetition.

One initiative from Independent which is designed to increase efficiency in terms of problem-control is the appointment of reporting incident officers.

Reporting incident officers – the RIO initiative

An RIO is an employee who is responsible for collecting information about an insured event. This includes gathering statements from those involved, taking photographs and completing a standard report form.

This process tackles the problem of late and inadequate reporting of events by policyholders and thereby improves the insurance company's ability to handle the claim effectively and efficiently. The availability of prompt, relevant and accurate information also helps in the risk management process so that future problems can be avoided.

If incidents are reported quickly, it cuts down on lost production time. Comprehensive reporting is also likely to reduce the incidence of fraud, simply because the procedure highlights anything unusual. And if claims are handled speedily and problems resolved with the minimum of interruption, it should also benefit morale in the workplace.

The beauty of RIO is that all these benefits ensue without the need for significant expenditure. Companies are encouraged to appoint an RIO at the rate of one per 25 headcount, train them and equip them with necessary documentation and a camera. For this modest outlay and effort, a new level of risk-management effectiveness can be achieved.

Conclusion

Developing risk-management awareness can lead to the creation of a more efficient organisation that is better positioned to deliver profitable performance. In today's competitive environment, risk management is a prerequisite for success. Businesses cannot afford downtime or disruption. Customers won't wait. Why should they, when they have so many alternatives?

Today's businesses understand the need to maintain constant peak performance. But they may not appreciate the role that risk-management has to play in keeping them competitive. Imagine a business producing goods for a major retailer. This customer has massive buying power and suppliers clamour for its contracts. Those working for it concentrate a disproportionate amount of resources on getting orders out on time. They know that any lapse in performance could result in the loss of the contract. They know, because it says so in the contract.

So what happens if there is a fire on the production line which knocks out essential pieces of equipment? Will the customer be content to wait for fulfilment? Or will it look elsewhere? Can the supplier afford to take this sort of risk?

Would it not be better to take preventive measures to reduce the likelihood of fire, thereby protecting the integrity of the production facility? Some fires are unavoidable, of course, regardless of sprinkler systems and extinguishers. But what about a plan to recover the operation following a disaster? Why are contingency plans not in place? Why has an alternative facility not been sourced before the problem arises?

The benefits to the business of undertaking an effective risk-management programme are clear. It pays to manage risk.

An insurance policy will always be a key element of risk management. Paying the premium transfers the risk to the insurance company and provides financial compensation if problems occur. But as has been shown, the viability of an organisation is best ensured by preventing problems from arising in the first place and having measures in place to solve them if they do.

When arranging insurance, a business should not be looking simply for the cheapest premium. It should be seeking to forge constructive relationships with a professional broker and an insurer of repute so that a fully-rounded, progressive risk management strategy can be adopted.

What is Independent Insurance's approach to risk management?

The cornerstone of Independent's approach to insurance is SAM: Source, Adequacy, Management.

SAM means that the broker who is the source of the business (Independent only sells through insurance intermediaries) must be a professional who shares Independent's philosophies and objectives.

It means that the premium must be adequate for the risk and must not be set artificially low merely to attract the business (there is no escaping the fact that the right insurance costs money and, as with so many things, you get what you pay for).

It means that the policyholder must be prepared, in conjunction with the broker and with Independent, to manage the risk to reduce the likelihood of insured incidents occurring.

The commitment to risk-management principles is reflected in every aspect of Independent's activity, from sales through to claims. We promote our risk-management expertise to brokers and policyholders when we are selling. We take account of risk-management practice when we are underwriting. We survey every risk and take the opportunity to advise on risk-management issues; indeed, we actually call our surveyors risk control advisers. And if there is a claim, we advise on ways in which the risk can be better managed in future to prevent recurrence.

Independent's extraordinary commitment to risk management and the wide range of initiatives and services it offers does not mean that its policyholders are required to pay extra. Services provided to existing policyholders are normally offered without a fee. This covers a wide range of industries and disciplines, from heavy engineering, mining and transport through to occupational health and hygiene and environmental issues.

Indeed, Independent is willing to work with the broker and policyholder to develop a bespoke risk-management solution for each case. This level of close cooperation is the best way to ensure genuine understanding and common purpose between all parties. It also ensures that a cost-effective premium is agreed which truly reflects the risks involved.

Clearly, this sort of relationship works best beyond the traditional confines of annual insurance policies. This is why Independent

Insurance has pioneered the development of long term policies lasting up to five years. These offer guaranteed premium rates for the term, allowing policyholder, broker and insurer to concentrate on risk-improvement work. Budgeting confidence means that resources can be committed to a long-term risk-management strategy.

Knowing that the policyholder has demonstrated this level of commitment allows Independent to take a much more constructive view of the risk, contributing towards the cost of risk-management measures and rebating part of the premium in appropriate cases. But even for traditional annual policies, where the premium is sufficiently large and the commitment is evident, Independent will extend its full risk-management capabilities to ensure that the risk is a success.

To find out more about Independent's attitude to risk management, talk to your insurance broker. If you would like details of a broker in your area, please contact the Independent marketing department.

1.5

Going for Growth

John Eggleston
National Head, KPMG's Owner Managed Business Team

Stories of how self-made businesspeople created and developed their businesses hold a powerful fascination. What drove them, what was their particular talent, how did they spot the goose that laid the golden egg? Are there any common signposts on their journeys that could direct others?

Let's consider if the type of business is the answer. Should the would-be entrepreneur focus his or her attention on a particular area? In the listing, 'The Top 100 Entrepreneurs', it's no surprise to see the high-tech sector well represented, as one of the new growth industries. However, it by no means dominates and leading entrepreneurs are to be found in every sector. Fortunes are to be made out of new products, but also out of very prosaic activities, such as coffee-making or carpet-cleaning.

UK Ltd, KPMG's study of the health of the private business sector, shows the strongest growth in real estate and communications. However, while real estate has converted this turnover growth into profit growth, communications is showing a deterioration in profitability and a decline in margins. While there are signs of a widening gap between the best and the worst profitability performances in manufacturing, overall it is too simplistic to talk of a two-tier economy, when the performance in some parts of manufacturing is better than in some parts of the service sector.

Is there a location where entrepreneurship thrives? The London streets are, of course, paved with gold for some, but there are also those running thriving businesses in areas that have generally been described as 'depressed'. KPMG has found that the towns demonstrating the greatest growth in turnover are in the South, in Southampton, Cambridge, Reading, Crawley and St Albans. The best profits are, however, returned in the North and the Midlands, in Leicester, Edinburgh, Huddersfield, Derby and Aberdeen.

Other economic studies, trying to predict the next hot spots, forecast the most growth in paper, print and publishing, transport manufacturing, other manufacturing and hotels and catering up to the year 2000. The regions which are expected to experience a growth in GDP are the East Midlands and East Anglia.

In looking for a pattern by examining the past and forecasting the future, what is evident is that there isn't one. New industries will grow more quickly than old, but success is as likely to be found in a different and better way of running an established commodity or service. Talented entrepreneurs have the ability to grow a business, to improve profits and margins, whatever the sector or location. The more appropriate quest is perhaps to find what sets these entrepreneurs apart and what distinguishes them. I believe that there are four fundamentals.

First is the ability to identify a new opportunity, whether this is through product differentiation, a response to new technology, the application of a new technology or the offer of a new service. If successful entrepreneurship relied on new inventions, growing businesses would be few and far between. Better instead to focus on identifying a new niche in an established marketplace.

Second is to be a leader. A leader needs a vision, but as important is the ability to communicate this. A leader also needs a team and, while the successful entrepreneur does not always demonstrate politically correct team behaviour, he or she does know how to act as a coach, in being able to attract a good team and bring out the best qualities in the members of that team. The entrepreneur uses the team to give the vision a solid foundation.

The third quality is a capacity to relish change, to see change as the norm and not as an irritation and inconvenience. External forces make change inevitable and, although a vision needs to be constant, the means of achieving this necessarily have to adapt to circumstance. An ability to respond to change helps the business make the cultural leaps from small to growing and from growing to sustainable, because it is a dynamic unit.

An entrepreneur with these qualities can set up a flourishing business, but it is a business without structure. The long-term entrepreneur, dedicated to developing the business he or she founded, also has a fourth quality. This is to recognise that, while starting up is very exciting, growing up means establishing processes that can deal with the complexities that development brings. It means setting up mechanisms to attract and retain staff, for example, to deal with tax more effectively, to put in place strategies that take change in their stride, to plan for the future.

Entrepreneurship is a state of mind; more a question of approach than a question of process. If entrepreneurs are born, not made, the ones who make it are the ones who shape this innate quality, systematically putting in place a series of measures that will create the platform for continued growth.

KMPG's Owner Managed Business Team is the leading provider of business advice for growing companies and is focused on identifying solutions that help owners develop sustainable and successful businesses.

John Eggleston is Head of KPMG's Owner Managed Business Team and is a member of KPMG's UK Management Team. He has spent the last seven years as senior partner of KPMG's Leicester office, which concentrates on serving the owner-managed business community in that area.

Part 2
Growth Mechanisms

2.1

The Challenge for the Owner-managed Business

Colin Perry
Owner-Manager, LTE Scientific Ltd

Who needs more challenges? Certainly not the poor owner-manager. By now he (or she) is suffering from a surfeit of challenges that have been chucked at him recently from all sides.

They include (but are by no means limited to):

- the high value of sterling;
- the threat of recession;
- increased costs of borrowing;
- the imminence of the euro;
- the millennium bug;
- the phasing out of retirement relief;
- abolition of tax credits on dividends;
- removal of the cap on unfair dismissal claims;
- strengthened union-recognition rights;
- prompt payment legislation.

At times, it is difficult to stand back and identify the *fundamental* long-term challenges – as opposed to the multitude of transitory ones – facing the typical owner-managed business. Even when they are identified, how many owner-managers really have the time to give them the attention they deserve? Owner-managers do not normally have a staff to assist them – very often they must do the whole job themselves.

And yet, the effort has to be made. The business cannot grow and prosper unless the long-term challenges are identified and dealt with effectively.

The challenge of successful innovation

The pace of change in business is increasing all the time. It is no longer enough to watch what your competitors are doing and then seek to emulate them. By the time you have done that, they will have moved on to the next idea.

Innovation means different things to different businesses. In a manufacturing business, the most obvious requirement is constantly to be developing new products. Even subcontract manufacturers must involve themselves in regular product-development initiatives, perhaps in partnership with their customers.

Then there is process development, which often interacts with product development – a process innovation can trigger a product innovation and vice versa.

A similar need to innovate applies to service industries – where the 'product' is the service offer and the 'process' is the way in which it is created and delivered.

Twenty years ago businesses could get by with long intervals between periods of innovation, no longer. It has to be a constant feature.

The challenge of increasing the value added

Value added is another name for increasing productivity, and it applies equally to service and manufacturing companies.

The 1980s saw great strides being made in British productivity by improved working methods. Yet we still lag behind our main competitor countries. To take the productivity improvements further will require enhancing the value – as perceived by the customer – of the services and products being sold, without a proportionate increase in the people employed to make and deliver them.

That again will need a greater emphasis on innovation.

The challenge of exploiting international markets

Not everyone can be an exporter. But even non-exporters should be looking for ways to tap into international markets, even if only indirectly by targeting internationally minded customers, because that is where the big growth prospects are.

The opportunities for SMEs to participate in international markets have never been greater. The single European market – imperfect though it may be – is potentially even more valuable to growth-minded small companies

(which typically operate from a single establishment in the UK) than for large multinational companies.

In this context, it is vital that SMEs get ready for the euro. If they do not, they risk losing the advantages of being part of a large single market and may find themselves on the outside of the *real* single market, which will undoubtedly be euroland. British businesses can, if they choose, become part of the euro area – whatever the politicians believe government policy to be.

Help and advice for SMEs with exporting aspirations are more readily available today than they used to be, often at local level through the Business Links.

The people challenge

Getting and training the right people is a particular challenge for the owner-manager. If the business is to grow, the owner-manager cannot expect to be able to handle all the important functions personally. But one function which they must supervise personally is ensuring the quality of the people who work in their business.

Small businesses have sometimes had a reputation for poaching well-trained people from larger businesses. True or not, that type of attitude is not viable today. Motivation is a key ingredient in the small, growing business. Increasingly, employees are most motivated by employers who offer them training which enhances their personal development and reward them for their achievements. The pay-off for the business can be remarkable, too – a well-trained, well-motivated management and workforce team is essential for an entrepreneurial business.

The challenge of electronic commerce

Just as the single European market has been a big new opportunity for the owner-managed business in recent years (and will continue to be so for some years to come), the next such opportunity coming quickly over the horizon is the single electronic market.

The Internet, e-mail and other forms of electronic communication and advertising are open to all businesses, regardless of size, and on the same terms. It is difficult to predict clearly where this new medium will take us, or which small businesses it will benefit most. But one thing is for sure – it is going to change the business landscape. There is a learning curve here, and the sooner the owner-managers get to grips with it, the better placed they will be to take advantage of its opportunities.

Colin Perry is an entrepreneur with interests in several private companies. He is also chairman of the CBI's SME Council, which represents the interests of small and medium-sized companies in lobbying and advising government on policy and legislation.

Perry is owner-manager of **LTE Scientific Ltd**, a small company which manufactures specialised equipment for microbiology laboratories. He is also chairman and an investor in Kenrick & Jefferson Ltd, a manufacturer of envelopes for the direct mail industry.

LTE Scientific Ltd manufactures microbiological incubators, ovens, autoclaves and other specialised equipment for laboratories. Customers are principally located in the pharmaceutical, chemical and food industries, as well as in research establishments and hospitals. With a turnover of £3 million, LTE exports 20 per cent of its output to around 25 countries. The aim is to raise exports to 40 per cent over the next three years.

2.2
Succession is a Healthy Business

Patrick Dunne
Director in charge of ID programme, 3i

Three types of succession help drive our business at 3i: ownership, leadership and technological. Much has been written about each of these forms of succession, but normally in the context of 'succession problems'. Nowhere is this more evident at the moment than in the German press, where it is regularly reported that 700,000 businesses face 'succession problems'.

It is true that unresolved leadership, ownership or technological succession issues are a frequent cause of boardroom disharmony and business under-performance. It is also true that these issues can rapidly become crises when the business climate becomes more difficult. For the business ghouls at the business schools, it can provide additional delight when ownership, leadership and technological succession issues combine to form that fatal cocktail so ideal for a case study.

There is, however, a more positive view and that is that succession issues are rich in opportunity. Ownership succession is the creator of immense entrepreneurial opportunity. Leadership succession and its consequential ripple through a business are how most people gain career opportunity. Technological succession from the wheel to the printed circuit board and beyond will continue to be a tremendous driver of commercial progress. So I believe that whatever our vantage point – owner, director or aspirant – we should start looking at succession more positively.

Another general working assumption in succession lore is that this is an issue for the older generations. My experience with entrepreneurial teams leads me to believe that leadership succession has a lot more to do with the rate of development of the business and the rate of development of the team than with their age. It can be great fun to discuss how to hand the leadership baton of a high-growth technology business on to the next generation, particularly when the founder is under 40. The corporate mergers and acquisitions market in the UK leads to approximately 2000 ownership successions, and this also has little to do with age. It might actually have more to do with CEO tenure and the human instinct to react against a predecessor's strategy.

So if I'm a talented manager, how do I become a victor of succession rather than a victim? A recent study by the 3i Venturelab at INSEAD showed many similarities between high-flying corporate managing directors and the entrepreneurial MDs who run management buy-out or buy-in companies. A major difference, however, is that the MBO/MBI managers seize their opportunity. Incidentally, the entrepreneurial group had a generally more positive outlook to business – they were far more inclined towards growth than rationalisation. A separate study in 1994 which 3i commissioned from the London Business School looked at the average lifecycle of ownership of a UK company – this study concluded that it was seven years. Even if you just added the number of companies you could be suitable to buy in to within your own sector, including the one you run, there is therefore a reasonable chance of success.

Getting good MD experience puts you in the best position to see opportunities, to be approached for them and to take them. Technological succession has led to a huge flux of ownership and the opportunity to carve out very entrepreneurial businesses within major corporates. Just look at the rise of the science entrepreneurs, particularly in the UK life science software industries. At 3i we can't find enough of them!

What about the owner's perspective? If I am an owner, whether I'm corporate or an individual, how do I get to feel good about handing my business on? Remembering, of course, that I want to maximise the cash at the same time! Being clear about your objectives for ownership as well as for the business will help enormously. Clarity of strategy leads to clarity of purpose. I know a very successful businessman who has just entered his seventies and can't bear to cease his involvement with his business. The reality is that if he doesn't he'll kill it, and if he does it may kill him. He doesn't know what he wants. He's a classic succession victim. The canny owner, the succession victor, gets the business in good shape to transfer with ease when an opportunity arises and doesn't get trapped. By looking out for the strategic shifts in their sector or economy, they get their timing right. By building good second-tier management, you build a team that is capable of getting venture capital backing to compete with trade buyers. By recognising technological succession, you seize competitive advantage or sell the business before it surpasses you.

Often owners have a gloomy view of the afterlife – they shouldn't. If they are entrepreneurially inclined and fear they may miss the buzz, there are plenty of opportunities. At 3i, many of the people we back in management buy-ins are second-time entrepreneurs. Many of the investing chairpersons or independent directors we introduce to younger entrepreneurs are also second-timers, who this time have got the 'MD bit' out of their system and are happy to provide the coaching, mentoring role.

To conclude: ownership, leadership and technological succession will drive opportunity for those who want it to and will continue to depress those who don't.

3i Group plc is Europe's leading venture capital company. The group invests in start-ups and in independent, growing companies with turnovers of between £1 million and £250 million. It provides funding for growth, recovery, management buy-outs and management buy-ins.

3i is an involved investor, not an owner-manager. It has a flexible exit policy aimed at maximising returns to all shareholders of the companies it backs.

3i has 28 offices throughout Europe and a presence in Asia. The group invests in companies from all sectors. Overall, 3i has invested more than £9.5 billion in over 13,000 businesses and currently has a portfolio of investments in around 3200 companies.

Patrick Dunne, a director at 3i, is in charge of 3i's ID Programme, founded in 1986. The programme has approximately 450 members and has made approx 200 appointments. Patrick is the author of the recently published book *Running Board Meetings: Tips and techniques for getting the best from them*, published by Kogan Page.

He also runs a series of fora for 3i portfolio companies on how to pick and use independent directors, manage board disharmony and run board meetings.

2.3

How to Buy or Sell a Private Company

Barrie Pearson,
Executive Chairman, Livingstone Guarantee

Little, if anything, is straightforward in the world of corporate finance, and the buying and selling of companies is certainly no exception.

In fact, it is a risky business with many pitfalls for the uninitiated who may embark on an acquisition or disposal without advice or previous experience. However, potential acquirers should begin the process without appointing an adviser by preparing an acquisition profile to describe the type of company they wish to buy. Otherwise, they could end up attempting to buy only those businesses that are for sale at the time, and not the businesses they could and should be buying.

The acquisition profile should only after rigorous evaluation embrace diversification by acquisition, because this is deceptively risky. For example, this may be acquiring a business with unfamiliar technology, or operating in a country where language difficulties may arise. Even attempting to take on a different customer base can have its pitfalls. For example, selling to corporate customers, as opposed to individual consumers, may prove to be a step too far.

For those prospective acquirers taking a safer route, searching for acquisitions in their own country and market sectors, I suggest that they conduct their initial search without paying fees to advisers to carry it out for them. It is unlikely that any adviser will have as deep a knowledge of their industry as they do themselves.

However, the adviser does have a valuable role to play in the early stages in making initial contact with selected companies to open dialogue. The most effective method of doing this is by a direct telephone call to the appropriate person rather than writing a letter, which may be treated with no more respect than junk mail. Further along the line, when heads of agreement have been signed – and these are literally letters of intent – it must be remembered that both parties have the right to withdraw from the deal, prior to legal completion. The acquirer should therefore always insist on a period of exclusivity following heads of agreement to ensure that the vendors are not pursuing other buyers in parallel.

Having made these observations regarding the pitfalls of conducting an acquisition, it must be remembered that there are equally as many concerns to be borne in mind by vendors. No matter on which side of the table one is sitting, the possibilities exist to be financially hurt.

The main advice to vendors of private businesses, and even groups when selling a non-core subsidiary, is to be wary of pursuing an unsolicited approach. Despite the fact that the approach may have come from a prestigious company with an obvious appetite to do a deal, reality may well reveal that this 'sweetheart' is looking for a bargain-basement price.

The way to maximise shareholder value is to run a covert auction whereby an experienced corporate finance adviser will identify six known, serious buyers from around the world and inform them on a confidential basis that the business is available for purchase. The corporate finance adviser will then provide sufficient information for detailed conditional offers to be submitted in due course within a two-week period so that an informed choice of the preferred purchaser can be made.

Experience has shown that when at least four offers are received, the highest offer is virtually always at least 50 per cent above the lowest, and in a significant number of cases the highest offer can be (even more than) double the lowest.

Ideally, none of this activity should have taken place before the company has been 'groomed' for sale – something that could take between six months and two years. However, this exercise does result in a maximising of shareholder value in making the company as attractive and profitable as possible by addressing potential problems and issues which, if left unattended, would seriously delay or jeopardise the sale.

As a final observation, I would make a plea to all potential vendors not to attempt a 'King Canute' attitude. Many owners of private businesses have the fixed idea that they will not contemplate an earn-out deal, but insist that the entire purchase consideration be paid on legal completion. This approach does not often succeed. More than half of private company acquisitions in the UK include an earn-out deal, which means that some of the purchase price is not paid for up to two years and is dependent on profit performance following acquisition.

This is not really surprising, since this is the only way in which a buyer is able to offer a tempting price to the vendor while retaining protection in the event that the post-acquisition performance does not reach expectations. With so many risks, the advice has to be 'take advice', whether you are considering buying or selling a company.

Barrie Pearson is Executive Chairman of **Livingstone Guarantee**, the UK's largest independent corporate finance house. He founded Livingstone Guarantee to provide independent strategic and corporate finance advice of unrivalled quality, and today the company specialises in acquisitions, disposals, MBOs and MBIs of unquoted companies valued at £3 million or more. Livingstone Guarantee is an active member of Euromerger, the international association of independent corporate finance houses.

2.4

Business Profits and Taxation

Andrew Jupp and Andrew Jones

KPMG Tax Advisers

Corporate and personal interests are inextricably linked in the growing owner-managed business. There are occasions when what is most tax effective for the company will not be what is most tax effective for the owners, and compromises will be required. But if we start from the premise that what drives and motivates an owner-manager is the creation of wealth within the business, then effective tax planning at the corporate level is fundamental to growth and success.

The well-known and often over-used phrase 'don't let the tax tail wag the commercial dog' is undoubtedly true. Decisions should never be taken purely to save tax. But tax is a real business expense that has a direct effect on the profits available for growth. After all, the funds available for future spending and hence future growth are those remaining *after* tax. While decision-making based purely on tax strategy can never be advocated, decisions taken without due regard to the tax consequences are short-sighted in the extreme. We highlight some of the key areas in which the successful owner-manager will seek to minimise tax.

Structure

What is the most appropriate structure – sole proprietorship, partnership, company or group? This will be determined by size, by the personalities involved, by commercial factors and by whether the protection of a limited liability company is required. But most businesses sooner or later will incorporate. When there is more than one line of business, is a group more appropriate? Consider this carefully – moving from one to two companies not only increases the administrative burden, but immediately introduces a restriction to the availability of the small companies' rate, and could create or increase a liability to make payments on account of corporation tax. Get it wrong and your tax rate increases from 20/21 per cent to 30/31 per cent, and if you are in the marginal rate, even higher. Maximising the use of the small companies' rate can provide a simple but very effective absolute tax saving and tax deferral over a number of years.

Funding

The possibilities of funding are covered elsewhere in this book, but what about the tax effectiveness? Will interest on debt be tax deductible? Is the debt in the company best able to use the deduction? Can longer-term finance be provided tax effectively?

Withdrawal of funds

How can funds be withdrawn most efficiently to reward managers and investors? This must be determined by the company's cashflow and working capital position. Should dividends be paid or would remuneration be more appropriate? Dividends can be more tax effective if the company pays at the small companies' rate of corporation tax, otherwise remuneration may be better. Where there are conflicting requirements, such as outside shareholders where the company would not obtain tax relief for 'remuneration', consider different classes of shares so that dividends can be paid on some but not others, or consider dividend waivers. Time the payment of dividends to maximise the time before shareholders pay the higher-rate tax liability. Consider payments in kind so that the company saves employer's national insurance – effectively another tax. Remember that remuneration must be paid within nine months of the year-end to obtain tax relief.

Acquisitions, disposals and reorganisations

For a trading company, an expense will be tax deductible only if it is incurred wholly and exclusively for the purpose of carrying on the trade. The rules for investment companies are different; consider whether there should be a group holding company that should bear the expenses incurred on corporate acquisitions, disposals and reorganisations. Not all expenditure will be deductible, but more will be than in a trading company. When acquiring a business, consider whether it should be an asset purchase or shares. Asset purchases usually permit greater tax relief, especially if the purchase price is allocated to qualifying assets, but consider whether there are any benefits in a share purchase such as brought-forward ACT or unused tax losses.

Overseas issues

The UK currently has one of the lowest corporate tax rates as compared to most of its main trading partners. Sooner or later, most growing businesses do business overseas. Simply dealing with an overseas customer or supplier – and getting it wrong – can in a stroke wipe out the benefits of all your careful tax planning. Sending a salesperson to another country for only a few days can inadvertently create an overseas tax presence.

Consider overseas tax strategies at an early stage. Moving from one structure to another months or years down the line can create significant tax costs. Is a formal overseas presence required and, if so, what should it be? Is a branch, subsidiary company, or a form of commissionaire structure the best for your company? Are there overseas tax-filing requirements?

Consider how the overseas operation should be funded to maximise tax relief and think about profit repatriation to minimise withholding taxes and to maximise cashflow. Set transfer prices to be as tax-efficient as possible but, in view of the extension of self-assessment to this area, ensure that they are defensible and fully documented.

Don't forget the basics

The most effective ways to minimise tax and maximise retained funds for growth are often the easiest. With an increasing trend towards profits for tax purposes being computed on the basis of the accounting profits, consider your accounting policies and the effect that they have on tax. Consider capital expenditure, whether assets should be leased or bought, and time the expenditure so that tax relief is obtained sooner rather than later. Are provisions sufficiently specific to be tax deductible?

In conclusion, this chapter highlights the importance of tax strategy in assisting growth. Tax is a major cost to growing businesses. Both absolute savings of tax and the timing effects in terms of cashflow advantages are vital in providing owner-managers with funds for growth and reinvestment.

Andrew Jupp is a senior manager and **Andrew Jones** is a tax partner with chartered accountants and business advisers **KPMG**. They lead the owner-managed business tax group in KPMG's Reading office and London offices respectively and specialise in advising companies expanding both in the UK and overseas.

Part 3
Building Competitive Organisations

3.1

Transforming the Business through Multi-skilling

Tina Mason

Chief Executive, Training Division, Dutton Engineering

Dutton Engineering was founded in 1972 with a handful of people, and today it employs 40 people with a turnover of £2 million. Having been bought out by its management in 1983, it went down the traditional 'quality systems' route of the 1980s, achieving early accreditation to BS5750 (now ISO9002). This was not, however, the competitive weapon that the organisation needed if it were not only to survive, but grow.

We believe that many companies waste 25–30 per cent of their efforts on activities that do not add a value, directly or indirectly, to the customer – because we have been satisfied with tinkering when we should be re-engineering. Dutton's founder, Ken Lewis, took a hard look at 'the way we'd always done it' and decided that it was time to move on.

The company embarked on its 'journey to excellence' in 1989 with a fresh look at what it needed – and it made some radical changes. The core values were of trust, of partnership with customers, suppliers and workforce, and the belief by everyone that 'quality starts with me'. We all had to learn to stop thinking in terms of tasks and individual performance, and start to think in terms of a team delivering customer satisfaction.

If I think about what our organisation was like when I joined it some 11

ACTION 2000

By Gwynneth Flower, Managing Director of Action 2000

There can be few business challenges that have prompted so much heated debate - and so little understanding - as the Millennium Bug. Some 'experts' are predicting economic meltdown while others are advising that the general populace stockpiles food and other essentials.

Against this background of mass hysteria, business people are expected to relate these stories of doom and gloom to their own organisations. Unsurprisingly, many are failing to make the connection. They want to know:

- What is the Bug?
- How will it affect me?
- What can I do about it?
- Where can I find help?

These are sensible questions requiring practical answers, and it is to fulfil precisely this role that Action 2000 was set up.

WHAT IS THE MILLENNIUM BUG?

The Millennium Bug has its origins in the early days of computers, when the cost of memory space was at a premium. To save space and money, programmers abbreviated the year to the last two digits. This meant 1998 featured as 98, and so on.

The problem arises because of the change from 1999 to 2000, which will be interpreted as 00. The impact of this on date sensitive systems and electronic devices could mean the generation of unpredictable or corrupted data or outright failure.

WHERE WILL THE BUG STRIKE?

It's not just computers that will be affected, but all manner of business equipment and devices that contain electronic chips which may have a date function. These include embedded chips contained in anything from process and environmental control systems to alarms and door entry mechanisms. Action 2000's advice is; if in doubt about a piece of equipment, get it checked.

BARRIERS TO ACTION

Action 2000 has conducted two sets of quarterly research to gauge what UK businesses are doing to tackle the Bug. The results were mixed, with awareness of the problem running at 100% but understanding and action trailing some way behind. There are a number of reasons for this:

- managers don't think the problem affects them
- firms think they can put off dealing with the problem until late next year
- some believe the problem has been hyped up by the computer industry to drum up business
- many companies don't have, can't find or afford the skills necessary to deal with the Bug

Action 2000 is concerned at the 'perception gap' between what companies are doing, and what they should be doing.

Every company in the country could be affected by this problem. It is a business issue, not a technical one, and needs to be addressed by senior managers. It is no good leaving it to the IT department - if you've got one - because the survival of your business is at stake.

In fact, for many companies, preparing a project plan and understanding their potential exposure to the Bug will involve little or no IT skill.

ACT NOW - A STEP BY STEP GUIDE

Action 2000 has devised a three stage plan to help businesses - particularly small and medium sized companies - to get to grips with the challenges presented by the Bug. They are:

Understand and assess - appreciate the importance of the subject by treating it as a boardroom agenda item, and a business issue with an IT flavour. Appoint a senior manager or director to oversee all Bug work, audit all systems and equipment that may be affected and list all critical suppliers and customers. Next, assess the information you have gathered and set priorities based on the extent to which your business relies on various systems and equipment. Then draw up a project plan, and continually check deadlines are met.

Implement - pursue the project plan, using existing skills and resources where they exist and hiring in help where needed. You will need to consider whether to repair, retire, replace, upgrade or rewrite equipment, systems or software.

Test and install - having made the necessary modifications and replacements, tests need to be carried out to ensure the changes work as planned. Testing is the most time-consuming element of most Year 2000 projects, and must be completed before final 'live' installation.

It is important for businesses to approach the Millennium Bug as they would any other business challenge, with the important proviso that, unlike nearly all other projects, the deadline for this one cannot be moved.

SUPPLY CHAIN ISSUES

Understanding the systemic nature of the Bug is crucial. No business is an island. All of us rely on elaborate and complex supply chains for our survival, and it is as important to check that your suppliers and third parties are taking the Bug seriously as it is to get your own house in order.

Action 2000 is urging companies of all sizes to work together to beat the Bug, and has drawn up a document that encourages a cooperative approach between firms.

Pledge 2000 comprises a six point plan committing signatories to sharing relevant information on their Bug plans with each other and advocating an approach to the problem that avoids legal action wherever possible.

To date, some of the UK's largest companies have signed Pledge 2000 including Unilever, Sainsbury's and Prudential. Hundreds of less well-known businesses have also signed Pledge 2000 or asked for further information about it.

Action 2000 has also launched a national TV, poster and press advertising campaign alerting businesses to the threat posed by the Bug and advising people to ring the action line (0845 601 2000) for further information.The action line provides callers with guidance and assistance by sending them a core information pack and help sheets as well as sign posting further sources of help.

There is no excuse for companies taking no action. Help is available and Action 2000 exists to provide it. This is an issue that they ignore at their peril.

ABOUT ACTION 2000

Action 2000 is a company set up with Government support to advise businesses on the potential impact of the Millennium Bug and how they can reduce disruption to an acceptable level.

This advice and guidance is delivered in the form of easy-to-understand information packs and help sheets, available by calling the Action 2000 action line on 0845 601 2000, or visiting the web site at www.bug2000.co.uk

Action 2000 also advises Government on the threat posed by the Bug to core public services that underpin the UK national infrastructure.

The personnel touch

Stephen Williams of Cedar International, the Human Resource consultants, sets out his views on the personnel issues that can be neglected when preparing for flotation.

AIM offers a very practical option for any company wishing to expand rapidly, but for whom listing on the main market may not be appropriate. Cedar International's experience has shown that these developing companies are usually highly entrepreneurial in their management style. They spend a great deal of time considering the financial, accounting and legal implications of seeking additional capital - including their admission to AIM - but often fail to take account for the other vital requirement for success: people.

This is where a properly developed human resources policy can help. Among the issues facing owners, directors and their advisers are succession, the need to strengthen operational management, the need to appoint proactive and relevant non-executive directors, and most importantly, the need to prepare a robust strategic plan.

Cash Injection

The potential for growth brought by an injection of capital raised on AIM has tremendous significance for the workforce as well as for the management and outside investor. It is often claimed that organisations succeed or fail largely as a result of their ability to manage resources. All too often the human resource is ignored.

Effective strategies for managing, motivating, training and retaining employees are always vital issues, never more so than when a fundamental change such as a move to public ownership is being undertaken. without the commitment, goodwill and enthusiasm of every member of an organisation, the future can be prejudiced.

The 'people' factor has for many years now been accepted as the single biggest reason for the failure of corporate change strategies, including many company mergers and acquisitions. Investigation has shown that failure is often based on the reactions and resistance of employees at all levels to a change being thrust upon them. The most frequently heard complaint is 'nobody talked to us about what was happening'. Any ambitious organisations with an eye to flotation on AIM must have a comprehensive human resource strategy integrated into the formal business plan.

Strategy

This strategy, which may take considerable time to devise and implement, must focus upon:

- Recruitment matters, defining business objectives and identifying the new skills required to achieve those objectives
- Development of existing staff through training and planned career management
- Communication and disclosure of all relevant information to key staff
- Renumeration geared to the new found status and profile of the company, acknowledging that the wider market will be only too pleased to obtain the services of your best performers if remuneration does not reflect contribution
- Retention of people by offering new challenges, and demonstrating a genuine interest in the aspiration of staff.

This strategy requires a commitment upon the part of management to the ideas of teamwork, openness and honesty. It also requires the creation of a cohesive culture often underpinned by external accreditation such as Investors in People and ISO9000.

All of these issues need to be clearly defined and expressed strategically to prepare the company for flotation on AIM. It would be a tragedy to fucus on the financial and legal aspects of AIM alone. By considering the people factor, the future viability of any new AIM company should be enhanced significantly.

For further information regarding the services of Cedar International, please contact Helen Pitcher or Leslie Newell on 0171 831 8383.

Cedar International is a full service HR consultancy offering support to corporate clients in executive recruitment, training and management development, career management and executive coaching Cedar is a member of IMSA, an international network of owner managed consultancies.

years ago, it was very different to today. Even in a small company, we had heavy hierarchical control, with people working in a 'one man, one job' culture, and an 'us and them' attitude between workers and management. And yet where was our money made or lost? On the shopfloor!

It made sense to try to unlock the potential of all the people in the company to improve our performance, instead of expecting the managers to have all the smart answers. We learnt that to stay competitive, the real trick is flexibility. We certainly did not have much of that in the early days. We began our journey with training, training, training, and bags of support from the top. We trained our people in the concepts of 'total quality'. We showed them the value of measurement and encouraged them to begin to set their own targets.

We began a programme of multi-skilling – breaking people out of the boxes in which we had kept them for so long. It was rewarding to see people blossom and grow and, as they started to see more pieces of the company jigsaw, their knowledge and understanding increased and they began to become more actively involved. We underpinned the goodwill for change with a process to capture the ideas and convert them into action – Kaizen. This is the cornerstone of continuous improvement, run by team leaders, not managers, and it allows everyone in the organisation to be involved in the elimination of waste.

We try to work *smart* instead of *hard*. We were staggered by the ingenuity of people who had for years 'just done the job'. The difference in employee attitude, and the achievements in terms of the elimination of waste, were more than we could ever have wished for. Building on these early successes, we moved from a functional company with dedicated skill centres to one built around multifunctional teams. This was a major step change for the shopfloor, and one about which in the early days they had some real reservations. They quickly saw the benefits of a small team of people owning a whole process – everything became much more visible, and fire-fighting and reactive behaviour were replaced by planning and cooperation. It also gave improvements in quality – the team 'owned' products and took on the responsibility of customer care – dealing direct with their external customers. This improved communication, gave increased flexibility, and the whole organisation became much more customer driven.

We went on to introduce production cells and a flexible 'annualised hours' contract that allows working patterns to move around to match customer demand. Communication has been vital and everyone in the organisation knows what is going on. Teams are involved in setting budgets, planning recruitment and training, and scheduling their own workload.

Change for us delivered real, tangible results: turnover up from £1 million to £2 million in a climate where prices are going down, not up. Our 1980s workforce of 40 included 13 people on 'indirect', non-value-adding activity. Our 1998 workforce of 40 includes only 5 on indirects. Stock and work in progress reduced from £250,000 on £ 1 million to £80,000 on £2 million – with a corresponding disappearance of a massive bank overdraft. Lead times on key products are down from six weeks to eight hours. Paperwork in the company has been reduced by 80 per cent. And it led to an unexpected business opportunity – a new training division has been launched to help other organisations embrace the challenges of the new millennium.

Dutton Engineering (Woodside) Limited is a small but growing subcontract sheet metal company, specialising in stainless steel fabrications and enclosures for a variety of high-tech customers. It also fabricates in mild steel and aluminium, and offers a full design-to-manufacture service, from production of prototypes to small batch and volume production. Dutton is based in Sandy in Bedfordshire and employs 40 people with a turnover of £2 million and growing. It is a host company for the Department of Trade and Industry's 'Inside UK Enterprise' scheme, winning the 'Best SME' accolade in 1996. Its new training division 'Business Excellence Training' offers advice, training workshops and assistance in the implementation of best-practice tools.

Tina Mason is chief executive of Dutton's training division, 'Business Excellence Training'. Tina has worked for the company for 11 years and has played a key role as 'champion' for the identification and implementation of change-management strategies. She is a trained assessor for the British Quality Foundation (1998 programme) and is actively involved with the Department of Trade and Industry in promoting best practice.

3.2

Leadership in Management

John Caudwell
Chairman, the Caudwell Group

In many ways I'm the wrong person to ask about leadership. It is, I believe, the people who choose to follow who ultimately create a leader. It is they who define the role and it is the quality of their support that allows an individual to be successful.

This, of course, in no way denies that a leader must have skills. To be in the lead one must have at least the foresight to recognise and exploit a market opportunity. Ten years ago, when I founded the company with my brother, Brian, few people would have predicted the enormity of the growth in mobile communications, nor our ability to impart to others an enthusiasm for the venture. However, this ability alone is not enough.

To build a group of companies like the Caudwell Group which now covers every aspect of communication in a global marketplace, needs not only persuasive, some might say innate, charismatic skill, but also the acquisition of people-management skills and an uncompromising belief in one's own judgment.

In the initial stages of any business, a leader needs a measure of single-mindedness, selecting only those who believe in his (or her) dream; those who can run alongside him as he thrusts the business forward. A business stands or falls by the quality of its managers and I have been uncompromising in collecting around me, from the very beginning, a very loyal and talented core of managers who have understood my vision and allowed me the freedom to pursue it.

By following a policy of internal promotion and a 'hands on' management style, borne of necessity in the company's early days and still actively encouraged, these managers have grown with the company. They have, in effect, grown the company. Taking the leadership skills that we have acquired together, they have been able to expand the organisation into different fields of operation in various parts of the world, with a uniformity of company style.

It would be naïve, not to say egotistical, however, to assume that positive leadership was achieved by collecting together 'like-minded' people. On the contrary, it is the very diversity of personality skills that makes today's businesses successful.

A group of companies such as ours is constantly in search of talented managers, many from blue-chip backgrounds, whose business culture is much older, less proactive than our own. These new managers look to the board for a different style of leadership – the leadership of encouragement. Excited by the freedoms offered by an industry still very much in its infancy, they are creatively motivating a young staff and evolving their own management structures.

It is, by definition, the role of a leader to lead, to forge ahead into the uncharted if not the unknown. However, I believe that the success of the journey depends on those who follow.

Ten years ago, **John Caudwell** sold cars. Today, he is Chairman and Chief Executive of the **Caudwell Group** and one of the wealthiest people in the country.

Built upon John Caudwell's exceptional flair for realising market opportunity, the Caudwell Group, which began life as a small Midlands-based mobile communications company, today sells a mobile phone every seven seconds, employs over 1,200 people and has a turnover in excess of £300 million.

With thirteen companies spanning five countries, the Caudwell Group is Europe's largest mobile phone distributor and is in a strong position to take advantage of the continued worldwide expansion in cellular telecommunications.

3.3

Management Development for the Twenty-first Century

Lesley Boyce
Senior Consultant, Chameleon Training and Consulting

Superior management performance will differentiate companies in the twenty-first century. Chameleon Training & Consulting specialises in management development, working with a wide range of clients in blue-chip industries, the public sector and education. Whether an organisation is looking to enhance the performance of an individual or its complete company, Chameleon can deliver measurable results through its consultancy and personal development.

The evolving role of the manager

The traditional role of the manager – controlling resources and acting as an information channel – has proved inadequate to manage people through the degree of change and ambiguity currently within organisations. The manager of today and tomorrow is faced with ever-increasing amounts of information and choices. They are required to motivate and energise their people to create an environment of continuous improvement.

Managing a team requires breakthrough thinking, encompassing greater capability and more effort than it did 20 years ago. It is not technical capability that matters but how managers carry out their role. The ability of the manager to choose the right behaviour at the right time is critical to creating a high-performance environment. Managers who can embrace this challenge have a real opportunity to gain competitive edge through their management capability.

The high-performing manager

Underlying drivers of thinking, emotional intelligence and achievement drive have been shown to differentiate the superior performing manager. Including all three underlying drivers as a core part of future management development programmes will help achieve high-performing teams and a culture of continuous improvement.

In recent years, many organisations have invested in developing unique competency frameworks. These are designed to outline behaviour that leads to outstanding performance within their particular organisation. Chameleon has found that many of the resulting competency models from different organisations end up looking very similar and, while some underlying behaviours do surface, there is an emphasis on skills and knowledge.

Although it is perhaps harder to develop underlying behaviours that lead to superior performance than it is to develop the traditional skills and knowledge, we believe that it is important for underlying behaviours to become the main focus of future management development.

What differentiates a high-performing manager?

As Cooper and Sawaf point out in their book on executive EQ (*Emotional Intelligence in Business*), among managers with identical IQs, skills and knowledge, some will still outperform others. Something beyond these factors is at work and they identify a large part of it to be EQ. Other business schools and management writers have also come up with similar themes.

Cranfield University recently undertook a research project involving 267 managers to identify factors determining superior performance. It observed that superior performance is demonstrated by managers who have developed a generic set of 'meta-abilities'.

For example, Chameleon worked with the client managers to:

- personalise their vision of a future;
- develop partnerships with clients rather than adopt an adversarial approach;
- consider what the changes in culture meant for other people and for them personally;
- think about their part of the business/implications for their own style and their own team;
- challenge how they saw themselves as managers and give them something to compare against by sharing examples of approaches in other industries.

Practical/experiential style workshops allowed individuals to see how they operate habitually and to define in more practical terms how they will need to operate in the service excellence culture. Feedback before and after each project was critical in developing individuals' self-awareness of the impact they have on customers. Workshops helped them move through the process of personal transition, stop doing some of their old habits and start demonstrating new behaviours.

Chameleon helped people prepare for a return to work and the almost certain, but regrettable, obstacles they would face from colleagues and even customers. They were helped through force field exercises to identify when and where they would be likely to fall down and how they would 'bounce back' – so people left the workshop with a plan of action points and a plan for worst cases.

The client organisation had a clear message that the success of the new culture was in the hands of the managers and strong levels of achievement drive were needed. Their modelling of new behaviours would be the deciding factor in determining success or a return to old ways. They were helped to analyse their personal motivation and drivers.

Methods used:

- Understanding drivers and inhibitors through a learning log.
- Identifying people who motivate and energise.
- Motivation questionnaires.
- Group exercises.
- Individual exercises.

The management knew that changing the company was going to be like shifting a massive boulder. The managers started the boulder rocking slightly, then more vigorously until the weight of their influence tipped the boulder over. It then gathered momentum and change was achieved. It was the development of the underlying drivers that enabled them to act differently, understand more accurately the impact they were having and thus achieve the desired change.

Self-development of underlying drivers

All the underlying drivers can be developed. Three steps for self-development have been identified:

- Understand where you are now and where you would like to be.
- Understand the underlying drivers and how you could demonstrate the various behaviours.
- Allocate time to development, trying to pick low-risk situations, and do not be discouraged by early setbacks.

Summary

The role of the manager has changed. To create organisational excellence and achieve competitive advantage it is important to develop managers so they are able to handle the complex and changing environments in which they now operate. Evidence from current research and recent people development projects shows that focus on the underlying drivers of thinking ability, emotional intelligence and achievement drive creates superior performance. The most encouraging findings for managers of today is that, with focus, these drivers can be developed and the necessary personal transitions can be made. This will enable managers to improve their management performance, equipping themselves for the inevitable changes that the twenty-first century will bring.

Lesley Boyce is a senior consultant with **Chameleon Training & Consulting.**

She holds a BA (Hons) Economics from Exeter and an MSc Management Development from Roffey Park.

She has 10 years' management experience in sales/service organisations and four years management consultancy experience, working with Hay Management Consultants and British Airways.

3.4

Unipart – a Learning Organisation

John M Neill CBE
Group Chief Executive, Unipart Group of Companies

Knowledge changes at a rapid pace today, and the application of that knowledge can change businesses and industries overnight. The competitive advantage sought by companies is increasingly arising out of state-of-the-art knowledge, technologies and continuous improvements to the business.

For any business to survive in this competitive environment, it is necessary continually to keep ahead of any new skills, techniques and technologies. However, as 80 per cent of the workforce for the new millennium is already in employment, companies are faced with the problem of a workforce whose knowledge and training are increasingly becoming obsolete.

At Unipart we believe that we must create an organisation where continuous learning for our employees is the cornerstone in the development of the business. It is clear that in the face of accelerating change, effort alone is no longer sufficient: the only sustainable form of competitive advantage is to learn faster than our competitors. To help us achieve this, and to drive our mission to become a world-class organisation, we have created the Unipart 'U' – our own company university.

Opened in 1993, the 'U' is an integral part of working life in Unipart – employees enter through the 'U' every day on their way to and from work and it is the first area seen by any visitor to the Unipart Group of Companies' (UGC) head office in Oxford.

The Unipart 'U's mission is to train, develop and inspire people to achieve world-class performance within the group's companies and among its stakeholders. It endeavours to create an entirely new approach to work which constantly reviews established practices and procedures, and this is reflected in the training that it provides.

There are around 180 different courses running in the 'U' which have been developed and are taught by Unipart managers and staff. Courses cover many areas such as IT skills, supplier management, team management, customer service, problem solving and lean production; these support the company's core philosophies and programmes. The courses are designed to be practical, so that attendees 'train for work' and can apply 'this morning's learning to this afternoon's job'. They use the expertise that comes from doing the job to transfer knowledge and best practice to other areas of the organisation.

While the philosophy of the 'U' is one of continuous learning and is not dependent on qualifications, many of the courses have NVQ accreditations. Contributions made by employees at each course enable the company to adapt its working practices and apply continuous learning principles. One of the key challenges is to capture this learning, critical to the growth of the group's business, and disseminate it across the organisation. This is being done by using intranet Websites as repositories of learning accessible to employees and key stakeholders.

Courses are mainly for employees, but increasingly, other stakeholders of the company such as suppliers and customers attend courses and use the facilities. This allows Unipart's stakeholders, and thus Unipart through its long-term shared-destiny relationships, to benefit from best practice and learning shared through the 'U'.

The 'U's direction is shaped under the guidance of a 'Deans Group', comprising directors of each of the divisions within the company. It is chaired by a principal, Dan Jones, Professor of Motor Industry Management at Cardiff Business School, and co-author of *The Machine that Changed the World*.

The 'U' boasts state-of-the-art facilities: the Learning Curve – the company's resource centre; the Leading Edge – a showroom and training centre for new technologies and the latest in computer hardware and software; and the Internet Discovery Centre – a centre designed to advise on the best use of the business opportunities provided by the Internet and intranet. These are all located next to the reception area at the company's head office. When you walk through the door, the first impression you get is the company's deep commitment to learning and to the use of IT to enhance the creative potential of its people.

The company's commitment to continuous learning has also led to a willingness to study the best business techniques in the world and adapt them to the Unipart culture. Learning from its partners and customers, Unipart has demonstrated consistent benefits from this process. Within the 'U', the ideas and theories taught by the best management thinkers, as well as the unique learning that comes from Unipart's customers such as Honda, Jaguar and Toyota, are put into practice.

One of the minor thrusts of the Unipart 'U' has been in the area of supply chain management. Over 10 years ago, Unipart recognised that in order to compete successfully in the future and deliver world-class performance, companies had to work across the supply chain to meet the needs of their customers better than anyone else.

Unipart challenged the traditional western adversarial approach to customer and supplier and embarked on a programme seeking cooperation with its suppliers to drive down cost in the supply chain. Before work could begin with suppliers, Unipart employees had to adopt a new and fundamentally different attitude towards supplier relationships. They needed to learn to work in long-term, shared-destiny partnerships based in mutual trust. This important step in developing attitude change in employees has been at the core of the Unipart 'U's offerings.

The Unipart 'U' runs courses on the philosophies and principles of the programmes, as well as providing practical courses to equip employees with the skills and knowledge required to implement the programme successfully. It has estimated that each point reduction on the Ten(d) to Zero scale – a feature of the supply chain management programme – as measured at a groupwide level is worth £500,000 to Unipart's bottom line, which seems a good return on the heavy investment in training and education. Another key area of Unipart 'U' activity is the company's drive for continuous improvement in every aspect of its business and across its stakeholder relationships.

Unipart practises continuous improvement principles that encourage employees to improve quality and reduce cost through individual efforts or in groups called Our Contribution Counts Circles. This programme is supported through the 'U' with skills training for areas such as problem solving, facilitation and effective meetings.

OCC Circles were first launched in the Unipart Group of Companies in 1991 and were developed by drawing on best-practice experience from Japan and North America, but then designed specifically to reflect the culture of Unipart.

OCC Circles empower employees to solve any challenges that might face them in the workplace. Any Unipart employee can form a Circle with other employees – across all levels and parts of the group, chosen carefully either for their skills or for the knowledge that they can contribute to the work of the Circle.

Once a Circle's work is completed, a closing ceremony attended by colleagues and senior managers is held in the workplace. The Circle leader explains how, using techniques learned in the Unipart 'U', the team was able to develop solutions and improve quality or productivity.

In 1993, the programme was extended with the launch of Stakeholder Circles, designed to involve suppliers, customers and the communities in which the group trades. Many Stakeholder Circles have been formed, enabling the UGC's employees to work with their counterparts on a wide range of issues dealing with environmental concerns, quality and customer service.

In the five years since it was established, the Unipart 'U' has gone a long way towards establishing a learning environment within Unipart. It has become a central part of the business, providing a focus for the development of our people and their skills, and now plays a key role in spreading best practice throughout the organisation. It fuels competitive advantage for the business through the development of new ideas and new ways of working and has become fundamental to implementing the company's guiding principle of 'understanding and serving the real and perceived needs of our customers better than anyone else'. We believe that through the 'U' we are steadily moving towards becoming a true 'learning organisation'.

The Unipart Group of Companies (UGC) is one of Europe's leading automative parts and logistics companies. In 1997, UGC's turnover rose to £1078.4 million, with profits before interest and tax at £28.6 million. Dividends for the year were raised to £7.7 million, up from £7.1 million in respect of 1996. Share value has now risen 46,000 per cent since 1987.

3.5

Managing Stress in a Growing Business

Tim Cuthell, Dip Couns,
PPP Healthcare

Stress in the workplace is a subject that has captured the attention of employers, employees and anyone involved in the well-being of people at work. It is now generally accepted that unmanaged stress or pressure will affect individuals and have a subsequent effect on performance and attendance at work.

Effective stress management requires an intervention on two levels – first to enable individual employees to understand and recognise their own response to pressure and to develop a range of strategies to prevent pressure from having a detrimental effect on their performance and mental and physical well-being. Equally important is the need for employers to be proactive in assessing the systems, culture and management style with regard to the demands made on employees. This approach will not only identify areas, situations and groups of employees where stress levels are such where individuals' ability to cope is threatened, but can also pinpoint the positive situations in which the systems and people are working particularly well. This is enormously beneficial, especially if these 'best-practice' conditions can be replicated elsewhere in the organisation.

So what needs to be considered in the case of a growing business?

One of the greatest stressors in modern life is change. If our work and home lives are reasonably stable and predictable, our ability to cope is greater – as long as we are not in a situation where we have insufficient stimulation. But when we are faced with change – particularly rapid and unexpected

change – we have to manage a situation where we feel less in control. This applies even when we perceive the changes as being positive: a new job, promotion, winning a large contract or opening a new business site.

When the changes are not necessarily perceived by employees as a positive event, such as takeovers and mergers, the setting up of new groups and divisions or the introduction of a new product range, the potential for too much stress – or distress – increases.

Employees' actual experience of working in a successful, growing business may be an increase in the demands made on them, heightened expectations of performance, changes in working patterns – for example changing to a shift system – or even relocation, which could involve a major domestic upheaval or a tough decision on whether to move with the organisation or not.

Clearly, all of the above have the potential to become significant sources of stress. An individual's reaction will depend on a number of factors, including personality, physical and mental health, previous experiences, the existence of friends or family for support, and the other stressors in someone's life which are also stretching their ability to cope at any particular time.

As the organisation grows, the nature of the challenges faced by those in senior positions evolves. New challenges include the pressure to secure finances to pay for expansion, the responsibility for managing a relocation exercise, setting and trying to achieve new performance targets, some of which may turn out to be unrealistic.

So stress needs to be managed in the successful growing business. But how can this be done?

A healthy organisation is one in which good communication between all employees is seen as essential. The more people understand about the needs and requirements of others within the organisation, the easier it is to develop a culture where teamwork and a sense of common purpose prevail. Providing as much information as possible during times of change will help reduce stress. The absence of information is fertile ground in which rumours and fantasies can grow. Many of these will be negative and may be more stressful and damaging than is warranted by the reality of a situation. No news will not be experienced as good news by the workforce.

Managers have a key role to play. First, they need to ensure that they are aware of the way in which pressure and stress affect people and how to recognise the signs and symptoms when people are nearing the limit of their ability to manage it. Listening skills are essential and need to be developed. Secondly, managers need to be aware of the support services available to employees and how to use them effectively. This may include identifying situations where an occupational health service can provide support both for a manager and their team members. Similarly, the human resources or personnel department may be able to provide help and advice.

Many organisations are introducing employee assistance programmes (EAPs) to ensure that employees are supported during their employment. This is particularly important for a growing company and helps ensure that the new and exciting challenges of today do not become the root cause of stress and stress-related symptoms which undermine performance and further growth in the future. An EAP offers a range of free, confidential information and counselling services for employees and their families, available 24 hours a day.

To find out the levels of stress within an organisation, it is possible to conduct a stress audit. This usually involves an external consultant collecting data through questionnaires and focus groups within the company. The resulting information can then be used to identify areas where stress and pressure are highest, enabling the employer to take action to reduce stress levels in the identified 'hot spots'. This approach makes it possible to target resources in the areas where they are most needed rather than a more costly blanket approach.

Lastly, the most helpful action an employer can take to combat workplace stress is to create and maintain a culture in which seeking help and flagging up problems are seen as a strength rather than a weakness. To develop such a culture, it is essential that the issue of stress is taken seriously throughout the whole organisation and that resources are provided to maintain the health and well-being of the most important asset within any organisation – its people.

Tim Cuthell is an employee assistance programme specialist. He has an advanced diploma in counselling and interpersonal skills from the University of London and has worked in the field for 12 years. He is currently chair of the UK Employee Assistance Professionals' Association and he recently joined PPP Healthcare, where he is responsible for account management in respect of the company's employee assistance programme, 'Employee Support'.

PPP Healthcare provides companies with a comprehensive range of healthcare products and services, including employee assistance programmes, health audits, screening and monitoring, medical and dental cover, sickness absence management and medical advisory services.

The National Education Business Partnership Network has a striking way of articulating what they are about. Their "2020 Vision", as they call it, is about the kind of future they want to see for the four year olds who will start school this autumn. They look forward to these young people at the end of the second decade of the next century being citizens playing a full part in society, being employees and tax payers, and being lifelong learners. This is a vision which should make sense to every business in the country, large and small. It is also a vision I think which schools should not be expected to achieve themselves: it will work so much better if business is fully joined with them in partnership.

What is the reality, though, behind the vision? Earlier this year I had the great good fortune to visit Benfieldside primary school in Consett, County Durham and I heard from the very enthusiastic head how pleased they were to get just £90 for a field trip. In this case the money came as a grant from Durham Business Education Executive, the county's education business partnership, which has funding for a limited period from central Government. The grant enabled the school to waive the charges to parents for the study trip to the local waterworks ñ and in a relatively poor community that small difference matters.

£90 is a pitifully small sum of money, of course, alongside the six and seven figure sums committed by some of Britain's largest firms to the Government's new Education Action Zones - but I am in no doubt that it made a difference. The head teacher also gave me other examples of small inputs from local business which helped her to enrich the experience for the children in her care. One local-born businessman came in to tell the children his experience in setting up a business locally. That will have cost him a couple of hours of his time and with luck will have sparked some of the children to believe that they could follow in his footsteps, that business was an exciting thing to get involved in and that local people do succeed.

I also visited the very much larger Kvaerner Cleveland Bridge, the world renowned heavy engineering firm based in Darlington. Kvaerner requires all their apprentices to spend a few days a year as a "Business Ambassador" under another programme promoted by the Durham business education partnership. Business Ambassadors get a couple of days preparatory training through the partnership, particularly to improve their presentation skills. They then spend up to two days in a school (ideally their own school: "one of ours makes good") talking about what they do and linking it back to what the pupils are doing.

Alan Ellwood, the apprentices' manager, is very enthusiastic about the programme, despite the cost in time and a payment to the education business partnership (and, as they progress, a cost in lost production). He believes that it helps to project a very positive image of the company (which, of course, helps them to recruit the best to their apprentice school) and gives the apprentices enormous self-confidence.

Some of the very largest firms in the country have responded magnificently to the Government's recent announcement of the first 25 Education Action Zones, which shone the spotlight again on how business can contribute to education. David Blunkett and his team at the Department for Education and Employment have been very successful in signing up the support of well-known companies such as McDonalds, Tate and Lyle, Barclays Bank, BT and the Halifax and every Action Zone has raised at least £250,000 in sponsorship. I think their initiative is greatly to be welcomed, but it would be a pity if smaller firms felt that this was a game they could not play.

What the Durham examples show is that you don't need to run a huge company to make a difference to your local education scene - or to get a great deal back from getting involved. Like the old Youth Hostels Association advertisement I remember which said "most of our active members are under 85", so it is with education business partnerships. Most active employer participants are from smaller firms, or local branches of our best-known firms, such as Marks and Spencer. This is a game every employer can play.

Of course smaller firms don't have the community education teams which the likes of a BT can support and busy head teachers don't have the time to devote to fund raising or making business contacts. It does take some time to set up the right links and to manage them in the right way if it is to work for both business and school.

That is why both Benfieldside School and Kvaerner Cleveland Bridge turned to Durham Business Education Executive (DBEE) to manage their education-industry links for them. Like most education business partnerships, DBEE is independent of both business and education and works in a very practical way to build bridges between them. There are similar organisations throughout the UK, though their names vary a good deal and so does the range of services they provide.

Ten years or so ago the Government provided reasonably generous funds to ensure that there was a national network with an education-business partnership in every part of the country.* Central funding ended some years ago, however, and most local partnerships now survive on a rather unhealthy "snack" diet, picking up what funds they can from here and there.

So it would be a pity if employers assumed that it all gets paid for centrally: it doesn't. It would also be a pity, though, if employers felt they were only welcome so long as they brought their chequebooks. Education business partnerships are about far more than that, and they are about employers gaining as much as giving. Call them today: your local education business partnership will be pleased to talk to you about how you can get involved.

***** *if you can't readily find your local education business partnership, call Jane Ritchie, Secretary, National Education Business Partnership Network on (01740) 652681.***

3.6

Delta Air Lines – Calling Customer Service

Michael Boynton
Regional Director, Reservation Sales Europe, Delta Air Lines

For many companies, including an airline, a good telephone reservations system is key to success. This is often the first contact a customer has with the company and how they are treated by a telephone sales agent can greatly affect their perception of the company. It is also an extremely important source of revenue for the company.

Delta Air Lines opened its Western European Call Centre in Ealing in West London just over two years ago. The centre has been such a success that in July 1998 Delta moved its German operations to the UK.

The Call Centre was the result of the consolidation of 14 different reservations centres across Europe. The economy of scale achieved by this consolidation is estimated to save Delta around £30 million in its first five years of operation.

The Call Centre currently handles calls from 13 European countries – Austria, Belgium, Denmark, France, Germany, Greece, Ireland, Italy, the Netherlands, Spain, Switzerland, Sweden and the UK. The calls are answered by sales agents in 12 different languages – German, French, Flemish, Danish, Greek, English, Italian, Dutch, Spanish, Swedish and Catalan.

This is how it works: a European customer calls a local phone number in their own country and is 'patched' through to the Ealing Call Centre where they are answered by a sales agent speaking the same language. The caller is generally not aware that they are being answered from outside their own country.

The attention to regional dialects is extremely important in guaranteeing a high standard of customer service. For example, callers from Madrid will be answered by Castilian Spanish speakers, while a caller from Barcelona will be answered in Catalan, the regional language. Similarly, there are different groups of German speakers answering calls from Germany, Austria and Switzerland in different German dialects. Even callers from the Republic of Ireland are answered by Irish-accented agents rather than British ones.

This policy of ensuring that customers are answered by native speakers meant that the labour pool was the key factor in choosing where to base the Call Centre.

Several countries were studied as possible locations, including Ireland and the Netherlands. Ireland, for example, had a large supply of language graduates, but Delta felt that only native speakers provide the level of country knowledge and communication skills required and this could not be achieved through a university degree in languages.

London became the obvious choice in this respect because of its size and cosmopolitan diversity. London guarantees Delta access to a large well-educated, multilingual, native-speaking labour pool. The company now has over 200 employees at the Call Centre and expects to continue expanding.

The key to maintaining a high standard of customer service among such a diverse group of employees is training. Many of the sales agents join Delta without previous experience in the airline industry, selling techniques or computer skills. So training them to a high standard in those areas and in each different language is quite a challenge. They go through a rigorous training programme followed by regular refresher courses as well as continuous monitoring and evaluation.

Delta sales agents are much in demand by other companies, but Delta manages to attract and keep high-quality employees through a generous compensation package that includes flight benefits, stock options and profit sharing. The company has successfully advertised London-based jobs in Dutch and Swedish newspapers.

One other reason for Delta choosing London as a base for its Call Centre was the high standard of telecommunications infrastructure, which is critical to the success of a sales-based call centre. If the phone lines were to go down, the company would lose money and customers become upset and frustrated. London has lived up to expectations in this field, leaving the company to concentrate on providing good customer service to its pan-European customers.

- Delta WECC opened on 15 January, 1998, in Ealing, West London.
- The Call Centre serves 13 European countries – Austria, Belgium,

Denmark, France, Germany, Greece, Ireland, Italy, the Netherlands, Spain, Switzerland, Sweden and the UK.
- Calls are answered in 11 European languages – German, French, Flemish, Danish, Greek, English, Italian, Dutch, Spanish, Swedish and Catalan.
- The Call Centre is open:
  Monday–Friday: 6.30 am to 10.00 pm;
  Saturday–Sunday: 7.00 am to 7.00 pm.
- There are more than 200 people in full-time employment at the Call Centre, answering an average of 4000 calls on a typical weekday.

Delta Air Lines is one of the world's largest airlines with a global route network. Its headquarters are in Atlanta, Georgia. Delta carries more passengers worldwide than any other airline – more than 103 million passengers boarded Delta aircraft in 1997. Delta's Atlanta operations comprise the largest hub operation in the world. Delta operates a total of 622 flights daily to 118 non-stop destinations from Atlanta's Hartsfield International Airport.

Delta and its partners operate 5112 flights each day to 352 cities in 60 countries. The company has over 60,000 employees worldwide and a fleet of 568 aircraft. For its fiscal year ending 30 June, 1998, Delta posted a record net profit of $1 billion, up 13 per cent, and record operating revenues of $14.1 billion, up 4 per cent.

Michael Boynton was appointed Delta's Regional Director Reservation Sales – Europe in January 1998. He is responsible for all of Delta's reservation sales activities in Europe and for the Western European Call Centre and is based at Delta's international headquarters in London.

Boynton has been with Delta for over 25 years and during that time has held various positions within the company. He worked in reservations sales in Atlanta and also in Marketing, where he was responsible for the sales and marketing activities of some of Delta's key sales locations. In 1997 Boynton was appointed Regional Director Sales – Atlanta, where he was responsible for increasing Delta's revenue and market share with over 700 travel agencies and corporate accounts.

3.7

Hewlett-Packard Tackles Information Technology Skills Gap

Hewlett Packard Education

The economy has benefited from a degree of prosperity over recent years. This, of course, leads to a new generation of articles and discussion on skills shortages. Is the current wave of skills shortages any different to those we've seen before? Or does the truth lie in the fact that we never really solved the skills shortages of the past – we simply stopped talking about them?

At Hewlett-Packard, we know that there have always been skills shortages, particularly in the IT industry. We also know that the situation is getting worse. Inevitably, as the issue of skills shortages once again becomes a focus for journalists and academics alike, we see a wave of scepticism creeping in.

Peter Robinson, chief economist of the Institute for Public Policy and Research, was quoted in a leading Sunday paper as saying that a greater investment in education is beginning to pay off and that there is a huge increase in the number of educated workers entering the market. His view is that, at least in some cases, the problem may not be so much a shortage of skilled workers, or those with the right kind of intellectual ammunition, but of jobs they want to do, in working environments that attract them.

In Bruce Talgan's 1996 book, *Managing Generation X*, he says that those entering the workforce now have totally different attitudes from previous generations. They think nothing of leaving a job, once they have been trained, to move on to something else. This highlights another problem –

while companies may be spending more money on training, they're not getting the long-term benefits.

In 1998 we heard that the government considers the skills shortage to be real and a serious threat to the nation's economic well-being in a global marketplace. 'Over £100 million extra will be allocated in the coming year to tackle the skills gap in Britain,' said Chancellor of the Exchequer Gordon Brown in his 1998/99 budget speech.

Fine words. But who will benefit from that investment? Is it enough to make a real dent in the skills gap problem? Will it really allow Britain to take centre stage in the world market? The only answer to these questions at present is that we'll have to wait and see. But clearly, if the issue is recognised at government levels, it's obviously viewed as a 'votewinner' and in time we will all hopefully benefit.

Information technology is suffering

It's fair to say that any UK business is only as good as its IT. This means that technology is now the backbone of any organisation's short, medium- and long-term strategy. With so much emphasis on IT, it's not surprising that the IT skills gap is having a dramatic effect on business productivity.

Leading research firm Banner and *Computer Weekly* recently conducted a survey among 500 IT directors to find out to what extent this skills shortage really exists, and to determine whether it is having any bottom-line impact.

The results were startling. The survey showed that the skills shortage is biting so deeply that one in five organisations has had to change its IT strategy to suit available skills. The survey also showed that IT directors in the public sector are the worst hit, where 36 per cent have had to alter their strategy due to lack of staff.

This means that many British businesses are failing to use technology strategically; they're just plugging holes.

HP Education trains and educates over 80,000 IT professionals each year. We know the trends, we see what's going on. In a market that changes at the speed of light, business success depends on the ability of staff to learn new technologies and align them to the organisation's long-term business goals.

It's not just training – it's the right training that counts

If through this article we've managed to convince you that there is a real skills gap and that training is important – that's great. However, it's only part of the story. As well as making a commitment to training and education, you also need to ensure that your people are getting the right training.

"Especially in a technical business where the rate of progress is rapid, a continuing program of education must be undertaken & maintained."
David Packard
Co-Founder,
Hewlett-Packard Company
HP EDUCATION
HP Education helps your employees transition to new technologies by providing training for the real world. In a world where things change at the speed of light, your success depends on the ability of your employees to learn new technologies and adapt them to your business quickly, efficiently, and confidently. Find out how the company that trains over 80,000 IT professionals a year can make a difference for you.
HP Education:
• Offers comprehensive solutions and customised programs for Windows NT, Enterprise Desktop Solutions, UNIX, Network & System Management, Internet and MPE
• Accelerates technology and system transitions
• Reduces the risks of transitioning to new technologies
• Provides experienced instructors and quality materials
• Offers over 2,000 scheduled course sessions per year
• Over 250 locations worldwide
makes the difference
Registration and enquiries:
01344 763311
Call today for a catalogue
HEWLETT® PACKARD
CBI98
www.hp.com/uk/education

Hewlett-Packard adopts a skills gap analysis (SGA) model that looks carefully at people and the roles they perform within the organisation. We look at what skills are required to perform that role, then analyse what skills people currently have. This information allows us to see clearly where the skills gaps exist. We then work with the organisation to fill the gap. We often find that the SGA process is used to produce accurate job specifications and skills requirements, helping the customer to develop a learning infrastructure for future training needs.

Taking responsibility for training delivered

HP is not in the business of just supplying courses. It's our responsibility to deliver the right level of education. We therefore take a holistic approach to any organisation's IT training needs, and become fully immersed in its culture. Only by getting under the company's skin can we hope to understand and empathise with the total picture – warts and all!

We've talked about the skills gap analysis (SGA) model. In addition, we also use a training needs analysis (TNA) model. TNA allows HP to design and deliver a training programme that meets the exact needs of the customer's business objectives.

Most companies are familiar with 'skills audits', but the TNA model takes this audit process into a different league by being accountable for the assessment, delivery/implementation and results of any training and education programme. In addition, we manage the overall project to eliminate the risks and achieve the desired result for the customer.

3.8

Payroll Basics – Another Look at Outsourcing

John Woodman
Payroll Manager, Accounting Centre Ltd

This chapter briefly discusses the advantages and disadvantages of the various options that SMEs have to process their payrolls.

In current terminology, the question is: is it time for your business to consider 'outsourcing' if you are not already doing so?

The importance of payroll

Lest we all forget, let us remind ourselves of the legal requirements. As an employer, every business must by law operate PAYE (Pay As You Earn) on the pay of all its employees (including directors for limited companies).

PAYE is the system used for calculating and collecting income tax and National Insurance contributions (NIC) from payments made to your employees. In addition to NICs for employees, the business, ie the employer, also has to pay NI contributions on wages and salaries paid.

The business, as the employer, has a duty to:

- calculate and deduct the correct amount of income tax from the employees' pay every time they are paid;
- calculate and deduct the correct amount of NIC from employees and record the amount of NIC payable by the business, the employer;

- pay to the Inland Revenue the above sums each month;
- send to the Tax Office a P35 return and P14s at the end of each tax year (by 19 May) showing the payments and deductions of the employees; form P60 is to be distributed to all current employees;
- keep a record of all pay-related documentation for a minimum of three years.

There are many other elements involved in the payroll production cycle, eg Statutory Sick Pay (SSP), Statutory Maternity Pay (SMP), pension deductions and, most recent, Attachment of Earnings Orders. Therefore, the choice you make regarding how you will carry out the business of payroll processing should be an important factor in your thinking.

Choosing your payroll provider

There are only two realistic options in how the business will have its payroll processed. The first option is to process the payroll internally (in-house), either by doing it manually or by using a PC package (manually would not be recommended unless the business is very small).

The second option is have the payroll processed externally by a payroll bureau, and for this purpose firms of accountants are included under this heading as being external.

There are advantages and disadvantages to both options, as follows.

Internally

Advantages

- *Direct access to own records.* The payroll and other authorised staff have direct access to all the payroll records at all times.
- *Overall control.* The control of the whole operation is within the business confines.
- *Possible links between software packages.* Software packages are being developed that could link your payroll to your accounting programs, so directly transferring the payroll costs to each relevant cost heading.

Disadvantages

- *Time consuming.* One/two members of staff have to spend time processing the payroll each payroll period.
- *Cost of hardware/software/stationery.* The total costs of a computer project are about four times the initial budgeted expenditure. These additional costs will include payroll updates, stationery (payslips, payroll report

paper, P60/P14s, ribbons, cartridges for laser printers) and hardware upgrades.

- *Dependent on individuals to process.* The organisation is dependent on one/two individuals being around at the right time of the month. What happens if the payroll 'expert' is away sick or on holiday?
- *Security.* Non-authorised staff may gain access to the payroll.

Externally

Advantages

- *Special staff (including helpline).* Most external suppliers of payroll services have excellent free helpline facilities and dedicated payroll bureaux employ full-time specialist staff who are there in case of query, assistance etc.
- *Computer back-up.* External suppliers of payroll services will have excellent computer back-up facilities. What happens if the business's 'payroll' computer or software goes down at the critical time of processing the payroll?
- *Security confidentiality.* Processing is performed outside the business premises so that prying eyes cannot see the pay of other members of staff.
- *Automated payments (BACS).* Although in-house PCs can have BACS software installed, the ease and simplicity with which the bureau can transmit, normally by direct links to BACS (Bank Automated Clearing Services), makes staff salary payments that much easier. Also, bureaux now routinely pay directly to the Inland Revenue, pension providers etc. by BACS, on behalf of the client.
- *Payroll administration.* Many bureaux now offer, in addition to purely payroll processing, an administration service whereby they effectively act on the business's behalf as the payroll department. This service should include dealing directly with queries from the Inland Revenue, DSS and other third parties such as pension providers.

Disadvantages

- *Can be more expensive.* On a strict basis of comparing bureau costs versus cost of software, obviously in-house apparently scores well. However, has the 'true' cost of in-house systems been evaluated, and when was the last time your business investigated outsourcing payroll processing?
- *Input deadlines.* Some bureaux, but not all, have strict deadlines which if you miss could result in late payment of your staff or additional charges being made by the bureau in order to process outside of the scheduled timings.
- *Standard input forms.* Some bureaux have standard input forms, although

many of the smaller, user-friendly bureaux have considerable flexibility over payroll input documentation (phone, fax, e-mail, for example).

Summary

If your business decides to outsource, consider carefully all the points discussed and obtain quotations from several bureaux, asking them pertinent questions in the following areas:

- Cost effectiveness (short term/long term).
- Payroll knowledge and expertise.
- Simple input procedures.
- User-friendly output.
- Automated payment methods (BACS).
- Computer back-up facilities.
- Helpline facilities.
- Set-up costs (some bureaux do not have any).

Obviously, the final decision of how you will have the business payroll processed is yours.

John Woodman has been in payroll for 17 years, the last 10 as payroll manager of The Accounting Centre. John is one of the original members of the IPPM (Institute of Payroll and Pensions Management).

The Accounting Centre is a small, friendly, national bureau, based in North London, and presently runs over 700 payrolls per month.

MITEL

3.9

Could Teleworking be Your Company's Future?

Mitel Telecom

Business dynamics are rapidly evolving. Recession, technological advance and competition from emerging nations are driving the need for constant improvements in efficiency and productivity. To stay ahead of competition and provide added service to customers, organisations must consider more flexible and adaptable business strategies.

Greater access to affordable, easy-to-use technology has given organisations the opportunity to benefit from these more flexible working patterns in delivering service improvement and innovation. No longer is it essential for knowledge workers to be located in the office, as more companies consider teleworking as the tool to carry them forward into the new millennium.

Teleworking – from home, at a local satellite office or on the move – is now a feasible, cost-effective and practical proposition. Remote access technology is now 'plug and play'.

This chapter is written for those considering the introduction of teleworking into their organisation and is by no means a universal remedy. Based on a study of teleworking commissioned in May 1998, and including case studies or quotes from forward-thinking organisations, who have adopted teleworking eg Scottish Widows, Canon UK and Enfield Council, the guide examines the business case for teleworking, discusses business benefits, and highlights some of the issues to be considered.

This chapter has been adapted from Mitel's publication *A Director's Guide to Teleworking in Britain.*

Teleworking is by no means an inexpensive solution; the initial capital investment and change management costs are undoubtedly high. However, savings on expensive office space, greater location flexibility, productivity gains and staff retention can be significant. An increasingly important objective for companies implementing teleworking is that of actually solving their skills shortage. With a recent research report by MORI claiming that British captains of industry view the issue of skills shortage as the third most serious problem facing their companies, the benefits of teleworking have become increasingly clear. Also, the environmental benefits of reduced commuter traffic and pollution are well documented and enhance the positive image of the company.

At Mitel, we have found the business case for teleworking increasingly clear. Services can be more easily provided outside normal office hours, employees can be located nearer their client-base, experienced and valued staff can be retained despite relocation or parenthood and recruitment of the best available staff can extend far beyond the traditional geographical limits.

Our senior managers have been teleworking for many years. Our early start can be attributed to having the specialist skills in-house to install and implement it. It is only in the last few years that affordable plug and play remote access technology has opened up practical cost-effective teleworking solutions for permanent employees in any type of organisation, not just technology companies. Competitive pressures mean that organisations of every kind can no longer afford to ignore the opportunities that teleworking can offer.

We hope you find this chapter helpful in assessing the business case for teleworking and in developing your corporate teleworking strategy.

Teleworking Britain is a study into the adoption and acceptance of teleworking within British business, based upon research commissioned by Mitel, conducted in May 1998. The research explores the changing methods of working. Both employers and employees were asked for their opinions and experiences of such issues as trust, control and evaluation, corporate policy, culture and feasibility. Both the Times Top 1000 Companies and a sample of SMEs were interviewed and the results reported independently. Within this chapter, for ease of reference, a mean figure has been used.

Facing up to reality

Workplace dynamics

The digital society has brought about a radical change in the dynamics of the workplace. Organisations are capitalising on information technology to gain added value and competitive advantage. Until recently, teleworking has only been feasible for the few; but the developments in technology now mean that teleworking is a realistic option for every type of organisation: for you – and your competitors!

The initial capital outlay may not be insignificant, but this can be outweighed by the added value in terms of delivering a better, more flexible service, increased competitive edge, and higher productivity, combined with inherent cost savings such as office space and staff recruitment. A management approach based on trust with clearly defined, measurable outputs creates the necessary basis for teleworking. This approach has the additional benefit of providing far greater understanding of the work being undertaken by teleworkers and managers.

Corporate and economic issues

Current working practices were designed to meet the needs of mass production, based on a large number of people in a centralised location. However, with the growth of information-based jobs, the reasons for working in the same place, at the same time, all the time, disappear. With the increase in high city rents, shortages of key skills and ever-increasing congestion, the concept of teleworking has excited attention as a competitive and economic market advantage.

Who is teleworking?

With various definitions of teleworking in common use, figures from different research studies cannot easily be compared. However, the general impression to be gained from a number of studies is that although the incidence of teleworking is still fairly low, there is a growing trend in the Western economies.

Here in Britain, the Spring 1997 Labour Force Survey counted teleworkers for the first time. Defined as someone who works at home or who uses home as a base, working with a telephone and a computer, and who has worked at home at least one day during the reference week, the survey reported that 987,000 people (four per cent of the workforce) are teleworking for their main employment. Mitel's study, Teleworking Britain, shows that 27 per cent of office-based employees telework in some capacity with a further three per cent soon to follow.

In the European Community as a whole, the incidence of teleworking appears to be low. A recent EC study on teleworking reveals that teleworkers form only 0.1 per cent of the European labour force. However, some European governments are beginning to play a central role in encouraging teleworking. For example, Norway is charging tolls on its roads to discourage commuting.

In the US, where government is actively encouraging the uptake of teleworking and where teleworking is considered an important element of its clean air policy, some 4.5 per cent of the labour force are already teleworking. Los Angeles hopes to have 10 per cent of its office workers telecommuting by the year 2000, in order to reduce commuting by car and thereby cut smog and other pollution.

There appears to be considerable scope for Great Britain to significantly increase its uptake of teleworking and to reap the associated rewards; as shown, preparedness for the idea of teleworking here leads the rest of the EU. For example, the specialist Oxford consultancy, Strategic Workstyles 2000, forecasts that 25 per cent of jobs in the UK could be done by teleworkers. The Telework, Telecottage and Telecentre Association (TCA) believes the scope is higher; it estimates that as many as 50 per cent of non-manual jobs in this country could be teleworked. Only 30 per cent of those interviewed by Mitel were unable to telework, as their roles involved direct customer interface. 41 per cent did not or had not considered teleworking, therefore potentially, a staggering 70 per cent of roles could be teleworked.

Getting ahead of your competitors?

Even if your own organisation is not yet teleworking, your competitors may already be realising the business benefits. In Teleworking Britain, over 30 per cent of companies interviewed identified improved competition from lower overheads as the most important benefit from teleworking.

In the US, Ernst & Young's hotdesking scheme turned its accountants and consultants into part-time teleworkers with the objective of reducing its office space by 50 per cent. Several major forward-thinking corporates in this country have introduced teleworking schemes for significant numbers of employees. These include Bass, British Gas, BT, Cable & Wireless, Canon UK, Coca Cola/Schweppes, IBM, National Grid, Royal Bank of Scotland and Scottish Widows.

BT has provided remote access capabilities to some 15,000 staff, including 2,000 home-based teleworkers. IBM supplied 13,000 UK staff with PCs, printers and fax-modems so that they could work remotely. Hewlett-Packard is typical of the growing number of organisations that are equipping their mobile workers with a portable teleworking kit – a laptop with modem, a mobile phone, and even a mini video camera!

Many more corporates are beginning to put a teleworking strategy in place or are undertaking pilot studies. The public sector is also taking an interest. According to the TCA, some 20 or more local authorities are operating teleworking schemes of one kind or another, including Birmingham City Council, Cambridgeshire County Council, Kent County Council, and the London Boroughs of Brent, Enfield and Sutton.

Teleworking Britain highlights that almost 50 per cent of those companies not currently teleworking do not because it 'is not company policy' with around 25 per cent stating that they had not thought of teleworking as an option.

It's no longer 'Off to work we go'!

Stuck in the past?

Talk of 'going to the office', 'commuter traffic' and 'the rush hour' seems such an inherent part of our culture that it is easy to assume that workers have always commuted, and that commuting is simply a fact of life. But commuting is a relatively recent phenomenon. It is only since the Industrial Revolution and the expansion of industry, when large numbers of people moved from the country to the cities, that it has become common for large numbers of workers to gather in one place to work – and for those workers to be constantly watched over by bosses to ensure that the work is done.

With increased emphasis on self-motivation and personal choice, better education levels, flatter management structures and management by results, the 'us and them' approach is no longer appropriate. There is no longer a need for knowledge workers to be physically overseen and they no longer need to sit at the same desk on the same site every day in order to do their work. Managers and their teams can work in different locations and still achieve their objectives. Indeed, in many instances, it has been shown that people can achieve higher levels of performance when they telework.

With the emergence of affordable, easy-to-use remote access technology, it is increasingly recognised that simply getting the job done is far more important than where it is done.

Gridlock

The Department of Transport recently predicted that road traffic will increase by 38 per cent over the next 20 years. In cities across the country, the speed of traffic is now slower than it was in the last century. Commuting is already having a major negative effect on employee productivity and costs.

According to the TCA, the average person in the UK takes nearly five hours per week simply to get to work. For London, you can double that figure to an average of ten hours commuting every week and nearly seven out of ten commuter journeys are by car. The situation can only worsen as congestion increases. More people working from home or local satellite offices will mean not only that time is not wasted in traffic jams, but that industry can travel the country much quicker and customers receive goods without delay.

Case study: Scottish Widows

'Productivity is high and work quality is excellent. The staff really enjoy teleworking and are constantly extolling the virtues'

Gill Price, Area Manager, Virtual Life Office, Scottish Widows.

Scottish Widows is capitalising on the benefits of teleworking to provide a first-class, flexible administration support service to its 24 hour, 7 days a week direct sales operation. The team of 30 teleworking staff are based at home 100 per cent of their time: 23 work full-time and seven part-time. They support a team of sales representatives and a call-centre based in Edinburgh.

The teleworking scheme started back in 1993 when Scottish Widows launched its direct sales division with a network of eight branches, each with its own on-site admin/support staff. Gill Price, who is now area manager of the Virtual Life Office, was its first full-time teleworker. Gill was responsible for the team of support staff in all eight branches. At the same time she began to build a small team of home-based support staff.

Constantly adapted, improved and enhanced as mistakes were made and learned from, the teleworking scheme proved so successful that the teleworking staff were able to take on tasks traditionally performed by the on-site staff. After two years, in 1995, the eight branches were closed, in favour of all the admin/secretarial support work being done by teleworkers.

Home-based teleworking makes it easier to support a round-the-clock function and allows Scottish Widows to recruit the best staff for the job. The company has been able to recruit staff who would not be available to work in the traditional branch set-up due to inappropriate location or to family or caring commitments.

The scheme is very popular. 'At the outset the big attraction for staff was the home-based flexibility and the opportunity to work part-time,' says Gill Price. 'Since teleworking has become more widespread, potential staff members are attracted to a very interesting job coupled with a different way of working.'

The essentials

Every teleworking solution will be different, depending on the organisation, its people and its objectives, but in essence, many of the principles of change management apply.

The following checklist highlights the main aspects that need to be embraced:

- Board level commitment from the start.
- Clearly defined objectives.

- A clearly documented scheme.
- Effective management.
- Mutual trust.
- Careful investment in technology and technical services.
- Data security procedures.
- Sufficient support for teleworkers.
- Continued communication.
- Full integration of teleworkers.
- Regular feedback and appraisals.
- Regular training and development.
- The flexibility to change, improve and re-evaluate.

Why teleworking makes sense

Although the initial investment can seem high, various studies undertaken over the past decade or so have demonstrated that teleworking can increase productivity and cut costs, as well as helping to reduce environmental pollution from traffic. These lower costs will be felt over a period of time, but only once the initial costs of setting up the scheme have been met. Undoubtedly there will be savings, but substantial ones will only be realised if significant numbers of employees become teleworkers, enabling premises to be closed or dispensing with the need for costly office expansion.

Increased productivity

Teleworking can have a marked impact on productivity. According to the TCA, teleworking can increase productivity by anything from 15 to 60 per cent. These productivity gains reflect the significant benefits to employees that teleworking can bring. *Teleworking Britain* emphasised this issue with over 20 per cent of employers feeling that their company either did or could expect an improved quality of work, and 25 per cent stating that it would definitely lead to increased productivity.

Teleworking avoids the time-wasting and often frustrating commute to the office and it is far more convenient. Teleworkers can start work feeling fresh, rather than worn down by traffic jams, inconsiderate behaviour on the roads and public transport delays.

Benefits to employers:

- increased productivity and quality;
- wider pool of skills;
- reduced costs;
- employee benefits;
- environmental benefits.

Working remotely, away from the office, can mean fewer distractions or interruptions – less background noise and fewer people walking by or dropping in. Teleworkers can therefore get more done. In addition, the quality of their work often improves and where in-work travel time can be reduced, that time can be put to more productive uses.

Another major reason for the productivity gain is that teleworkers tend to lose fewer days off due to illness than office workers. Their exposure to germs may be lower; commuting on crowded public transport and working in crowded offices can spread illness. In addition, where an office worker might take the day off for a cold, teleworkers will often carry on working.

These factors can lead to increased motivation: more effort is put into teleworking than office working, resulting in a rise in productivity.

Benefits to teleworkers:

- start work feeling fresh;
- fewer distractions;
- less time off for illness;
- less time wasted on in-work travel;
- freedom to juggle home and work commitments;
- freedom to work at own pace;
- freedom to dress casually;
- more time to enjoy life;
- increased motivation;
- better quality work.

Wider pool of skills

Where circumstances change, teleworking is a very effective way of recruiting and retaining skilled, experienced and expensively trained employees. The US telephone company Pacific Bell calculated that if they had introduced teleworking a number of years ago, they could have kept a third of the systems analysts they lost through relocation and other problems. In Mitel's research, 30 per cent of companies felt that teleworking gave them access to a wider pool of skills that often were not available within a reasonable location to offices.

For example, if your office is relocated due to a merger, teleworking allows you to continue to employ staff who cannot or will not move home. Or where a valued employee has to move further away, for example because of their partner's job, that employee can continue to work for you remotely. It allows you to recruit the best candidates available, even if they live outside your traditional catchment area – in a different region or even overseas. And teleworking also offers a viable solution to existing and prospective employees who are housebound or who have domestic commitments, such as parenthood, during normal office hours.

Securing the best candidates

- If you have to relocate.
- If an employee has to move away.
- To fit work around domestic commitments.
- To recruit housebound workers.
- To recruit skilled candidates living too far to commute.

'Teleworking has allowed us to recruit the best people for the job, regardless of location or domestic commitments.'

Gill Price, Virtual Life Office, Scottish Widows

More resilient and reliable workforce

If your workforce does not have to commute to work, they are guaranteed to be at their desks at a certain time. They are not affected by bad weather or transport problems. So you don't have people turning up late – or not at all – with the inevitable excuse of traffic jams, cancelled or delayed trains, snow drifts or public transport strikes.

Flexible service

Teleworking makes it far easier to vary the number of hours worked each week, and easier to spread these hours over any time of the day or night. This means you can offer your customers a more flexible and responsive service that meets their needs at any time and in any place.

Reduced costs: office

If teleworkers are working even part-time from home or on the move, then central office desk space can be shared under a hotdesking system; less office space is needed, along with less parking space, and costs come down. For an expanding business, the introduction of teleworking can provide a practical alternative to the upheaval and costs involved in moving to a larger office space. It can also allow smaller companies to expand more quickly, without incurring major capital investment costs.

In the long term, the cost savings will normally outweigh the costs of setting up systems in employees' homes, and any heating and lighting costs reimbursed to home-based teleworkers. The savings will normally also outweigh any costs incurred in establishing and using a local hub or satellite office, as these will normally be situated in lower cost locations than the central office.

Reduced costs: travel

A study undertaken in 1997 on behalf of the Department of the Environment, Transport and the Regions, by the Home Office Partnership, analysed the work patterns of 2,367 Cambridgeshire County Council staff. It was found that by using a range of teleworking opportunities these staff could in total reduce their commuting time by 70,000 hours a year and their in-work travel by 900,000 miles.

Teleworking can dramatically reduce an organisation's in-work mileage and therefore cut fuel costs, especially for mobile workers such as service engineers and representatives. Instead of being required to start work at the office before going out on the road and to go back to the office to collect the paperwork for their next assignments or meetings, mobile teleworkers can access information remotely and thereby cut down on their in-work travel. There may also be a saving on company cars – fewer vehicles and lower mileage will mean lower maintenance costs.

Where are the major savings?

- Less office space.
- Cheaper local hubs/satellites.
- Lower in-work mileage.
- Lower company car maintenance.
- Fewer company cars.
- Reduced parking.
- Avoidance of losses due to public transport strikes.

Environmental benefits

Teleworking is a practical and immediate solution to some of the environmental problems associated with commuting and car use. A massive 85 per cent of UK travel is by car and 40 per cent of that is travelled by commuters. BT's *The Economics of Teleworking* estimates that if the proportion of full-time teleworkers increased to 15 per cent of the workforce, fuel consumption would decrease by a dramatic 2.7 million gallons every working day. The result would be a massive reduction in the volume of exhaust fumes polluting the air we breathe.

Teleworking tends to use less energy resources than conventional office environments. It also encourages rural development with employees able to work from homes, local telecentres and satellite office in rural areas. This in turn is cheaper for the employer.

In time, it is claimed that every UK organisation will have to produce an environmental policy statement and establish their own environmental auditing team. It is likely that teleworking will form a major element. In addition, future governments may introduce other measures to reduce congestion. In preparation for this, organisations would do well to put new ways of working in place that reduce reliance on the car.

Meanwhile, organisations that are seen to be initiating practical action to protect the environment and minimise pollution are likely to enjoy a more positive corporate image, particularly among customers, shareholders and suppliers. Teleworking can therefore form a valuable part of your environmental policy.

Is it worth it?

It is important to assess in advance the costs and benefits of your proposed teleworking plan. A formal cost-benefit analysis may be difficult to achieve as many of the costs and benefits are hard to quantify, and they may vary from one individual to another. But an informal assessment of the costs and the benefits can be made as far as is possible.

Firstly, it is necessary to assess how likely it is that your proposed scheme meets company objectives – the financial and productivity value of that achievement to your organisation, the motivational benefits to your employees to make it succeed. A value can also be put on any office cost savings, travel cost savings and productivity increases delivered by teleworking.

These benefits need to be balanced against any costs associated with the changes being introduced, the likely levels of heating, lighting and telephone costs reimbursed to employees, and of investment in equipment. The cash costs and benefits of changing to teleworking will also need to be calculated for each individual employee. In most instances, teleworking results in financial savings for the teleworker, even if these are relatively small.

Costs and benefits

Corporate:

- financial savings;
- competitive edge;
- value of achieving objectives;
- productivity increases;
- equipment costs;
- costs of change;
- reimbursed teleworker costs.

Individual:

- travel costs savings;
- value of extra time;
- value of flexible working;

- reduced clothing expenses;
- any associated extra costs.

The most common objections

Why managers are careful

'They'll be out of control!'

When teleworking is discussed among managers in non-teleworking organisations, one of the most frequent fears is loss of control. However, a study for the Department of Employment showed that 75 per cent of teleworking managers interviewed found no major difficulties in managing their teleworking schemes. Mitel's research shows that under half of employers perceive this as an issue.

A climate of mutual trust is essential. Managers must trust their team's commitment to their jobs, to quality, and to the organisation. Where managers are still managing the work process rather than the outcome, successful teleworking will require a change of management style. But those who already manage by results will be well equipped to manage teleworking, as the main techniques will already be in place.

In *Teleworking Britain* approximately 80 per cent of employers were found to feel that they could trust their teleworking staff.

> *'The staff members are very well pleased to be appointed. They are not likely to risk a job opportunity such as this by being untrustworthy.'*
>
> *Gill Price, Virtual Life Office, Scottish Widows.*

'Surely teleworkers will be less motivated and less loyal'

Many managers predict a fall in employee motivation and loyalty for teleworkers compared with on-site employees. However, the reality seems to be that teleworkers are more loyal and more motivated than their on-site counterparts and according to the research only 15 per cent saw this as a problem.

> *'At the heart of our success with home-working are our enthusiastic, committed staff'*
>
> *Colin Bullworthy, Homeworkers Leader, Enfield Council*

'It will be hard to monitor productivity and performance'

In many teleworking schemes, productivity has risen dramatically and less than a third of employers were concerned about this issue judging by Mitel's research. Management by results allows productivity and performance to be measured more easily, and where there are particular issues individual teleworkers can be evaluated more closely.

'I can foresee problems with technology'

Knowledge workers already rely on technology to carry out their work. As long as organisations invest in proven technology and put in place sufficient technical support, there is no reason why technology should be any more of an issue than it is for on-site employees. The research shows that under a quarter of companies are concerned about this.

Why employees are hesitant

'I will feel left out'

When prospective teleworkers are asked for their views on teleworking, isolation is one of the most common fears, approximately 80 per cent in Mitel's research. They believe they will miss out on the corporate culture – finding out what others are up to and sharing ideas. But with regular scheduled team meetings and informal gatherings, there is no reason for teleworkers to feel left out.

'I'll lose out on training development and promotions'

A successful teleworking scheme will put in place clear and regular procedures and structures for assessing individual training and development needs, providing the necessary programmes, discussing the opportunities, and informing teleworkers of vacancies as these arise. Teleworking Britain shows that under a third of employees fear that they will lose out on personal and career development.

'I won't have all the information I need'

Where employees already use the Internet and corporate intranet to obtain information, it will be just as easy to access information remotely, once the right technology is in place. Where employees are relying on paper-based information for their work, this will probably need to be converted into digital form so that it can be made available remotely.

'They won't think I'm as important if I'm not at the office'

For teleworking organisations, teleworkers are just as important as office-based employees. Organisations need to make every employee aware that it is corporate policy for off-site and on-site workers to be treated equally. Teleworkers should be invited to meetings and social gatherings in the same way as their office-based counterparts, and given the same opportunities.

'I won't be able to keep home and office life separate'

It is preferable for teleworkers to create a separate work area – in a spare room or little-used space. 73 per cent of those interviewed for Mitel expressed this as a concern. Teleworkers quickly learn to adopt strategies to keep others out of the way while they are working. Initial training can highlight the most effective and appropriate strategies to use. Where it proves impossible, employees may need to stay on site.

First things first

Why introduce teleworking?

If you are to get everyone committed to the idea from the start, you'll need a very good reason for your organisation to introduce teleworking – or you may need several good reasons. *Teleworking Britain* shows that of companies not currently teleworking, 10 per cent had plans to do so in the near future.

Set clear objectives

- Keep ahead of competitors and increase competitiveness.
- Reduce office space and overhead costs.
- Increase employee productivity.
- Increase flexibility.
- Gain access to a wider pool of skilled workers.
- Retain employees.
- Base employees nearer to clients/customers.

The fundamentals

Organisations of any size and in almost every industry sector can take advantage of teleworking for their office-based knowledge workers. Many organisations already think nothing of having location independent field sales forces, yet they remain unconvinced of the rationale behind allowing more of their employees to be based independently.

Once you have decided to consider teleworking, you need to make sure there's a corporate willingness to change. Widespread teleworking represents a fundamentally new approach for most organisations. Even if your organisational chart is already flat, and you already manage by results, there will still be significant changes to be made throughout the organisation.

One of the biggest issues affecting the adoption of teleworking is a lack of corporate willingness to change, and around 70 per cent of companies interviewed for Mitel have not thought about teleworking or have a negative corporate policy.

As with any fundamental change to corporate policy, it is essential that it is driven from board level. Once commitment at the most senior level has been agreed, an organisation must work to ensure that employees at all level understand the rationale and business drivers behind the new policy. Without this commitment and clear understanding, the chances of success are considerably reduced.

As the scheme is developed, each stage needs to be agreed, so that it can be integrated within the corporate culture, via a documented teleworking programme that includes details of best practice techniques. The objectives must be clear and concise and the scheme needs to be discussed with employees to gauge their general reactions as well as their individual reactions and attitudes to teleworking.

Get people on board

- Corporate willingness to change.
- Commitment at the top.
- Director level responsibility for teleworking initiative.
- Top-level agreement at each stage.
- Part of corporate culture.
- Documented programme highlighting best practice.
- Employee involvement.

'Enormous support from my immediate manager was of paramount importance.'

Gill Price, Virtual Life Office, Scottish Widows.

What type of work is suitable?

- Office-based, particularly knowledge workers;
- any level;
- anything not requiring daily office-based face-to-face contact with customers or other employees;
- results-led;
- varied, not monotonous.

Teleworking can embrace every level of office job; from clerical to senior management. Organisations have developed teleworking schemes for many different types of work, even work that has initially been considered completely unsuitable.

Any role that does not require continuous face-to-face contact with other people at your central office is suitable for teleworking. However, the work needs to be suitable for management by results – for example the achievement of mutually agreed targets, deadlines or stages. If the work requires 'time-sensitive' exchange of information and work (ie the time constraints would not allow for it to be exchanged by courier or mail), it must be capable of being exchanged by phone or electronically.

It is best if the work is varied rather than monotonous; teleworkers have found that repetitive routine tasks can lead to feelings of isolation and demotivation, even where there is plenty of contact with colleagues and central office.

In control and in touch: remote management

Set clear targets

Managers need to agree responsibilities and targets with their teleworkers. Studies show that deadlines and target dates should be relatively short – between one to six weeks – to provide sufficient motivation and maintain productivity. The ideal timescales will vary according to the individual and the project. A longer-term assignment can be broken down into a number of short-term goals and deadlines.

Trust

Trust is one of the most important ingredients for successful teleworking. Managers need to be able to develop and maintain a relationship of openness and trust with their team despite not seeing them on a daily basis.

As most humans tend to try to live up to other people's expectations of them, a relationship of trust and of high expectations in terms of their loyalty and commitment to the organisation is likely to generate increased trustworthiness, loyalty and commitment. Only 20 per cent of employers in Mitel's survey felt strongly that they couldn't completely trust their staff.

Integrating the team

It is vital to take active steps to ensure that all teleworkers feel they are an integral part of their team and just as highly valued as every other member. Managers must encourage a sense of equality between all team-members, wherever they are based. An important element will be regular communication and meetings with all members of a project team.

Evaluation and motivation

Like everyone else, teleworkers need to know where they stand and whether they are doing a good job. Not only should teleworkers remain part of regular staff appraisal and development schemes, managers should also give frequent feedback and positive reinforcement to teleworkers. Without regular feedback, performance may be affected.

Support systems

Teleworkers need to have just as much back-up and support when things go wrong as their office-based colleagues. So, systems need to be put in place to help them cope with anything from equipment failure or information overload to deadlines they cannot meet or difficult clients. The introduction of a mentor would be useful to help new teleworkers through the first few months. This will be someone to share concerns with and who will provide a direct link with what's going on in the office.

IT support

Your IT department will have to change the way it works to be available to provide help remotely. No longer can the IT department be called up from the basement to resolve any technical hitches. Solutions will need to be provided clearly and concisely over the telephone, from relatively minor questions to upgrading software.

Agreeing the hours

You will need to decide how many hours each teleworker should spend where. Studies have shown that it is often best for teleworkers to spend at least one or two days a week in the office in order to keep in touch with what's going on.

Training

With teleworking it is no longer possible to lead by example as staff could be many miles away or on a different continent. Training needs to be built into individuals' appraisals and reviewed to ensure that teleworkers are apace with their site-based colleagues.

Tips for managers

- Trust your teleworkers.
- Keep in regular communication with team meetings.
- Give regular feedback on performance.

- Offer frequent positive reinforcement.
- Set clear targets and short-term goals.
- Ensure integration with organisation.
- Establish teleworker support systems.

> *'For a good manager, managing a home-based team is no different to managing an office-based team. The staff are appraised and managed in exactly the same way as office-based staff: ie on attitude, productivity, etc. We have had no problems with managing our teleworkers.'*
>
> *Gill Price, Virtual Life Office, Scottish Widows.*

Of the companies currently implementing teleworking that were interviewed for *Teleworking Britain*, a quarter have made specific arrangements for staff to be supported by senior management, with other companies ensuring director-level responsibility for the initiative.

Who will be right for teleworking?

Selecting those employees most likely to succeed with teleworking is not a clear-cut matter. There is no real way of knowing whether a particular individual will be suited or unsuited to teleworking until they try it. However, there are a number of qualities that can help with teleworking.

For example, teleworkers need to be self-disciplined enough to get down to work rather than be distracted. They will need to be able to motivate themselves to do not just the tasks they enjoy or find easy, but also the work that they would rather not do. They'll need to have a mature independent approach, rather than relying on others to solve problems for them. Above all, they must be trusted to do the work properly and with the organisation's interests at heart.

> *'Having recruited both office-based and home-based staff for many years within the financial services industry, I maintain that the qualities required are one and the same, ie hard-working and a good work ethic. But a self-motivated, disciplined worker who is able to work alone is more likely to succeed in (full-time) telework'*
>
> *Gill Price, Virtual Life Office, Scottish Widows.*

Teleworkers must be able to manage their time well so that they achieve their goals in the agreed time, by prioritising their tasks and avoiding time-wasting activities. It goes without saying that good communication skills are essential.

Nevertheless, an employee may have all these qualities and simply be unable to function well when they are away from the constant human contact of the office. Some teleworking organisations make use of trained career development counsellors or psychological tests to help assess whether

- social gatherings or outings;
- intranet site;
- special clubs and newsletters;
- encouragement to network informally;
- office as 'pop in' centre.

'In addition, as head of the division, I meet up with our teleworking staff at regular half-yearly team meetings. I also ensure that staff are kept well abreast of such things as divisional and corporate goals and developments. And meet personally with the supervisors at least once a month – both individually and as a group.

Gill Price, Virtual Life Office, Scottish Widows.

Hotdesking

Hotdesking encourages a sense of belonging. It helps to ensure that teleworkers feel that they have the same right as everyone else to be in the office. A hotdesk provides a place where the teleworker is entitled to be when in the office, where they are not in the way or wasting time.

Time in the office affords them the opportunity to discuss issues with colleagues, solve problems, exchange ideas and contribute to the success of the organisation. It gives managers the time to discuss evolving issues and changing corporate objectives.

Ongoing evaluation

It can be tempting for managers to feel that teleworkers may not be as productive as they would be in an office environment, where their work can be supervised more closely. But managers should be reassured by the fact that teleworkers tend to be more productive than their office-based counterparts and often produce better quality work. If work is measurable then evaluation is simple.

Since the introduction of teleworking Rank Xerox has reported productivity improvements of up to 60 per cent, and a 1992 survey of 250 major organisations by Oxford-based Strategic Workstyles 2000 found that those organisations employing teleworkers saw an average increase in productivity of 45 per cent. Mitel's research validates this, with approximately half of those interviewed stating that increased productivity and improved quality of work were two of the most important benefits from teleworking.

In the final analysis, just like any other employee, teleworkers know that if they do not perform, then their teleworking position will be reassessed.

Evaluation methods

1. Feedback from clients/customers: you may already be assessing the service you give to clients, for example via telephone research or questionnaires, or on a more ad hoc basis If appropriate, this type of research can also be used to highlight individual performance.
2. Time sheets: if the work is difficult to monitor in any other way, you can ask teleworkers to fill in time sheets on-line.
3. Analysis of output: work can be analysed for a period of time to ensure it meets the agreed standards and timeframes.
4. On-line evaluation: in some circumstances, it is possible to evaluate productivity by on-line monitoring. This should be agreed in advance with teleworkers.
5. Regular progress reports: managers may find it helpful if teleworkers write up regular progress reports, weekly or monthly.

A suitable environment

The only physical requirements for teleworking at home are to have sufficient space for a desk and a chair where the teleworker can work safely, comfortably and undisturbed, and with adequate light. They may also need space for any reference manuals and for storing any paperwork, perhaps in a lockable filing cabinet.

It is preferable, but not essential, for the working area to be kept entirely separate from the living area. Noise and disturbance levels should be bearable and other members of the household must be prepared to accept the teleworker working from home.

Normally the teleworker will assess for themselves whether their home would be suitable for teleworking, perhaps via a self-assessment check list. This will help to ensure compliance with health and safety regulations.

> *'It is important to ensure that the home-based location is suitable. Every home-worker's address is visited before an appointment is offered, to satisfy us of the suitability of the working arrangements'*
>
> *Colin Bullworthy, Homeworkers' Leader, Enfield Council.*

Dealing with information

Avoiding information overload

The amount of information available today is colossal. A recent report by Reuters claimed that around 1,000 books are published internationally every day, and the total of all printed knowledge doubles every five years. However, Reuters pointed out that too much information can lead to information overload, occupational stress and dramatic loss of productivity.

When organisations have teleworkers, information overload can be even more of an issue. With employers keen to ensure that their staff are fully aware of everything that is happening, numerous emails can be created to keep everyone up to date. This can actually cause more problems.

Creating an effective information strategy that extends to teleworkers is vital. It will help minimise the exposure to irrelevant data and ensure that your teleworkers have just the right amount of information needed to do their jobs effectively. An information audit will reveal the information they actually need, where this information is, and how teleworkers can access it in the most efficient and cost-effective way.

Where a corporate intranet is used to publish information, a corporate policy with strict rules, procedures and formats should be agreed and adopted. This will allow the information to be indexed and cross-referenced just like a library, with a built-in search engine so that employees can quickly identify the information they need.

Email is also another area of concern. Reuters reports that at present it is not unusual for someone to receive 60 emails a day, and senior people in large multinational organisations may typically find more than 200 emails waiting in their electronic in-baskets in the morning.

While email can represent a vital communication tool, if people receive large numbers of messages, they may simply go unread. A corporate email policy detailing guidelines on email use will help to avoid email overload. It is best to limit the use of email to specific and urgent messages between individuals, rather than as a means of circulating information of general interest to groups of people. And incoming emails can be categorised into urgent, file, or ignore.

Knowledge management

Knowledge management should also play an important role in your information strategy. The accepted wisdom is that much valuable knowledge lies trapped inside employees' heads. This includes know-how, workarounds, solutions and other relevant information.

If this knowledge can be made easily available to others it will avoid other employees needlessly re-inventing the wheel, and everyone will then be able to move forward on the organisation's collective experience.

The casual opportunities for knowledge-sharing are likely to be even fewer for teleworkers than for office-based workers. Knowledge-sharing should also be encouraged across the organisation, possibly through a knowledge management scheme which offers incentives such as increased status – knowledge-sharers should be held up as good examples to be admired and emulated.

Protecting your information

Precautions over data security and confidentiality will need to be taken, just as for office-based work, and teleworkers will obviously need to comply with the Data Protection Act.

To protect sensitive corporate information, strict security procedures will need to be put in place so that confidential files and records can only be accessed by those authorised to do so. Teleworkers will need to be trained in any security procedures.

To protect their work over time, teleworkers will need to be trained to save their work regularly and to back up all files held on the hard disk before switching off their computer. In addition, it is advisable to invest in equipment with in-built protection from power surges and power cuts.

Hooking up to the office

Teleworking schemes rely on technology for communications and information exchange. It is developments in the remote access arena, the use of ISDN (Integrated Services Digital Network), the Internet, email and the integration of computers and telephones, which make teleworking a practical alternative.

Your teleworkers may be able to work wherever they happen to be by simply taking out their laptops, plugging them into the phone system, and logging onto the Internet, and thereby accessing the corporate intranet, with its library of data and information. The nature of the role will dictate the equipment specification and, in general, any piece of equipment used for teleworking should be supplied by and remain the property of the employer.

Before you buy, check the equipment is:

- essential for the work;
- easy to use;
- reliable;
- easy and quick to maintain and repair;
- compatible with your organisation's other systems;
- ergonomic and safe.

Connection with the outside world

It is recommended that in addition to an employee's private home telephone line, the employer provides a separate telephone line for work. This not only enables the employee to distinguish between personal and work calls, but also allows the employer to pay directly for work-related phone calls, ensuring against any perceived tax benefits to the employee.

Call forwarding

With teleworkers often travelling a great deal, it is recommended that the organisation invests in a call forwarding or a 'hotdesking' application. This ensures that all calls made to the individual's DDI (Direct Dial Inward) line are automatically routed to where they are located. If this is not felt necessary, a 'find me anywhere' personal numbering service, offered by one of the many telephone service providers, serves the same purpose.

Mobile communications

For more mobile teleworkers, there may also be a need for a mobile phone with data facilities to enable communication and access to information from any location. This ensures that the employee is always contactable, that urgent information reaches them and that they are able to respond immediately.

Voice mail

To provide cover when the teleworker is not at their desk or available on their phone, a corporate voice mail system is essential to take messages. Not only will this ensure that all calls are answered, but it will also provide another way of messaging colleagues. Many of the more advanced voice mail systems allow users to set distribution groups on their systems – just like with email. It is now also possible to integrate or unify voice mail and email messages so that users can access both message types at a PC or using text-to-speech from a phone.

Fax

Many PCs now offer an integral fax facility. This is likely to be the most cost-effective way to proceed, rather than investing in a separate fax machine.

Remote access technology

Remote access technology, in the form of an intelligent remote access card, can connect a PC or multiple PCs, phones and fax machines to an ISDN line in the most cost-effective way. An ISDN line allows faster dial up into other networks, including the Internet, and faster voice and data transmission. The business drivers will dictate the amount of integration required – single or multiple users needing high speed file transfer; database, email, Internet and e-commerce, either via the corporate intranet or externally through the Internet.

The corporate intranet

A corporate intranet is a secure internal corporate network that uses similar technology to the World Wide Web. An intranet can form an important and invaluable part of a teleworking scheme and can hold vast amounts of corporate information. Acting as an instant-access corporate library, it offers a highly efficient way of giving teleworkers access to all your up-to-date internal documents – from company reports, industry intelligence, and supplier contact details to company handbooks and internal telephone directories to operational data stored in your data warehouse. It can also offer access to external subscriber information services.

An intranet can serve as an electronic filing cabinet. Information to be shared by teleworking teams or workgroups can be posted at separate dedicated sections of your intranet. It can also act as an electronic notice board, so that all your news items and staff notices can be posted up. In addition, a news flash facility means you can highlight urgent information or messages on-screen for teleworkers.

Webcasting is another useful way of sharing news and information to teleworkers over your corporate intranet. Webcast software automatically monitors large numbers of Websites and other information sources for content that matches the user's agreed requirements. This information can then be 'pushed' to the teleworker's desktop at agreed intervals: once an hour, once a day, once a week.

Information can include press cuttings, articles of interest, and news footage on video. Content can be tailored to each individual's specific needs. And an alarm can be set to be triggered automatically by certain events or changes, for example if share prices hit a certain level.

The Internet/World Wide Web

The Internet offers access to information wherever you happen to be based. When used with a good search engine, the Internet offers an easy-to-use and convenient way of researching and retrieving information. To make use of the Internet a viable proposition for your teleworkers, it is essential that they each have a powerful PC and high-speed modem to minimise the time spent accessing and downloading information.

You may also want to consider other software tools such as filters and storage management systems to help limit the amount of information your teleworkers have to sift through to obtain the data they need.

Technology issues

Avoiding technology problems

The software used by teleworkers should be managed in just the same way as that of on-site employees. As new upgrades become available, these should be installed on teleworker and on-site equipment at the same time so that all employees are using the same version.

Help!

It is vital to give teleworkers easy and fast access to immediate technical assistance and support over the phone via a helpline, be it your own internal helpdesk or a service that you outsource. This should provide extended cover so that help is available whenever your teleworkers may be working. Whereas office-based workers may be able to ask a colleague to help them solve a technical problem, teleworkers will rely heavily on telephone support.

Who should invest?

It is best for the employer to supply any equipment. This makes it easier to arrange maintenance and insurance, easier to ensure health and safety standards are met, and easier to minimise compatibility issues.

Equipment maintenance and insurance

A maintenance contract will need to be put in place so that equipment can quickly be fixed if it fails: normally your office maintenance contracts can be extended to cover equipment used elsewhere. All equipment will also need to be fully insured: equipment can normally added to the employer's insurance policy.

Getting started

Will it work for you?

Introducing such radical changes demands a step-by-step approach.

Feasibility study

Conduct a feasibility study and outline the business case, including the strategic, operational, competitive and cost advantages to be gained. If it appears that gains are insignificant – don't introduce teleworking! The objectives of the study are to develop a business case to identify any main problems that will be encountered and afford solutions; gain top level management commitment and support and assess the overall potential for telework

Identify suitable roles

Before developing the pilot, clear ground rules need to be established and clearly defined. Research into the legal and health and safety needs should be conducted.

Pilot project

An experimental pilot project will enable you to assess the benefits of the scheme more accurately. You can use it to trial different scenarios for different users and different demands. This will help to highlight the most appropriate approach to meet your needs, and will pinpoint any adjustments that need to be made before finalising the details. You can then implement a permanent scheme on a gradual roll-out to different departments, different levels of workers, or different work-groups.

Select suitable staff and train them

The best workers to involve in a pilot scheme will be the 'old hands' – valued employees with plenty of experience of your organisation and who are keen to try teleworking. They will have the enthusiasm to help make it work and to suggest modifications and improvements where necessary. They will also be the first to outline their training requirements!

Monitoring and evaluating the pilot

Even if your ultimate aim is for a full-time teleworking scheme, it may be preferable to begin with a part-time scheme: with staff spending two or three days a week based at home, at a local centre or travelling about, and the remaining time in the office.

Training and preparation

Teleworkers and their managers need to be prepared for the requirements of teleworking through a programme of training. This can consist of workshops, shadowing experienced teleworking colleagues and mentoring. Staff may need training in the following areas:

- how to manage teleworkers;
- how to communicate effectively on the phone;

- how to use the technology;
- how to find the information needed;
- time management and work prioritisation;
- self-motivation;
- avoiding information overload.

What should go into the employment contract?

In essence, contracts for teleworkers and on-site staff should be broadly similar as they are often undertaking the same role. However, the following aspects may need to be added to your teleworkers' contracts:

- hours when the teleworker is expected to be available at their remote desk;
- hours when the teleworker is expected to be in the employer's office;
- health and safety considerations;
- claimable expenses eg for heating, lighting, postage, stationery, etc;
- responsibility for the employer's equipment;
- equipment maintenance/service contracts;
- equipment and liability insurance.

Tax issues

For a full assessment of the tax implications of teleworking, it is best to consult your accountants regarding current legislation. One example is that for tax purposes it is essential that the employer formally instruct the employee to work from home rather than from the employer's offices, and to use the employer's equipment at home. The employee will then be able to claim a deduction for related heating, lighting and telephone costs or travel expenses, or for any equipment they provide: these should not form part of the teleworker's taxable income.

Is it meeting your objectives?

Long-term monitoring

It is important to set up a system for monitoring your teleworking scheme and reviewing it over time so that changes and adjustments can be made to improve the scheme – be it in the pilot stage or an integral part of your corporate philosophy. You will need to set up benchmarks so that you can compare the status quo before you start a scheme with the results achieved.

You can also conduct regular research among your customers, your teleworkers and their managers to obtain feedback on the general principles of the scheme as well as each individual's experience and levels of satisfaction.

You can circulate regular questionnaires, use telephone research, and also get your teleworkers and managers together for informal group discussions.

This approach will help to highlight any adjustments that need to be made, for example in procedures, technology, data accessibility or information sharing. It will also help to assess the longer term benefits and implications of teleworking for your organisation. You may find that some teleworkers will want to revert to being office-based if their circumstances change, or when they reach a different phase in their lives.

Improving the scheme over time

- Make changes where necessary.
- Establish benchmarks.
- Measure results.
- Regular questionnaires.
- Telephone research.
- Group discussions.
- Assess long-term benefits.

Mitel Telecom Limited is the UK subsidiary of Mitel Corporation. Founded in 1971, Mitel is a major international voice and data communications supplier with headquarters in Ontario, Canada. In 1998, turnover reached 888.5 million Canadian dollars.

The company employs over 6,335 people worldwide and has 56 regional facilities, including manufacturing operations in Canada, the UK, the USA and Sweden.

An early pioneer of computer telephony integration, Mitel's core competency continues to be real-time voice communications. With more than twenty years' experience, Mitel ranks among the world's leading suppliers of real-time call control solutions. It is also an industry leader in the growing trend toward voice and data network convergence.

Mitel's Gandalf division provides a range of remote access solutions, which provide ISDN connectivity for individuals, small organisations and larger organisations.

Part 4
Expanding the Marketplace

4.1

Targeting New Markets to Maintain Export Momentum

Dr Allan Groden
Managing Director,
Sanmex International

We are proud of the dramatic progress we have made at Sanmex International since embarking on a major expansionist strategy in 1990.

Over the past eight years, we have broadened our sales horizons across the globe and at the same time enhanced significantly our position in the domestic market. Sanmex now exports to over 40 countries and supplies charm-label and own-label to most of the UK supermarkets.

A combination of innovative production techniques and astute marketing has underpinned an outstanding sales performance at home and abroad. But despite this impressive track record of sharp growth in a highly competitive sector, we have no intention of resting on our laurels.

It is essential to guard against complacency and to be alive to the possibility of new business opportunities, wherever they arise.

The strength of sterling in recent months has had serious consequences for many exporters and illustrates the danger of focusing on a narrow range of markets. At Sanmex we responded to the currency challenge with a flexible and energetic strategy.

A swift response

We quickly identified the economies where the strong pound was likely to stifle business prospects and set our sights on emerging markets with more favourable monetary conditions.

Morocco, Brazil and New Zealand are now among the countries where Sanmex products sell strongly as a result of the decision to widen our export net.

We have not deserted countries in Eastern Europe which have served us so well in recent years. Russia, for instance, remains an important market and the demand for Sanmex products there continues to rise.

In 1997 the Russian market still accounted for a substantial part of total export turnover, which increased 42 per cent on the previous 12 months.

But it was crucial that we successfully broke into new markets to broaden our export base and minimise the danger posed by a strong pound in established European markets.

Our export team has also investigated the possibility of market entry into Far Eastern countries, but depreciation in local currencies has temporarily halted plans for a concerted sales campaign.

We are now gearing up for the next challenge to face the export industry – the introduction of the 'euro.' From as early as January 1999, companies may be required to trade in the new currency of the European Union in certain markets, and our team of executives is already investigating the likely impact of this historic reform.

In order to sustain our high level of export activity we have increased investment in personnel and technology. Service to our customers has been improved with the appointment of an export executive who is fluent in German and French and of an assistant who is skilled in ensuring that our products reach their destinations speedily.

They have joined our Russian- and Czech-speaking export director in driving forward a sales strategy that continues to exceed set targets.

Investment in technology

Recruitment of key personnel has been coupled with the adoption of leading-edge technology to strengthen the performance of the department.

We have recently installed state-of-the-art software that will streamline complex documentation and accelerate the processing of information to customers and officialdom.

Sanmex's decision to launch a sales campaign in 'cyberspace' is also paying dividends, with the rate of serious enquiries from potential overseas customers to our Website increasing all the time.

Our commitment to developing a world-class export strategy has been recognised in prestigious competitions. In 1995, Sanmex received the TrailBlazer Award, partly sponsored by the *Herald* newspaper, for the steps we took in developing new markets to replace those in decline. In the same year, we also won the International Executive Scheme, a competition run by the Glasgow Development Agency designed to boost export potential.

These accolades encouraged us to develop our proactive approach to export activity. The heightened level of activity in the face of tough market conditions, particularly over the last year, emphasises that the decision back in 1990 to pursue new international markets vigorously was correct.

Establishing a high profile at the sector's leading international trade show has been vital in promoting our products in the global marketplace.

We have gained substantial new business and many new customers from maintaining a strong presence at the annual Private Label Manufacturers' Association Exhibition in Amsterdam. The 1998 event produced many positive leads that will result in further export growth.

A joint project with the University of Strathclyde has also helped us build up our export expertise and provide valuable experience to tomorrow's marketing executives.

Firms, all small to medium-sized, were chosen to take part in the pioneering programme in which six international marketing students worked with company executives to devise a detailed export marketing plan.

It has been a valuable learning experience for both sides in the partnership and we will continue to seek new ways of assisting marketing students and increasing our own bank of export knowledge.

The Sanmex strategy for further export success

We have made great strides in our campaign to increase our customer base throughout the world. Expansion plans to enable the plant to cope with the increasing demand are well advanced and we can look forward to the future with confidence.

But we know that success is not guaranteed and we will continue to pursue new markets, invest in skilled staff and the latest technology, and study the movements of the money markets to ensure that Sanmex stays one step ahead.

Managing director, **Dr Allan Groden**, is the son of Mr Louie Groden, who founded the British Products Sanmex Company in 1932.

Sanmex International has built an outstanding reputation for producing and delivering high-quality goods to an ever-increasing portfolio of clients in Britain and overseas.

The firm is a family-owned business and one of Scotland's fastest-growing manufacturing companies, specialising in the production of liquid and aerosol household and personal-care products.

Sanmex currently employs a workforce of 220 and is planning to increase production following the acquisition of land adjoining its plant in Rutherglen, Glasgow. The purchase brings the total site occupied by the company to 12 acres and plans are well under way to build a new facility that will increase warehousing, liquid and aerosol filling capacity.

4.2

You Don't have to be Big to be Global

Express Engineering

North-east company the Express Group has ambitions to be a world-class organisation working on a global basis.

It is already one of the most dynamic companies in the precision engineering industry. It is also one of the fastest growing, with aims to almost double its current annual turnover to £60 million and more than double its workforce by the year 2001.

Managing director Chris Thompson believes that this is a very achievable goal for the group of specialist businesses which has a strong focus on profitable growth through 'delighting' its customers with a fast, cost-effective and efficient service.

Based on the Team Valley at Gateshead, one of the UK's most successful business parks, the group will grow over the next few years in two direct channels: first by increasing market share within existing sectors, but secondly by targeting industrial and manufacturing markets around the world – that is, by operating on a global platform.

'This may be unusual, possibly unique, given the size of the company and the conservative sector in which we operate,' said Chris Thompson. 'But with the advent of modern digital communications, particularly compact disks and the Internet, it is perfectly feasible. A key part of our future development will find Express cooperating with a growing number of other like-minded business partners at home and abroad in strategic alliances.'

The group is already collaborating with partners in the USA, Europe and the Far East.

'We are working virtually globally by creating a bridgehead to new and bigger markets using a low-cost and shared-risk strategy which a few years ago would not have been possible,' added Chris Thompson.

The pace at which such alliances can be set up has been facilitated by the capability of the Internet to compress time and distance. But it has been enhanced by the fact that the companies are small enough to enjoy an open and honest dialogue at the highest level.

'The speed at which negotiations can take place in such circumstances leaves other, usually larger, companies standing. At the end of it all you need a legally binding document, but the lawyers are in the background rather than at the forefront,' said Chris Thompson.

The group's first joint venture was set up with Omega Plastics of the USA, based in Detroit. It took 18 months from Express first setting out to find a partner company to establishing a joint office in the UK. Six months later, after joint marketing, training and skill swapping, the joint venture's turnover was approaching £1 million.

Omega is one of the world's leading companies in the field of rapid tooling and the venture brought its special 'time compression' and 'bridge to market' techniques within the reach of Europe for the first time. 'At first we had difficulty persuading would-be customers that we could deliver machine tools for new products within weeks rather than months. Pretty quickly we built up a bank of satisfied clients who could confirm the inconceivable was indeed possible,' said Chris Thompson.

The benefits are obviously reciprocal and Express has made inroads into US markets through its product design arm, xpd. The company has already set up an office in Minneapolis.

'While Omega's rapid tooling expertise has astonished companies within Europe, our ability to develop products from concept to manufacture within the group has impressed the Americans,' said Chris Thompson. 'It may seem an obvious point, but it is essential from the outset to be up front about what's in it for both sides of the alliance.'

When it comes to going global, there are a number of important elements on which Thompson and his team at Express will not compromise. Partners must have their own strategy for growth, they must have excellent IT capabilities and they must have a cultural synergy.

'The cultural fit is crucial,' said Chris Thompson, 'and we have turned away from potential partnerships because the fit did not feel right. But when I first walked into Omega in the States, I actually felt at home.'

He is careful not to let the group forget that there are fundamental trading factors behind its global strategy – the fact that companies are shedding non-core activities and reducing their supplier base, and the need for customers to get their products to market quickly and to reduce costs through value engineering.

'Utilising the strength of the Express Group and our trading partners, we can provide engineering solutions that can add value to a customer's business wherever they may be in the world,' he said.

The ability to make a difference globally is indicated by the group's amazing performance in the export market. In 1995, Express had zero exports, yet three years later they represented over 20 per cent of group sales, with business growing in such countries as the USA, Germany, Switzerland, Russia, Egypt and India.

Express Group is a solutions-led precision engineering organisation comprising ten companies that offer world class services to manufacturers. Based in Tyne & Wear, the group has started to expand globally in the past two years via strategic alliances and joint ventures.

Express was established 27 years ago by the father of the current group chairman, Chris Thompson, and now has a turnover in excess of £30 million and more than 220 employees.

4.3

Exploiting Intellectual Property

Karen Ngo
Head of Legal Affairs, Copyright Promotions Licensing Group plc

Recently, even the most pragmatic of professions has come to acknowledge the value of a company's intellectual and industrial property (IPR). The Accountancy Standards Board has introduced in a short space of time Financial Reporting Standards 10 and 11, which together make it mandatory for companies to classify separately their intangible assets on their profit and loss accounts. FRS 10 and 11 also acknowledge that, while it is difficult to ascertain the market value of certain IPR, some of the most volatile IPR, eg brands, patents and technology knowhow, are also potentially the most valuable assets of a company.

Today's companies all own a combination of a variety of IPR, ranging from patents, registered designs, registered trade marks, copyright, confidential information and so on. How a company manages and exploits its IPR could lead to its success or eventual downfall. Recently, trading simply on its name, British Airways was able to obtain valuable discounts on its purchase of a new fleet of aeroplanes from Boeing, while cosmetics company Yardley's demise was generally attributed to the mismanagement of its brand.

IPR Audit

If a company wishes to manage and exploit its IPR effectively, it has to make time in its management agenda for periodic IPR audits, find out exactly what IPR it owns and ensure that records of such IPR are constantly kept up to date. With respect to patents, industrial design, trade marks and service marks, consider if new registrations should be applied for and if existing registrations should be renewed or updated. Always keep in focus the company's current business as well as future direction, and a close eye on the industry in which the company operates and on the international arena. For example, if a company distributes copyrighted material to the USA, such copyright could be registered with the United States Copyright Registry, thereby affording the copyright owner with additional protection not available in the UK.

Or, if a company is looking to trade within the European Economic Area and Turkey, it could consider the advantages of applying for its trade marks to be registered as Community Trade Marks. A traditional company with standard distribution structures should not forget the world of e-commerce and should consider the implications of not registering its company name as a domain name.

Exploitation and advertising

Some of the most successful and growing industries – media, entertainment, pharmaceutical and luxury goods – are founded on IPR. The value of a company's IPR, unlike its tangible assets, often greatly appreciates through use. Successful brand management achieves a careful balance in building an advertising agent's dream brand that is a household name, and yet not so famous that it becomes generic and no longer identifies its origin, ie the company that makes the product or provides the service.

Conversely, a company's management knowledge and confidential information should be kept close to its corporate chest. Confidential information and knowhow can range from production methods to client databases to proposals for advertising campaigns and so on. Less sophisticated types of confidential information, though often still as valuable, may not be adequately protected by copyright law and companies must rely on breach of confidence. Hence, it is essential to put in place management systems for clearly identifying and classifying confidential information. There should be procedures for employees to treat confidential information with appropriate care and respect, ensuring that all third parties provided with such confidential information sign well-drafted confidentiality agreements with the company. All third parties commissioned by the company to develop commercially valuable material should provide the company with appropriate copyright assignments of such material. Understanding the most efficient way of exploiting a particular type of IPR is crucial to maintaining and increasing its value.

Management and enforcement

With the advent of new electronic media and the World Wide Web, IPR are becoming increasingly vulnerable to copying, theft and a variety of infringements. Where a company owns a valuable portfolio of trade marks, retaining the services of a trade mark watching service can be a necessity. Taking decisive action against infringers, including sometimes costly legal action, is an expense that successful IPR owners deem essential. Fortunately, due to the global awareness of the importance of protecting IPR, most national legislation provides varying degrees of protection for IPR owners. In the UK, trade mark owners are assisted by Trading Standards Officers, who have statutory powers to seize counterfeit articles and bring proceedings against their manufacturers. Owners of valuable IPR should also consider enlisting the assistance of national customs departments globally.

Finally, IPR owners should always endeavour to keep pace with new technology developments. Products to watch out for in the near future to assist in the monitoring and protection of IPR include digital tags, codes and watermarks, ie identity codes embedded in, for example, a piece of music, a digitised photographic image or a software program which will enable IPR owners and the police to track down counterfeit material and distinguish licensed material from counterfeit material.

The **Copyright Promotions Licensing Group plc** (CPLG) is one of the world's leading entertainment, sports and brand licensing agencies. The company has the only independent pan-European licensing operation in existence, with dedicated offices in every major city in Europe. Its extensive structure also includes international agencies servicing the rest of the world. CPLG is divided into three operating divisions: Entertainment, Sports and Brands.

The nature of CPLG's business is to select appropriate licensees (usually manufacturers or retailers) for properties or characters owned by licensors (film studios, sports bodies or brand owners).

CPLG generates revenue by receiving non-refundable advances from licensees followed by royalties per product line. The licensee benefits from a higher rate of sales from the licensed product and the licensor gains additional revenue as well as increased exposure for its character.

CPLG represents the rights of some of the world's largest entertainment and media companies, such as Lucasfilm, Twentieth Century Fox, MGM, Marvel and D.C. Thomson. It acts as agent for a considerable portfolio of entertainment properties including Star Wars, The Simpsons, The Pink Panther, Spiderman and Dennis the Menace. In

sports licensing, CPLG holds exclusive worldwide licensing rights to the EURO 2000 European Football Championships, the England and Wales Cricket Board, the 1999 ICC Cricket World Cup, the National Federation of Anglers and Holland's football World Cup player, Dennis Bergkamp.

Karen Ngo, Head of Legal Affairs, joined Copyright Promotions Licensing Group plc as an in-house lawyer in 1995. She previously practised law with City law firm Druces & Attlee, whom she joined in 1993. Karen was called to the Bar in 1991 and has a Master's Degree in Intellectual Property Law from the London School of Economics.

4.4
Brintons means Fashion for Floors

Michael H Hardiman
PR & Advertising Manager,
Brintons Ltd

Brintons launched its first ever advertising campaign in 1993 after over 200 years in business. Five years later, with three acclaimed consumer campaigns under its belt and a fourth on the horizon, the company is today the most prominent brand in its market. This success was achieved through a mixture of courage, recognition of what branding is all about, a decent advertising budget and, as a private company, the ability to take a long-term view.

The value of brands

A strong brand has an unfair advantage. Consumers make an effort to seek out known brands and have positive expectations of the product beyond the visible. For the producer, it offers increased power with retailers and attracts a price premium. Competitors can copy products but not brand values.

Back in 1993, carpet lay within a virtually unbranded market. The UK market was pretty static, with cheap imports and a great deal of price competition chasing sales. Consumers were bewildered by what was on offer, buying on price. A strong brand could attract a bigger slice of the cake, and more realistic prices. If Pilkingtons could brand glass and Perrier do the same with water, it was surely possible to brand carpet. And Brintons had positive company characteristics to justify the effort of brand building: a good reputation with the trade for quality and reliability, wide product range, good distribution, leadership in design, company heritage and a Royal Warrant. It also had the ability to take a long-term view, a benefit of its private status.

Whom to target?

According to TGI, 15 per cent of the population bought carpet each year. Five per cent spent over £500 and 2.4 per cent spent over £800 – that was 600,000 households to target with the company's high-quality products. But what sort of people were they? The company undertook market research and discovered that they were ABC1 women, aged over 35, who valued quality, were interested in the home, enjoyed the creativity of decorating, read home interest magazines and bought leading brands.

With this knowledge, a new brand positioning statement was conceived. Brintons would mean uncompromising quality and style, fantastic colours and designs, beautiful finish, top-quality materials and long-lasting, hard-wearing products. The tone of voice of the ads should be confident, aspirational, contemporary, and the consumer take-out 'beautiful carpet I could get excited about'.

The concept

With this brief, it was time for an advertising agency to be appointed. A number pitched for the lucrative business – but who should get the account? Advice received was to go for an agency that felt right to work with, not just one with a good idea. Three were shortlisted, but Cowan Kemsley Taylor came up with a ground-breaking idea, seeded by a chance remark that 'Brintons' carpet was good enough to wear'. The fashion theme was born. A dress was run up with the help of art students, Brintons' board boldly accepted the idea and CKT won the account. The vehicle for Brintons' brand building was to be imagery showing clothes made out of carpets, designed by a top designer, worn by a supermodel and photographed by a top fashion photographer. Vivienne Westwood agreed to design the six garments required for the campaign and David Bailey to take the photography. The resulting images were clean, uncluttered – and absolutely eyecatching. A small logo appeared in the bottom corner of the ads.

The initial media plan included top home interest titles and high-circulation weekend magazines, together reaching a monthly audience of 16 million readers. The ads hit the streets with much acclaim and received an industry award for advertising.

To support the advertisements, there was a limited poster campaign, an 0800 number was set up to deal with enquiries, a supporting brochure produced along with show cards showing the imagery for in-store use, and a there was a great deal of PR support. A press cuttings service proved invaluable for tracking this activity. The inspired 'clothes' theme produced huge spin-offs into the fashion world and the carpet clothes were much sought after for exhibitions, fashion shows, window displays and other promotions. This all resulted in equivalent PR value being obtained for the advertising spend. Follow-up research showed vastly increased brand recognition and improved public relations.

Moving forward

After 68 weeks and over 10,000 responses, a second campaign was launched in January 1995. This built on the fashion theme and attached it to the company's heritage. The resulting '1783' campaign ran for 81 weeks and attracted nearly 16,000 responses. Of these, 41 per cent were carpet buyers and 29 per cent bought Brintons. There was an improvement in brand recall – spontaneous recall jumping from 4 to 13 per cent, prompted brand recall from 13 to 30 per cent and recall of the ad images came in at 55 per cent (68 per cent among magazine readers). Anecdotal evidence supported this improvement, with 70 per cent of top retailers reporting increased requests for Brintons by name, a reported growth in market share and an increase in competitor activity.

A third campaign was launched in October 1996. The advertising brief was to keep the popular and valuable fashion element, but to link it with carpet in use and to increase direct response. There was an opportunity to promote small motif designs. These elements together made for almost surreal imagery, with a model perched 14 ft above the ground, her mountainous dress merging into the room set beneath. Due to the discrepancy between brand and ad recall from the last campaign, the size and positioning of the logo were changed further to make it more prominent.

The third campaign reached 7.5 million readers each month and continues to generate enquiries, though no more space is booked pending the launch of a new campaign in early 1999. The campaign was supported through advertorials in home interest titles, competitions and brochure panels to increase response. The link of the imagery into the retail environment could have been better and this will be addressed in future.

The lesson for any aspiring brand builder is to research your product, know its values, make a plan and remain focused. Market research to measure results is crucial.

Established in 1783, **Brintons Limited** is the world's largest producer of woven axminster carpets. The £100 million company has a global sales network and manufactures in the USA, Australia, New Zealand and Portugal, and shortly will do so in India. Its first Queen's Award for Export was announced in April 1998.

4.5

To Franchise or Not to Franchise?

Keith Smith
Allied Domecq

The traditional pub has been around in Britain a long time, since the Romans brought their inns to the roadsides. In recent years there has been a tremendous upsurge in the development of English and Irish pubs overseas. Many of these are run by individual entrepreneurs, whose success has attracted the attention of the big British pub retailers and brewers who, faced with limited opportunities for expansion in a very competitive domestic market, have seen international expansion as a panacea to their ills. Here we look at the experience of one company, Allied Domecq, and see if there are lessons to be learnt.

Allied is certainly no stranger to international operations. It produces and wholesales worldwide such well-known spirit brands as Ballantine's, Beefeater, Sauza, Courvoisier, Teacher's and more. Through Dunkin Donuts and Baskin Robbins ice-cream it operates an 8000-strong worldwide franchise network. Operating 4000 pubs in the UK, it is one of the biggest independent pub operators, with well-known retail brands such as Firkin, Big Steak and Mr Q's.

Allied's initial ventures into overseas pubs came in the late 1980s, a long time before it became fashionable, and were largely built up in Eastern Europe, a legacy of the fact that Allied was heavily involved in exporting beer to that region. Over a period of five years, Allied built its John Bull Pub franchise to 60 pubs in Scandinavia, France, Italy, Russia, Hungary, Poland, the Czech Republic, Ukraine and even Beijing. For the franchise Allied supplied the beer, a reproduction English Victorian pub, training, promotions and expertise in pub retailing.

In recent times, Allied has moved away from John Bull franchising and concentrated on building its own owned and operated Firkin pubs. It now has two in the Netherlands (Utrecht and den Haag) and three in Paris. In an era when many retailers look to franchising as a way of international expansion, why does Allied pursue a different route?

It was really a number of factors and experiences coming together that made us reassess the strategy.

John Bull was not a brand that Allied operated in the UK. It was a caricature of an English pub for export only. A potential franchisee could not see a JB pub in operation in the UK to begin to understand the concept.

Allied had also never run an international managed pub system and thus had no evidence that the concept would work overseas. It is difficult for a franchisor to prove to a potential franchisee that this is a sound investment.

Allied also took the brave step of selling its UK brewing interests to Carlsberg. It could thus no longer tie up a franchisee on a beer supply agreement, while its UK competitors could supply an integrated beer and pub package overseas.

So why did it take the Firkin chain overseas as a managed system? Firkin is a tried and tested UK pub brand now numbering 200 outlets in its home market. With its real ale, often brewed on the premises, traditional fit-out and caring but casual and unpretentious staff, it represents all that foreigners love about English pubs. Through the JB experience, Allied had also learnt the crucial lesson of focusing in on a limited number of markets and building critical mass to cover the local overheads quickly, so further development is currently being limited to the Netherlands and France, with tentative exploration of neighbouring regions.

Allied does not rule out some sort of franchise or joint venture in the future. But it feels that it is important to establish the brand successfully in those markets first, not only to prove that it can be a financial and consumer success but also to establish its own credibility as a competent international operator.

Keith Smith is Director of Operations for the Firkin Brewery (Europe) and John Bull Pub Company at Allied Domecq.

Allied Domecq plc is a major international branded drinks and retailing company employing 55,000 people and providing hospitality and enjoyment around the world.

Part 5
Sources of Finance

5.1
Finance for Growth

Norman Price

A successful business needs enterprise, a good business proposition, capable people and a market. But without finance these are not sufficient. Growth will require more finance; the faster the growth, the more the need. The simple questions that need to be answered are:

- 'What exactly do you need the finance for?'
- 'Where will it come from to achieve that growth?'

Uses of finance

Consider the 'real' balance sheet, not to be confused with the accounting version. Money goes into:

- long term tangible assets – buildings and machinery;
- short term and revolving tangible assets (working capital) – stocks, debtors;
- intangible assets – investment in products, markets, systems, people.

Specific sources of finance

Some finance is unallocated to particular uses, such as equity and overdrafts. However, there is a growth in specific funding where the cash is tied to the asset. Asset-based finance is becoming more competitive and imaginative, particularly as new entrants from Europe and the USA without a branch structure see it as a way into commercial lending.

Long-term assets

As far as possible it is not wise to fund fixed assets with equity or overdraft. The former is too scarce and expensive and the latter too precarious. Mortgage, lease or HP options are preferable but will not normally cover all the cost. It is probably better to avoid buying and to rent if possible, even if it is slightly more expensive, rather than use scarce money. Note that this is contrary to the view of an established individual or business not short of cash for 'growth' and wanting safety.

Working capital

The cheapest cash is credit from suppliers who, as they have a vested interest in your success, may be prepared to advance credit if they share your vision. It may be worth paying more for this financial support. A cash-starved company I know was importing a cheaper component for cash compared with 60 days' credit from a local supplier!

Debtors are becoming easier to finance (up to 80 per cent), with factoring and invoice discounting growing rapidly both in activity and acceptance, although you need to shop around to get support for small debts, capital goods or services. This can fund rapid growth of turnover and may even make it cash positive. Become the equivalent of a retailer who sells for cash and buys on credit!

Stocks are more difficult to fund, but some specialist factors will consider finished goods separately, or as part of a package.

Intangible assets

When a business is growing, it is nearly always investing, ie spending money now for some future returns. This may be a salesperson who takes six months to generate new customers, designers working on the next generation of products or employees being trained. These are all investments with little tangible worth, even when they are about to generate a return. They are not susceptible to asset-backed funding and need finance based on future cashflows, which requires judgements carrying risk and requiring reward. Equity is the major finance source, but others exist.

- Grants support some product development, like the DTI Smart scheme or European programmes. Local initiatives may provide minor sums for productivity improvement, systems and exports. Your local Business Links will probably be the best adviser.
- The Department for Education and Employment small firms training loan scheme (SFTLS) is available from banks for up to £5000 per person and is underwritten by the government. It is not well publicised. TECS and Investors in People also have many schemes.

- Other companies may not only be involved financially but also provide other resources. This corporate venturing can be in the form of research contracts for new products, distribution agreements with shared benefits, equipment suppliers contributing to development etc.
- Intellectual property rights (such as patents) have a real value and can be used as security, although there are risks for both the borrower and the lender. They could also be licensed or assigned for a fee and a royalty paid.

Your intangible assets have a value, even if they are not on the balance sheet. Keep a record of their cost of generation.

General sources of borrowing

Overdrafts

These continue to be the most popular form of borrowing, often nominally calculated against the value of particular assets, eg 50 per cent of debtors, 10 per cent of stock, and secured as a floating charge. They are convenient, flexible and reasonably cheap – but only pay for what you need. They are not reliable, as they are repayable on demand and they are also conservative in valuation. They are tending to be replaced in part by some asset-backed finance.

SFLGS

Using the DTI small firms loan guarantee scheme, banks may lend money up to £250,000, depending on circumstances and backed by a government guarantee. The proposal must be soundly based, with a sensibly predicted cashflow for repayments, but does not require asset backing.

Sources of equity

Borrowing alone will probably not be able to fund growth needs and, indeed, should not, as unprofitable activity could rapidly lead to insolvency and collapse without the cushions of equity. The sources are as follows.

Own

The prime source of equity is, of course, the founders. Unpaid work provides 'sweated equity' and its value should be noted, because it demonstrates commitment and investment. The new CGT regime means that any capital gain after 10 years may be taxed at only 10 per cent.

Buying Out or In

Asset-based finance, including factoring and invoice discounting, was used in over 20% of all UK management buy-outs and buy-ins during 1997 - an increase of 8% on the previous year. A company's book debt is very often one of the largest assets on its balance sheets. Converting book debt into available cash is what factoring and invoice discounting are all about; and the cost of using these services can also be extremely attractive - often on par with a bank overdraft facility. Small wonder that many financiers are looking increasingly at using factoring or invoice discounting when they put together a buy-out or buy-in deal.

Factoring or invoice discounting in management buy-outs is very much part of a tailored package. The purchase of a business can leave a new management team with very little working capital with which to drive a business forward. As Smith & McLaurin found (see story below), factoring can provide a substantial cash injection at the very moment it is needed most.

Factoring Labels
Smith & McLaurin's Buy-Out A Success

Scottish-based Smith & McLaurin has stamped its independence on the world of label manufacturing. Using factoring to help fund a management buy-out, Chief Executive Dr Peter Emerson and his management team made the successful purchase from parent company Rexam Plc.

Smith & McLaurin was founded in 1849 as a family business. After being bought and sold by a number of companies during the last thirty years, the firm was eventually purchased by Rexam in 1993. The company's main plant at Kilbarchan employs over 145 people and Smith & McLaurin labels can be found on containers and bottles in stores across Europe.

During 1997 Smith & McLaurin began to consider a management buy-out from Rexam. Price Waterhouse, the company's accountants, agreed that factoring could be one method to help finance a buy-out and Lombard NatWest Commercial Services stepped in to offer their expertise.

Factoring is a means of funding based on the value of current invoices rather than past performance or fixed assets, so it is ideal for buy-outs and providing the new company with essential working capital which increases as business increases.

Lombard NatWest offered Smith & McLaurin Non-Recourse Maturity Factoring which guaranteed credit on 100% of sales proceeds on a pre-determined date. The deal was struck and Smith & McLaurin successfully completed their buy-out from Rexam in March 1998.

The company already has plans to focus on a host of new markets throughout Europe including event and travel ticketing.

To do this the new Smith & McLaurin has recently invested around £1million in new technology, and revamped its working practices to optimise efficiency.

The firm, with forward-thinking now watch-words in the boardroom, intends to position itself at the cutting edge of its industry.

Dr Peter Emerson says: "Smith & McLaurin has a long and successful past but our attention is firmly fixed on the future.The new Smith & McLaurin is technologically advanced and has a myriad of exciting projects on the horizon. Thanks to the management buyout we have a new look in the boardroom and a fresh and innovative perspective on our future."

Ian Knox, the Lombard NatWest's Area Business Manager for Scotland says:

"I am delighted that Smith & McLaurin will be working with Lombard NatWest. The factoring solution we provided played a major part in the success of the management buy-out. Our expertise will now be concentrated on running the sales ledger and helping Smith & McLaurin to build for the future."

LOMBARD NATWEST CAN BE CONTACTED ON FREEPHONE 0800 711911

The decisive factor
THINK BIG
When drawing up a list of potential suppliers of factoring or invoice discounting, size and stability are important considerations.
And, for the record, Lombard NatWest are currently one of the biggest. In 1997 we handled invoices worth over £7.5 billion for our clients. We expect to handle over £8 billion in 1998.
And we enjoy the support of NatWest, one of the largest financial institutions in Europe.
But, while size is certainly reassuring, it is by no means conclusive.
We are also fast – speeding cash to clients as much as three days faster than conventional payment methods.
We're advanced – with the most up to date factoring computer system and computer links with clients in the UK.
And we're experienced enough to know all the sensitivities that are involved with trade credit – and how to handle them.
Does all this mean that we only attract big businesses? Far from it. The majority of our clients are growing small and medium-sized businesses, for whom a healthy cashflow is absolutely vital.
In other words, they think big.
For more information about Lombard NatWest Factoring and Invoice Discounting call 0800 711911.
www.lombardnatwest.co.uk/lombard
Lombard NatWest

Family and friends

It may be possible for family and friends to invest with tax relief under the EIS scheme, which is easy in documentation, saving income tax and free of CGT after five years.

Business angels and private equity

Individuals are often prepared to invest in business and their involvement may also fill an expertise gap. Networks exist – check Business Links. Again, tax relief may be available.

Enterprise funds

Many localities have small venture funds that invest up to £50,000 in equity.

Venture capital trusts

VCTs allow tax relief to individual investors and cannot lend more than £1 million to any one company. Depending on size, their minimum is usually £300,000.

Venture capital funds

The minimum tends to be £500,000 but some do less. 3i is, of course, by far the biggest and it has a regional presence. Contrary to some popular opinions, VCs do not normally take control (greater than 50 per cent forces them to consolidate) and they also invest more money (in the form of ordinary shares, preference shares and loans) than a straight pro rata to the owner's cash investment.

For serious growth they are almost a necessity, unless the company is extremely profitable.

Public offering

The AIM market, London Stock Exchange, NASDAQ or EASDAQ all allow the public to invest, but disclosure and listing requirements are onerous.

Summary

Growth requires cash. There are many sources and each company must balance them to its particular needs. Take advice and shop around, but remember that part of success is better than the whole of failure.

Table 5.2.1 summarises forms of funding.

Table 5.2.1 Forms of funding

Assets	**Specific Forms of Funding**
Long term tangible	
Property	Mortgage, rental, sale and lease back
Plant and machinery	Leasing, hire purchase, rental
Working capital	
Stocks of raw materials	Supplier's credit
Work in progress	Supplier's credit
Stocks of finished goods	Selected factors
Debtors	Factors, invoice discounting
Intangible assets	
Intellectual property	Licences
Product	Grants (Smart), customers
Process development	Equipment suppliers, local support
Market development	Minor grants, allied distributors
Training	Small firms training loan, TECS
Systems	Local grants

Norman Price is an investing chairman in growing businesses, including Bede Scientific Instruments and Pashley Cycles, and a Director of the Business Angels Bureau. He chaired the CBI working party on barriers to growth in high-technology businesses, Tech Stars, as a member of the SME and national council. He is also a part-time adviser in the DTI Innovation Unit, concentrating on finance, tax and investment issues, particularly but not exclusively for small businesses.

5.2

Getting the Best out of the Banking System

James Larholt
The Bank Relationship Consultancy

British clearing banks have recently woken up to the realisation that the margins and fees they are able to extract from their larger corporate customers have been declining. Foreign banks are not only undercutting their pricing, but have been proactively offering products that suit companies' requirements, often involving the use of sophisticated derivatives. A survey carried out early in 1998 showed that two (English) clearing banks have opened several regional dealing centres, with the object of dealing directly with customers who have foreign exchange business or surplus funds to deposit, but who wish to keep their accounts at the local branch. Customer relationship managers go out to find new business, looking for companies whose existing banking service may be regarded as only satisfactory, and who might be receptive to new banking products.

It is at this point that '*caveat emptor*' arises: how is the finance director to judge whether or not the products on offer will be sufficiently greater in value than the additional charges that their use may incur? A careful costing must be made, taking into account such situations as likely changes in business volumes, cashflow, borrowing requirements and expected periods of liquidity when estimating the extent to which the products are likely to be used. There is no point in paying high commitment fees for services that would reduce borrowing costs (or enhance yields) but would only be used for low volumes. Remember that the banker's job is to increase income from fees and interest, so if there is any doubt as to the true value of a product being recommended, independent advice should be sought.

Nothing comes for free. If the bank proposes something new that costs nothing, the customer's suspicion should immediately be aroused. Independent consultants have carried out many successful banking reviews for companies which believed that they were paying no bank charges at all, only to discover that subsequent investigations revealed huge 'hidden charges' that the banks were taking.

How can a medium-sized company best manage its own banking? Efficient cash management is the immediate area that should be addressed; surplus balances should always be invested, either by making short-term deposits or by arranging for credit balances on all accounts to bear interest. Cashflow forecasting should be broken down to differentiate between cleared and uncleared funds; a dedicated terminal link to the bank might pay for itself many times over if used effectively. The aim should always be to *leave the minimum cleared working balances on all current accounts*. A company that runs a permanent overdraft need not worry quite so much about the cleared balance, although careful management will keep the size of the debit balances to the minimum. Companies whose balances fluctuate between credit and debit need to take particular care over their cash management, otherwise they will be making unnecessarily large contributions to their bank's annual profits.

Charges for payments and receipts of foreign exchange should be monitored and be compared to those of other banks; here the use of a consultant will save time and resources. Exchange rates applied should be checked and compared to those on Ceefax or, if the budget allows, a more sophisticated screen-based service. When getting forward exchange rates from the bank, the customer should ask it to compare the forward rate to the spot and to explain any premium or discount.

If possible, foreign exchange deals and money market deposits should be done directly with the nearest regional dealing centre, rather than with the local branch. A relationship can easily be established, with no need to open any new accounts. The local branches get rates from the centres and then take a spread from the customers, in addition to their regular charges. Branches never negotiate rates – their staff are not authorised to do this – but the dealing centres are far more flexible.

The bank's advice can be sought when deciding whether or not to hedge foreign exchange and/or interest rate risks, but it should not be forgotten that the banker will want to get a deal on the book and will usually advise the customer to take some sort of immediate action. A modest fee paid to get independent advice may turn out to be a lot cheaper than using the bank's free counsel! The bank can, however, be quite useful when asked to suggest ways in which hedging can be done once the decision to do so has been taken, although the customer should only proceed to buy the product if the degree of cover obtained is absolutely clear, and if all best- and worst-case scenarios have first been considered.

Preparations for EMU by British banks should have been completed by the autumn of 1998. The better-organised banks will spend the last few months visiting customers who trade with any of the 11 participating countries, or who have medium-term borrowing or investments in any of the 10 euro currencies, giving them details of all changes to accounting and reporting systems, as well as advising them how best to amend their own accounts in order to comply. There is no reason to go overboard on this; the euro may be just another currency to a UK company. The old currencies will immediately become a sub-denomination of the euro and, under the 'no compulsion, no prohibition' rules, either can be used for payments for three years, after which comes the phasing-out period of six months. By that time, everyone should be completely at ease with it.

Companies that maintain foreign currency bank accounts may wish to open a dual currency account in those euro currencies in which they do business. This account will be able to pay and receive both the national currency and the euro. A debit entry in a national currency which is offset by a credit in the fixed equivalent amount in euro will result in an unchanged balance; the format will be for the account to be denominated in one main currency in which it will report, referring to the other currency (ie reporting in euro with reference to the national currency, or reporting in the national currency with reference to the euro). A maturing ex-forward purchase or sale of a foreign (participating) currency may be settled either in that currency, or in its fixed euro equivalent; the bank where the funds are moved will be happy to accept payment in either.

To keep costs down, a company with payments to and from the euro-zone should make sure that its bank is able to pay and receive the euro using the lowest-cost systems, as these costs will, naturally, be passed on to the customer. European payments systems are likely to become highly competitive and charges should come down as the euro makes progress. A European system for small retail payments (such as standing orders and cheques) will eventually be developed. However, many companies are using the euro as a driver to reduce the use of currency cheques or drafts. These are administratively expensive to issue, unpopular with recipients, and cheques may be prone to fraud. Companies should try to follow press reports that cover cross-border inter-bank payments systems, and refer to them when negotiating lower scales of charges with their bankers, especially if the bank takes the liberty of attempting to increase its fees for remittances.

In conclusion, growing businesses must realise that the market is going their way, and that as different banks compete for their business, there is every reason for them to play one off against another. The fact that you might have a hefty facility need not deter you; remember that the bank's business is to lend money and, by agreeing to borrow from it, you are in the position of the consumer, while the bank manager is the retailer, trying to sell you his or her wares. Further, because the bank may already be earning considerable amounts of interest from your company, there is even more reason for you to ask for item charges to be reduced. Just as the bank looks at the overall earnings it makes from each customer (interest, fees, charges and spreads), the company must look at the total amount it pays to its bank in a year, and remember that the larger the amount, the greater is its value as a customer.

5.3

Factoring for Growing Companies

Ian Fitz-Harris

Chief Executive, Euro Sales Finance

The factoring case for growing companies is easy to make when compared with the other major source of finance, the overdraft. When they look at their capital/cashflow requirements, business people are looking at their *projected* sales, needs and debts. Bankers, when they calculate how much they can lend on an overdraft, look at the *historical* audited accounts. That is, there is likely to be a two-year gap between what the business needs and what the bank will provide. This may not be so bad if the company is growing at less than 10 per cent, but successful young companies are often growing at twice that rate, which makes the situation untenable. Two years for a successful young company is the difference between a pupa and a butterfly.

Factoring and invoice discounting form the only system of raising finance based on current sales. They are the only source of finance based on the here and now and future business. The major banks have realised that the overdraft is more of a straitjacket than a support for the fast-growing company.

The Factors and Discounters Association announced a 20 per cent growth in 1997. The figure is now six times the 1988 level. The Association's figures show that there are now 22,000 British businesses using this kind of finance. In a survey by a major international accountant into small and medium-sized enterprises throughout Europe, 70 per cent said that part of their short-term plans was to find new markets for their products. This figure has been growing for the past five years. New markets are increasingly seen as being within the EU; 86 per cent of companies identified intra-EU trade as their number one target.

When you're waiting for an invoice to be paid, throw your calendar away and buy a stopwatch.

There's no need to wait months to be paid, as Barclays will settle up to 80% of your invoices within one working day. We'll free your cash so your business has the funds to grow and you stay in control. The service is available to businesses with sales of £100,000 p.a. or over. For more details telephone Barclays Sales Financing sales support team on 0800 227222.

BARCLAYS

SALES FINANCING

However, at present international factoring is only 5% of the factor and invoice discounting market. Many of the major banks are reluctant to get involved, not least because the growth on the domestic front has been so healthy.

The survey also highlighted that one of the main brakes on growth is the lack of skills, typically in the financial sector. This leads to the argument for outsourcing the sales ledger, which makes even more sense in the export area as less than 30 per cent of British businesspeople are capable of a detailed conversation in another language.

Before a growing company gets involved with a finance house, there are certain questions that should be asked:

- Does the finance house have year 2000-friendly systems?
- Can your company deal directly through an Internet link?
- Can the finance house deal with the euro?
- Does it require directors' personal guarantees, and if so why?
- How long does it tie you in, how does it justify that time?
- Does it make you pay interest on its cheques?
- Does it provide the same service on exports?
- Are you dealing with a decision-maker or just a salesperson?
- Are you impressed with the person who will talk to your customers and is it always the same person?
- Are there hidden charges?
- What do other businesspeople say about the service?

Euro Sales Finance was one of the first companies launched on the AIM market in 1995 and has been one of the most successful start-ups on that market. Its purpose is to help fund the trade of small and medium-sized enterprises, a market significantly under-serviced by the traditional players. The company was originally founded by senior managers from Kellock, the factoring arm of the Bank of Scotland. Significantly the BoS is one of ESF's principal bankers. It has grown fast, both organically and by recruiting some of the best teams and managers in the factoring industry. It now has offices in London, Manchester, Leeds and Birmingham and is about to open in Germany and the Netherlands. At present, it is lending at the rate of more than £500 million a year to over 200 companies. Largely through recommendation, the company is recruiting around 15 new corporate clients a month. This success has been recognised by the share price tripling since launch.

Ian Fitz-Harris is the chief executive of Euro Sales Finance. He is 37 and qualified as a chartered accountant with Grant Thornton. He became a director of the Bank of Scotland subsidiary at the age of 28. He left three years ago because he wanted to establish a finance house with a forward-thinking strategy.

5.4

So You Want to Have Your Cake and Eat It Too?

Paul Gee

Director of Marketing & Strategic Development, Lombard Business Finance

Asset finance could be that vital ingredient

So your business is on the up and you are experiencing the pleasure and the pains that expansion inevitably brings. Advisers and consultants of different shapes, sizes and philosophies have lectured you on strategy, hectored you on IT, preached product development and evangelised the latest management accounting thinking. But when it comes down to it, the main thing your business needs to see you through the growth barrier is more cash. Solve that little challenge and everything else will slot into place.

Financing growth is probably more of an art form than a science, and no doubt you have studied the financial runes in an attempt to decide which form of funding would be best for your business – anything from venture capital to winning the lottery. Clearly, different forms of finance have different and important roles to play – the real skill is in getting the mix right. But to bake this particular cake to perfection without cooking the books, one ingredient is often overlooked – asset finance.

In a nutshell, asset finance can provide the assets your business needs for growth:

- without blowing a hole in your capital reserves or straining cashflow;

- which allows you to work within capital expenditure restrictions or bank covenants;
- where the security is in the asset, not in any business or personal property;
- which does not take a single crumb of equity;
- which can be highly tax efficient;
- and which can be free of 'residual value' risk – you don't have to be left holding a potentially outdated asset at the end of the agreement;
- what is more, the asset can be placed 'off balance sheet' (subject to auditors' approval, naturally), thus improving your gearing, liquidity, return on assets and possibly even profitability.

That is asset finance. Once the Cinderella of the corporate finance world, asset finance not only goes to the ball, it often steals the show with a performance that can leave more traditional forms of funding looking rather staid and inflexible.

Asset finance provides growing businesses with the opportunity to acquire plant and machinery, vehicles, office equipment and so on beyond their normal ability to borrow in the conventional sense. This is because payments are made from revenue and, as finance houses are specialists in managing and funding capital equipment, their security is in the asset, ie they underwrite against the value of the asset, which does not always happen with conventional lending. There is a range of different funding options to choose from, each offering different tax, cashflow or balance sheet advantages. The up-and-coming option, particularly for larger assets, is operating leasing.

Operating leasing – the icing on the cake

Hire purchase has, of course, been around for years, but more recently the financing of fixed assets has moved up in terms of sophistication and flexibility. Advances have been very much spearheaded by market leader, Lombard Business Finance, part of the Lombard Group and Europe's largest lessor. Where previously businesses found that financing high-value and 'one-off' assets – production plant, port-side cranes, fleets of earth movers and so on – could be a real problem, Lombard's operating leasing expertise ensures that funding packages can be 'flavoured' to individual requirements. This means taking into account factors such as the pattern of your cashflow, tax year, a choice of fixed or variable rate and whether you want varying levels or initial rentals and/or a final lump sum payment – or balloon – at the end.

Strengthening the balance sheet

So why is operating leasing particularly good for growing businesses? The fact is that most forms of asset finance can benefit a company experiencing rapid growth. All have the straightforward ability to pay for assets out of revenue rather than capital reserves – so the asset contributes to the company's upward mobility and is paying for itself at the same time. Asset finance helps preserve working capital, so overdraft limits, loans or inward investment can be minimised. It is well documented that as many businesses fail due to too much growth (overtrading) as too little.

Where operating leasing really comes into its own for growing companies is its 'off balance sheet' capability. You can have the assets you need, while leaving your gearing unencumbered by the acquisition – a clear case of having your cake and eating it. Clearly, if you are trying to attract venture capital or planning to go public, the shape of your balance sheet will be critical.

What makes a lease an operating lease is the 'residual value' of the asset that is built into the calculations. Essentially, *the lessor takes the residual value risk*, and so whatever the equipment is worth in, say, five years' time does not have to be your problem. And, of course, the beauty of all forms of asset finance is that the security is in the asset, so third-party collateral is usually unnecessary. Owing to the in-built residual value with an operating lease, monthly rentals are effectively reduced, thus benefiting working capital even more.

Contract hire, so popular with vehicle fleet buyers, is a form of operating leasing. For companies that place little importance on ownership, want maximum cashflow benefits and wish to divest themselves of the burden of managing fleets of cars, trucks or vans, contract hire is the perfect solution. The saving in the administrative overhead alone is often substantial and ensures that growing companies do not have cash needlessly tied up in heavily depreciating vehicles.

Different tastes for different palates

Operating leasing is one option; here are the other main ones.

Hire purchase

Hire purchase, or lease purchase as it is also known, is more flexible than it used to be, with the provision of variable deposits and/or balloons, fixed or variable interest rates and more besides. Where ownership is preferred, hire purchase is the simple, straightforward option – you pay a deposit and at the end of the agreement the asset is yours. With hire purchase, you control the value of the asset, ie you can sell it and pay off the outstanding balance at any time. As it is a purchase agreement for capital equipment you, the customer, can claim the writing-down allowances. Here, recent government policy has provided an added benefit with the increase in First Year

You can't touch it, see it, smell or taste it.
It makes no sound, so you can't even hear it

Allowances currently 40 per cent as opposed to the more familiar 25 per cent. This is available for small to medium-sized companies* on plant and machinery (it does not cover cars) and was designed to give a boost to investment.

Finance leasing

The July 1997 Budget reduced the tax benefit granted to lessors, which could be passed on to customers in the form of lower rentals. The result was that finance leasing became less attractive. However, it still holds its own with cars. This is because rentals are calculated on the cost of the car minus the VAT. Particularly for cars with low depreciation levels, if residual values are built in as a final lump-sum payment, rentals can be surprisingly low. VAT is then charged on the rentals, which many businesses can claim back (either 50 per cent or 100 per cent depending on the usage of the car). This VAT treatment is unique to leasing.

IT equipment is another area where depreciation is rapid and finance leasing tends to be a good option, as 100 per cent of the rentals can be offset against profits and the lease is matched to the depreciation period.

Contract purchase

In the Lombard Business Finance stable this is called Triple Choice, owing to the extra options built into the end of the agreement. With Triple Choice, you have all the flexibility of hire purchase, but at the end of the period you can choose to:

- keep and own the asset, paying off any outstanding balance;
- sell the asset, pay off any balance and keep any surplus;
- return the asset with nothing to pay.

In a climate of commercial uncertainty, it often pays to keep your options open.

Sale and leaseback

Businesses can often secure an injection of capital by selling and leasing back their own assets – vehicles, machine tools etc. The cash generated can then be used to fund expansion, while the same assets are paid for out of revenues.

---

* Small to medium companies are defined by fulfilling two out of three of the following criteria: annual turnover not more than £11.2 million, assets not more than £5.6 million and not more than 250 employees.

Just deserts – matching finance to the asset

Matching finance to the nature and expected lifecycle of an asset is the strategy most likely to maximise cost-effectiveness – overdrafts for working capital, term loans for premises and plant, factoring or invoice discounting for cashflow and venture capital for new or young businesses.

Asset finance should be seen as one of a whole raft of different options. Whereas a commercial mortgage may be better for buying premises, or an overdraft for day-to-day working capital, neither of these options may offer the flexibility and manageability of an operating lease when it comes to acquiring machine tools or a fleet of vans. Certainly, the cost of funding a £50,000 machine tool or £75,000 truck would be punitive on the business – and probably hold back rather than fuel growth.

This financial specialisation can break down further. Just as certain types of banks or investment houses focus on particular financial instruments or property, so leasing companies have their specialists in particular types of fixed assets.

Here again, Lombard leads the field with a cluster of joint-venture companies, subsidiaries and special units that operate independently from, but complement, the core Lombard Business Finance operation. For earth-moving equipment, trailers, fork-lift trucks, cars, van and truck fleets, boats, technology assets, farming equipment, buses and coaches and more besides, Lombard has, or can plug into, specific expertise in the financing, managing, maintaining and disposing of these assets. Customers can be reassured that they are getting precisely the right funding for the assets they need to create growth.

Lombard also boasts the UK's largest factoring and invoice discounting company, which offers very direct finance for growth through accelerated cashflow and improved credit-management services. Both factoring and invoice discounting can be a very effective alternative to conventional lending. Equally, this kind of current asset finance can complement a typical bank overdraft (and is generally no more expensive). A combination of overdraft, fixed asset financing and invoice discounting can be a powerful cocktail for growth, as most financial eventualities are covered and the business can generate enough cashflow and working capital to keep the show on the road.

Latest market trends show an annual decline in bank lending since 1993 of 3.7 per cent, while finance house lending has grown by an average of 12 per cent during the same period. Plainly, businesses are switching to funding that can be better tailored to make the most of cashflow and tax allowances. The fact that asset finance does not usually take a charge on business or personal property must give it a certain warm, reassuring glow.

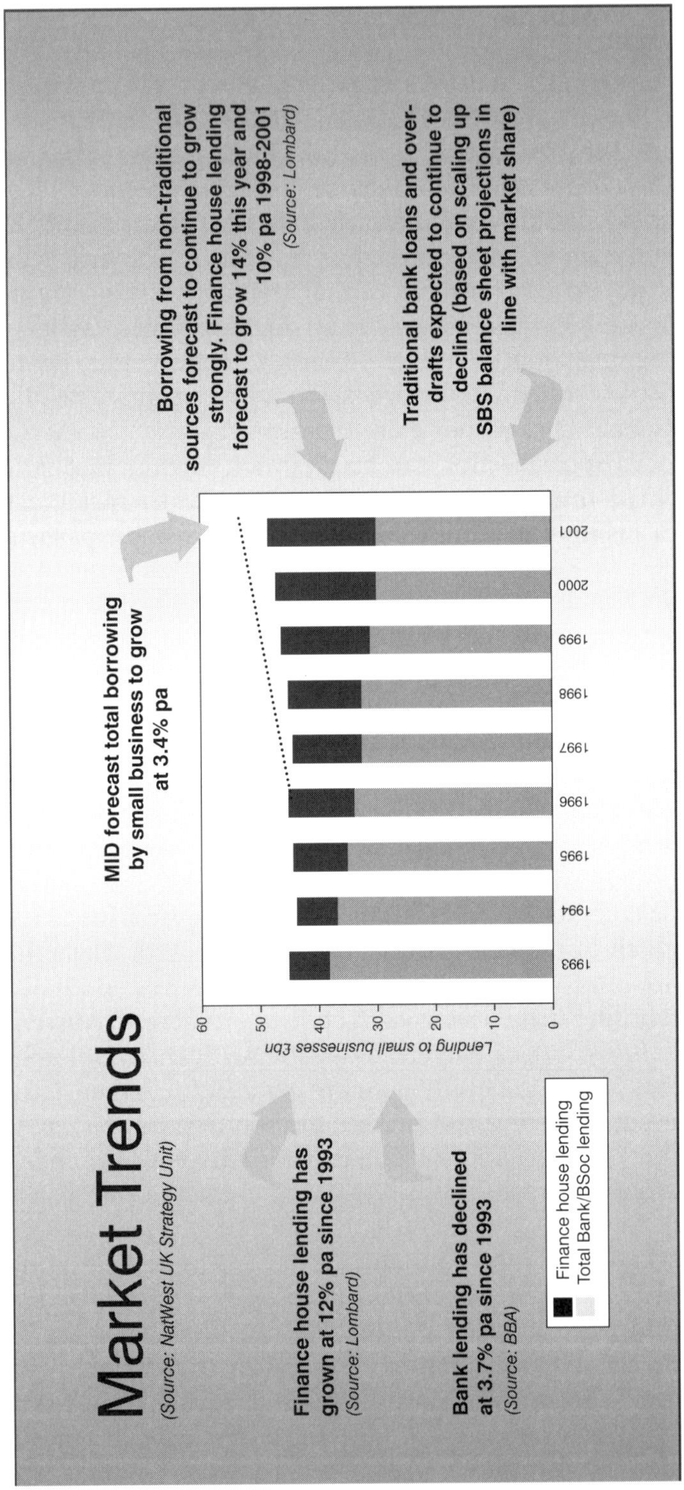
Market Trends
(Source: NatWest UK Strategy Unit)
Finance house lending has grown at 12% pa since 1993
(Source: Lombard)
Bank lending has declined at 3.7% pa since 1993
(Source: BBA)
Finance house lending
Total Bank/BSoc lending
Lending to small businesses £bn
0
10
20
30
40
50
60
1993
1994
1995
1996
1997
1998
1999
2000
2001
MID forecast total borrowing by small business to grow at 3.4% pa
Borrowing from non-traditional sources forecast to continue to grow strongly. Finance house lending forecast to grow 14% this year and 10% pa 1998-2001
(Source: Lombard)
Traditional bank loans and overdrafts expected to continue to decline (based on scaling up SBS balance sheet projections in line with market share)

Gaining a bigger slice

There is another angle to asset finance for growing businesses that manufacture, distribute or retail plant, machinery and equipment. Providing finance at the point of sale can give your operation a competitive edge. Not only are you creating the desire for your customers to buy, you are also providing them with the means to purchase. For your customers, it makes buying simpler and less time consuming and, where rates are competitive, possibly cheaper too.

In the final analysis, asset finance offers the cashflow advantages, tax efficiencies, risk management and off balance sheet capabilities (operating leasing only) that hungry, growing businesses need to feed their growth ambitions. As part of a mix of finance options, it has a key part to play in the funding and management of fixed assets.

With bank lending in decline and asset finance very much a growth industry, the pressure is on the major clearers to work in tandem with their respective leasing arms. Lombard is a member of the NatWest Group and together they hold a commanding position in the UK business market.

What customers say about operating leasing

For the right kind of assets, operating leasing can provide the right kind of funding environment for growth. Not only does it offer lower payments compared with other types of instalment finance, the lessor carries the 'residual risk' of the asset. So equipment that becomes outdated or obsolete by the end of the agreement need not be the customer's problem. But its real advantage is its off balance sheet capability. For businesses which want an attractive balance sheet while still having the assets that create growth, operating leasing is the 'cake and eat it' option.

Here is what three customers had to say about Planned Rental, the operating lease facility marketed by Lombard Business Finance, in association with their joint-venture company GATX Asset Residual Management PLC (GARM). GARM specialises in the valuation of high-value assets.

Joyce Whitham, financial controller, Classical Circuits Ltd (part of Symonds Group PLC), manufacturers of printed circuit boards, said:

> *Planned Rental allowed us to buy a lot of plant at a reasonable cost and it was advantageous on our gearing that it was an operating lease. Because we are part of a publicly quoted company, it helps create the right perception as we could keep all the plant off the balance sheet. And because it is an operating lease, this was obviously an advantage for cashflow. With a lot of equipment to buy, if we can pay for all of it within cashflow, we are not restricted in choosing between different items – we can have everything we need.*

Terry Kemp, finance director, James Latham PLC – timber importers and distributors, commented:

> *In the last few years we have acquired mainly internal mobile plant on Planned Rental – heavy trucks, side loaders and fork-lifts, around £2 million worth. Our objective is to keep our capex on our balance sheet down. In fact, we have to as part of a covenant I agreed with the bank. Now these are all off balance sheet so they don't constitute part of the capex going onto the balance sheet.*
>
> *We also had continual difficulties turning profit into cash. To reverse this process, I needed to spread the investment out over a longer term – Planned Rental gave us the best possible cashflow enabling us to strengthen the balance sheet and give us a platform for developing the business further, which I did not want to do on too much highly geared borrowed money.*

Rod Garland, finance director, WT Foods plc (La Mexicana), food manufacturer, described his experience.

> *We financed a complete tortilla manufacturing line through Planned Rental. Lombard were very good at coming in and looking at the sort of machinery we needed to buy and putting a package together over five years. I didn't want to put it onto the balance sheet so we could gain a cash advantage – keeping the cash on the balance sheet whilst not showing too many fixed assets. We are cash generative and we like to use that for expansion and funding small acquisitions. Planned Rental helped us fund larger asset additions without using up our cash reserves.*

Lombard Business Finance supports business customers from sole traders to plcs through a national network of 32 Business Centres and a central Telecentre. Specialist markets are serviced through Corporate Finance and Point of Sale teams.

Paul Gee is Director of Marketing and Strategic Development, Lombard Business Finance. Previously he spent four years as Sales and Marketing Director of NatWest's factoring and invoice discounting subsidiary.

5.5

Pricing Power – a Vital Ingredient for Ambitious SMEs

Charles Breese
Managing Director, Larpent Newton

In periods of high inflation, such as the 1980s, companies were able regularly to increase the sales prices of their products and services. Provided that they were profitable (ie revenues exceeded costs), the impact of these regular sales price increases was to produce a record of growing profits without the need to achieve growth in the volume of products or services being sold. Since the City was generally obsessed by growth in earnings per share (without looking in great depth at the factors underlying such growth), this state of affairs led to a large number of companies with very ordinary management and underlying businesses looking highly attractive to the City.

This picture changed dramatically with the arrival of a period of low inflation. Many businesses are finding it very difficult to increase sales prices in line with the cost increases that they are having to bear. Indeed, in industries such as the automotive industry, deflation is already an established way of life with suppliers to OEMs (original equipment manufacturers) being expected to achieve price decreases of, say, 4 per cent per annum.

In this new environment, the financial media have recently started to identify that most companies do not have pricing power and that companies which do have pricing power are those which are likely to be most attractive to investors. A recent article in the *Financial Times*, 'Survival of the fittest', identified 'solutions companies' as being the most attractive in the economic climate expected to prevail for the foreseeable future.

At Larpent Newton, we have been encouraging our portfolio companies to develop as 'solutions companies' for a number of years without using that title. A key feature of a solutions company is that it is able to sell its products or services on the basis of payback rather than price. Key features to enable a company to sell on the basis of payback are shown in Table 5.5.1.

Table 5.5.1 Key features of a solutions company

Feature	Comment
Innovation (this includes, but is not limited to, product, technology, marketing or company organisation)	Companies must be capable of providing solutions tailored specifically to potential customers' needs The culture required for a solutions company is very different to that required for a shrinkwrapped products company. For example, it should develop, where practicable, the various components of its products as standard modules, so that the provision of a bespoke solution comprises, say, 85 per cent assembly of standard modules and 15 per cent bespoke engineering. The latter may well generate another standard module.
Operating in business-to-business marketplace	It is much easier to develop and sell solutions based on payback to businesses rather than to non-profit organisations or to private individuals.
Providing performance products or services	This means that the supplier has a good understanding of the customers' business processes and can incorporate into its products or services features that bring measurable financial benefits to customers, thereby enabling the products or services to be sold on the basis of payback to the customer rather than on price. A recent example of this is one of our portfolio companies which develops non-destructive test instruments for incorporation within production processes in order to improve process control – one recent installation at a selling price of £200,000 generated a four-month payback for the customer. It is quite difficult for customers not to buy (even in tough economic times) when products bring this level of financial benefit!

continued overleaf

Table 5.1.1 *continued*

Feature	Comment
Achieving above average margins in relation to sector	This enables the company to continue innovating and hence maintain the virtuous circle described above. Quite often, very able engineers are good at delivering clever solutions but do not charge prices that fully reflect the value that the solutions bring to the customer and hence jeopardise a business' capability for continuing to deliver innovative and value-based solutions to its customers.
Operating in growing and/or changing markets	It is impossible to develop ambitious companies providing clever solutions if the market being addressed does not provide good scope for growth.

The UK has enormous capability for developing great platforms for innovation, the most recent, well-publicised version being the impotence drug Viagra. However, it has a poor track record of successfully exploiting these platforms commercially. I believe that the number of successes would increase if the teams involved in such innovation focused more on the measurable financial benefits that such innovation can bring to customers and developed business organisations around the innovation platform so as to deliver those benefits. The customer is primarily interested in the benefits that products or services can bring to them, not in the features.

Larpent Newton is a company focusing on investing in and helping to develop companies with the potential for:

i. above-average and sustainable growth;
ii. a solutions business culture (rather than a shrinkwrapped products business culture);
iii. capitalisation in a range of up to £100 million.

5.6
Public Equity Markets

David Browne
Corporate Finance Director, KMPG

Why consider public equity markets to fund development?

There are many reasons for growing companies to consider raising money through these external markets. These include access to funds at the time of the initial public offering and subsequently through secondary issues, an extended shareholder base, a trading facility for the company's shares and a recognised market value for the company's shares. These shares can be used to incentivise employees and issued as consideration for acquisitions. For the potential investor, the main attraction of these smaller companies is the opportunity that they present for substantial growth, although this has to be balanced against greater risk and concerns about liquidity.

The options

Other than the main stock exchange, there are additional options that growing businesses can consider.

AIM (the Alternative Investment Market) has celebrated its third birthday and has 308 quoted companies. It was set up to provide an alternative to full listing, with rules and entry criteria more appropriate to the smaller or relatively new company. For example, there can be fewer shares placed in public hands than is required for a full listing and entry and ongoing costs may be less.

OFEX is not a formal market, but a trading facility to allow trading in the shares of unquoted companies. Together with AIM, it is an increasingly popular route for small firms. Companies looking to raise small amounts of equity, usually between £0.25 million and £1.5 million, may do so through a broker who typically places shares with private clients. An OFEX facility is obtained to allow shareholders to track their shares more easily. Trades are performed off market and Stock Exchange regulations do not apply.

Other options for high-growth companies, although not widely used, include the American *NASDAQ* and its European equivalent *EASDAQ*. In line with other US markets, where companies register with the Securities and Exchange Commission, the regulatory environment is onerous and the cost of compliance high. EASDAQ targets businesses with a potential market capitalisation on admission of at least £30 million.

EURO NM is worth mentioning. It is a partnership of the junior European stock exchanges and is aimed at innovative companies with a high growth potential. Current members are the exchanges of Paris, Brussels, Frankfurt and Amsterdam. Its intention is to operate as a single 'virtual' market, providing companies with easy access to a much larger, pan-European pool of investment funds.

Owners need to be clear about their objectives and ensure that any decision is based on sound commercial judgement. The equity markets represent an excellent mechanism for facilitating the realisation of a company's real potential. However, they bring a higher degree of accountability and less flexibility that can be difficult for an owner used to a large amount of freedom.

Companies should choose the market that gives them the appropriate profile and comparatives in terms of their business sector. They also need to be able to satisfy the criteria for entry to the market. Capitalisation can be a stumbling block and not all markets are available when a company does not have the required trading record. Companies should assess what proportion of the company they want to take to the market and if their choice of market is consistent with those plans. Ongoing compliance and reporting requirements can outweigh the benefits to be derived. Flotation can be expensive and the costs need to measured against the size of the company and the funds to be raised.

Managers and shareholders should also consider the impact of a float on their own tax position. AIM, for example, preserves many of the unquoted tax reliefs, such as inheritance tax exemption, and tax-free gift of shares, but these disappear if a full listing is being sought. Once listed, companies should remember that tax planning is an important part of their new responsibilities and has a direct impact on many measures of shareholder value. Investors will judge the performance of management by their ability to handle the tax opportunities effectively and minimise tax cashflow outlets.

The smaller company sector is currently under-valued, with the result that it has been difficult for companies to float and for existing public companies to raise new finance. Furthermore, smaller companies tend to offer only a limited number of shares, which hinders their liquidity, the ability to buy or sell their shares. While private investors may be content to buy only a few hundred or a few thousand shares, fund managers usually require more and the smaller company cannot satisfy this need. Consequently, public equity companies have not been the first choice for smaller companies as a way of raising funds.

However, equity markets and listings bring profile and status and can be the ideal route for some. While there is no standard answer to the question of which route and which market, there is a logical process of decision making, where corporate and personal ambitions should be examined closely to find the right approach for each individual situation.

David Browne is a Director of KPMG's Nottingham practice. He is a corporate financier who specialises in advising the owner-managed business community.

5.7

Simply Replacement Capital

Lloyds Development Capital

In 1979, Graham Simpson and his wife founded Simply Travel, a successful, independent specialist travel business. Growing and consistently profitable, eventually they had to face the issue of how to take the business to its next phase of growth.

'Simply Travel appeals to a niche market of professional people who want a more personal service,' explains Simpson. In 1996, the company carried 26,000 customers and made £1 million profit. In 1997, it was 32,000 and £1.5 million. At year-end 1998, it should be 43,000 and £2.1 million. In 1999, the projections are that Simply Travel will carry 55,000 people.

Simpson and his wife owned virtually the whole company but for a few share options. The business was growing fast and people who wanted to buy it had approached them, but the timing was not right. What, for example, were they going to do next? It was then that a non-executive director of the company suggested bringing in an outside investor and they really started to think about the advantages that replacement capital could bring.

'You can be financially secure,' he said to the Simpsons. 'You can gather your retirement relief ...' – Graham Simpson was coming up to 50. 'And then you'll have big brother and if we can find the right kind of people, as and when you need to develop the company you'll have someone on board who can give you financial help. This will be a great help if you want to make an acquisition, sell the company or whatever you want to do then.'

'We spoke to several venture capitalists,' says Simpson, 'and it was really a question of what my gut feeling was as to who I felt comfortable selling shares to. And I felt very comfortable with Lloyds Development Capital.

'I liked their approach. It was very down to earth. They didn't try to oversell their involvement with the company. They asked a lot of questions and listened to us. I felt that we had a mutual understanding of each other, of what each was trying to achieve in this deal. And my gut feeling was that they would be supportive but would not interfere.'

One of the things Simpson did not want was to join forces with shareholders that were going to restrict him too much. 'I felt that I had a lot to offer to take the company forward; I had lots of ideas. Although I understood that a partner needed to come along and be on the board, I didn't want this to stop me growing the company. And LDC gave me the feeling that I would still be able to go ahead with my plans and ideas. I gave them a three-year projection of what I planned to do and they were very excited about it.'

He was, nevertheless, fully aware that development capitalists have the interests of their investors to think of as well. 'Every venture capitalist has an exit idea, whether it's long term – over 20 years or short term – over four or five, and Lloyds is no different to anyone else. I think there are a number of scenarios and we will consider these in the future. We are always looking at how we are going to develop and we are very much still progressing. We are continuing to expand and, for example, right now we're looking for acquisitions.'

Simpson says that if he had some advice for other entrepreneurs in growing companies like his, it would be that the most important ingredient is to find somebody – the person who represents that organisation and who sits on their board – that they can relate to: 'a partner who is in sympathy with you.'

'Sure it's got to be profitable and it's got to work, but it's also useful involving, in a sense, an outsider. It makes you justify things more,' he added. As a result of having LDC on board, Simpson says that he felt 'a little bit more keyed up' than he might normally have been. 'You can't just say that you're doing this or that because you think it's right. You have to justify it a little bit more.'

Having LDC as an experienced and sympathetic partner to work alongside proved to be a new and valuable spur for the company, as Simpson concludes: 'To be honest with you, it's made us even keener than before to continue growing a prosperous and fast-growing business here at Simply Travel.'

Following a record year in 1997, **Lloyds Development Capital** (part of the Lloyds TSB Group) has continued to expand in 1998 and is now the third most active venture capitalist in the UK mid-market sector (source: Corpfin UK, August 1998).

Targeting the UK mid-corporate market, with a typical deal size of up to £35 million, LDC supports experienced management teams operating in growing companies.

LDC provides equity funding of up to £12 million for management buy-outs, management buy-ins, institutional buy-outs and expansion financing for growing businesses across a wide range of market sectors, of which IT, Pharmaceuticals, Outsourcing and Aerospace have formed a large proportion.

Part 6

Developing Innovative Products and Services

6.1

The Inventor, his Ideas and the Pitfalls

Trevor Baylis
Baylis Generators Ltd

Many of us have skills that are useful to the inventor. For example, an accountant may have an invention, in which case his accountancy training may well be able to help him produce his own business plan. He may, like James Dyson, be an industrial designer. In such cases, those special skills would not have to be purchased or obtained when working on the overall business strategy. There are very, very few people who have all the skills that are needed to push the product, however. The inventor seems to be travelling steerage class on the *Titanic* of the economy for, as the ship sinks, he or she has to make his or her own arrangements.

The emergence of the Clockwork Radio – the options

In the case of the BayGen Freeplay radio, affectionately called the clockwork radio, I certainly had few skills which I could call on after I had created my first working prototype. I had applied for a patent as soon as I had a working model and I paid for the services of a patent attorney to put the papers together. I then started to make approaches to British companies which I thought might have had an interest in my invention. But I was horrified by the number of rejection slips I received. I started to examine myself, thinking that perhaps I was the problem and not the solution, or that the invention itself was no good. I even had a letter from an august engineer telling me that the clockwork radio, which was merrily playing in my left hand, couldn't possibly work unless the spring weighed 100 lb – and I am not Hercules.

The solution to my problem had to be sought somehow, but I was getting to the end of the 12 months' honeymoon period during which activity on my patent application could be facilitated. I, rather foolishly with hindsight, simply threw my rejection letters up in the air and went public on British television, hoping that perhaps someone would watch the programme and come to my rescue.'

Had this foolish gamble not paid off, I would not have found my business champion, Christopher Staines, who purely by chance was watching the programme. Within four days I had struck a deal. It was perfect. Christopher worked for a very large company of accountants, of which he was an acquisitions and mergers director. He made complete sense. He said that his company would work for me to fulfil my objectives, providing that it could share in the profits that might come from future opportunities. I still owned the intellectual property, my parents' name was on the product, a royalty-receiving company was formed and a large share of an international company, bearing my name, was in my ownership.

The important thing, however, was that my product champion was able to fulfil his promises to me by raising the capital needed, developing the product, establishing a manufacturing plant and, as a great compliment to me, insisted that people with disabilities of one kind or another participated in the enterprise. Christopher now works with me and our new partner, Rory Stear, full time on the BayGen Freeplay radio. Chris and Rory were able to raise a huge sum of money from the Overseas Development Administration, through Baroness Linda Chalker, and the bulk of the development capital came from Liberty Life of South Africa.

The need for greater recognition of the value of invention

Usually, the best sort of money to be obtained, is not, unfortunately, to be found in the UK. The British economy is currently losing £156 billion a year through British inventions going overseas (Hansard, House of Commons Debate, 1 May 1996). My own project has its base in South Africa. This is even though 56 per cent of the world's greatest inventions come from the UK. The Japanese tell us and we only have to look at history to see how British inventors have been shoddily treated by government and industry. If we do not finally recognise the social and economic opportunities that are being wasted purely on the basis of the nation's ignorance and indifference, then we as a nation do not deserve a future. We spend disproportionately large sums of money on what is considered to be our heritage, yet we are not prepared to make some sensible effort to reclaim the £156 billion.

Trevor Baylis is the inventor of the BayGen Freeplay radio and is establishing an Academy of Inventors.

6.2

The Value of Design

Sean Blair

Design & Communication Director,
The Design Council

Can you believe it is nearly 2000?

It seems only yesterday that coalminers were on strike, Margaret Thatcher was laying into her enemies and John Major was nervously stepping into her shoes.

Tempus fugit – and particularly so over a decade like the last. Only a few years back, 'Business Link' sounded like a filing system, 'Pentium' a 13-carat engagement ring and an 'extranet' something used by fishing enthusiasts.

Design has also changed a lot, in that time. It is more important than ever before, but still many small businesses don't seem equipped to compete in the ultra-fast, ultra-competitive, global market where, to quote Edward de Bono, 'If you don't design your own future, someone else will design it for you.'

Last year in this very same handbook we talked about Dyson, trying to inspire you all to 'Do a Dyson'. My guess is that most of you didn't, so I'm not going to bother with another inspiring case study. All I would like to do is ask three questions – perhaps for discussion at your next management meeting:

- Are you using design to move up-market, into new growth markets and to add quality, features and performance? Or are you simply using design to restyle and remove costs?
- Are you increasing the number and skills of your research, development and design capability? Or does the MD do all the NPD?
- Are you accelerating your introduction of new products and services? Or is your introduction rate declining?

These questions emerge from Design Council research into more than 200 small businesses who used design through the DTI's Enterprise Initiative.

The research, called MADRID (**Ma**rket **D**emands that **R**eward **I**nvestment in **D**esign), clearly shows that those projects which were profitable used design to improve product performance, features and quality.

Conversely, in projects which made a loss, design was used only for product styling, cost reduction, range unification or customisation.

MADRID also shows that profitable design projects used design strategically to move up-market by creating genuine improvements in product features. Loss-making projects, however, tended to move up-market merely by extending the product range, rather than improving the design.

The winners employed a higher proportion of R&D staff; more often used external expertise for product development; and introduced new products more frequently than slow-growing or declining firms.

But make no mistake – designing your own future is not easy. Using and doing design is hard. You know it; we know it.

It helps to know, of course, that for small businesses, virtually every single Business Link has a dedicated Design Counsellor who can help advise on how best to exploit the full potential of design.

However, the fact remains that in a new decade and a new millennium, organisations have to be better at designing value if they are to compete and survive.

The Design Council is the UK's national authority on the effective use of design. Its aim is to get leading organisations in business education and government to champion effective design.

Sean Blair is the Design & Communication Director. He was previously Principal of Octo Industrial Design, a consultancy he founded in 1989, with international clients including Black & Decker, Panasonic and Philips. Sean has won a number of awards for his work in design and business including the 'Livewire' Young Entrepreneur of the Year Award in 1990. He is a fellow of the RSA, and serves on the Business Link Accreditation Advisory Board.

6.3
Technology Transfer

Tim Cook
Managing Director, Isis Innovation Ltd
and Jim Shedden
Independent Technology Consultant

Challenges and opportunities to growing business

All over the world there are researchers and developers in academic, government-funded and privately funded establishments, inventing new products and processes (generically known as intellectual property or IP), some of which will be applicable to your growing business. The costs of using third-party IP are the sum of three components:

- the cost of identifying and contacting sources of relevant IP;
- the time spent developing a relationship with them and doing a deal which is usually management intensive and may well include some lawyers' bills; and
- the cost of the deal itself, which may include a downpayment, picking up patent maintenance costs and/or a royalty.

Depending on the style of management in your company, there may also be a cost in demotivating your brightest technologists, who may see some of the fun work going elsewhere or even see third-party IP as a threat.

The benefits of transferring IP to your company are that you can access technology which you may not have time or resources to conceive or develop yourself and, in general, the technology is available on a shorter timescale. An additional benefit to the company, some would say the major sustainable business benefit, is the relationship that develops between the technical staff in the company and the researchers in the academic institution.

Stages in an effective technology-transfer operation

Decide to do it

The key stage, which is often performed too late or not at all, is for the strategic managers in the relevant part of the company to decide that they really do want to license in some technology. Sometimes it is a last resort when an internal development programme has failed to deliver, in which case internal management is crucial to avoid the 'not invented here' effect, whereby the company's technical staff are not committed to the acquired technology and so its chances of successful exploitation are reduced. The skills of those managing the operations are critical. If you do not have staff with both technical and commercial skills, experienced in technology-transfer methodology, you might consider contracting in, at least for the first time you try it.

Identify the IP required

It may be that one step in a process is proving difficult, or that the company needs a new manufacturing technique to make a new component, maintain a competitive position or perhaps a completely new product is needed to add to the range. Alternatively a research breakthrough may allow a whole new area of products for the company to make and sell to diversify its offering.

Identify potential sources of this IP

Academic establishments all have an industrial point of contact (called variously industrial liaison, research support, contract office etc), so if you know an institute it is relatively easy to find the right person. Some universities, eg Oxford University which, through Isis Innovation Limited, manages the Oxford Innovation Society, are proactive in building networks and relationships. Similarly, commercial organisations will always have a contracts or commercial office to start you off. If you are not aware of the relevant research groups there are published directories of research which will point you in the right direction. Trade associations, professional associations and business libraries have also proved good sources of leads.

Unless the particular piece of IP is to solve an isolated, once only problem, we suggest that an ongoing relationship with relevant researchers may provide a valuable asset. Such relationships can be built up from trading or conference contacts, from employing graduates from the institution or from industrial-sponsored research students. We have found this latter very rewarding because, in addition to the work the student performs, the contact with senior research staff is very valuable.

Doing the deal

The stages in purchasing IP are the same as any other deal and negotiating skills are the key tools. First, ensure that you are negotiating with someone who can sign off on the deal. It is very frustrating to spend time negotiating prices with an academic and then find you have to do it all over again with the licensing officer. The more you know about your own and the researcher's negotiating position the better. For example, if there is a rule that some institute has a defined minimum deal below which the officers are not allowed to act, there is little point demanding that they do. If, on the other hand, you are negotiating on a patent that expires in a few months, you always have the option of waiting and saving the licensing costs. Similarly, you need to know the cost of the alternatives to your company so that you know when to get up and leave the negotiations. Do not expect these negotiations ever to be easy. Occasionally they are, but even then you are left with the feeling that you could have done a better deal!

After the deal

Having bought the licence, it is important that, where possible, you continue to cultivate your relationship with the inventor. A great deal of additional value can thus be extracted. This relationship can be nurtured through consultancy, formal meetings or even informal chats. However you do it, we are sure, based on numerous experiences, that both your company and your academic partner will benefit.

Tim Cook is Managing Director of **Isis Innovation Ltd,** a company owned by the University of Oxford specialising in the licensing of intellectual property developed in the university to existing and new companies. **Jim Shedden** is an independent technology consultant.

Part 7

Getting Better Value from Suppliers

7.1
Energising Your Business

Richard Taylor
Business Manager, Industrial and Commercial Sales, Eastern Electricity and Eastern Natural Gas

The competitive energy market has been evolving for some years and major users of gas and electricity have already been enjoying the benefits of buying their energy from a choice of suppliers. From September 1998, many more energy users, including growing businesses, will be able to buy their electricity competitively. Richard Taylor, business manager, Industrial and Commercial Sales at Eastern Electricity and Eastern Natural Gas, gives some guidance on how businesses can benefit from this new emerging market.

The energy sector reached a milestone in 1998. During 1999, the electricity market will join the gas market and become fully open to competition.

This deregulation means that domestic customers and those business customers not in the existing competitive market will, for the first time, have the freedom to choose which company supplies them with power. So, if your business is located in Scotland, for example, you could choose to buy your energy from a company based in Ipswich.

Since the beginning of the 1990s, the electricity supply market has been progressively opening up to competition, culminating in full deregulation over the next year or so. Currently, business customers with a maximum electricity demand in excess of 100kW (equivalent to an annual bill of around £12,000) can source their electricity from any licensed supplier.

The gas market has been open since 1989, with large customers, those using 25,000 or more therms of gas a year, being able to buy competitively. In cost terms, this equates to an annual gas bill of around £10,000 and would cover very large manufacturing sites, for example.

In 1992 the gas market expanded further with the opening up of the credit tariff sector that allowed businesses with an annual spend of approximately £1000–£10000 to buy their gas competitively.

Although the competitive energy market has been evolving and has indeed matured considerably over the last decade, it is in the last few years that we have witnessed the most change, with the gas market now fully open and in 1998 the electricity market opening up on a phased basis to all consumers and businesses.

Figure 7.1.1 shows the expected timings for the phased deregulation of the electricity market. Even if your area is not covered for some time, it can still be worthwhile getting information from suppliers at an early stage to see if switching supplier is right for your business.

The benefits of buying energy competitively

Any business, of whatever size, has a requirement for energy within its operation. Whether you're a manufacturer, market gardener, hotelier, shop owner, or run your enterprise purely from office space, you will need electricity and gas to keep your business operating efficiently. In some cases the energy costs may be quite small, in others they can be a substantial part of the company's running costs.

Whatever the individual circumstances, as with so many areas of business life, it is worthwhile looking at your energy needs to see if buying competitively could help you save money and help run your operation more efficiently.

The following are the key benefits that you as a business user can enjoy by buying your energy on the competitive market.

- *Increased customer choice.* The gas market has opened up steadily since 1986, following the privatisation of British Gas, and there are now 10 main suppliers in the market. The gas market has been open to smaller business users since 1992 and the full deregulation of the market, including all business and domestic users, is now in place. The electricity market is currently undergoing full deregulation and, once the market opens fully, you will have the option to buy your electricity from any licensed supplier in the UK. As the market matures even further, it is likely that business will wish to take advantage of dual-fuel contract options with a single energy supplier. Eastern Group is already working with many companies to meet their total energy needs, providing this service through Eastern Natural Gas and Eastern Electricity.

Electricity deregulation activity

Electricity roll-out	May 98	Jun 98	Jul 98	Aug 98	Sep 98	Oct 98	Nov 98	Dec 98	Jan 99	Feb 99	Mar 99	Apr 99	May 99	Jun 99
Eastern Electricity					●			◆			■			
Manweb					●			◆			■			
Seeboard					●			◆			■			
Yorkshire Electricity					●			◆			■			
Midlands Electricity						●			◆			■		
Northern Electric						●			◆			■		
Scottish Power						●			◆			■		
Scottish Hydro-Electric						●			◆			■		
East Midlands Electricity								●				◆		■
London Electricity								●				◆		■
Norweb								●				◆		■
Southern								●				◆		■
Swalec								●				◆		■
SWEB								●				◆		■

Key to electricity roll-out

- ● STAGE 1: 10% by postcode area + ALL maximum demand customers + ALL half-hourly metered customers
- ◆ STAGE 2: (+13 weeks) ALL remaining business sites + 40% of domestic market by postcode
- ■ STAGE 3: (+13 weeks) remaining 50% of domestic customers market by postcode

Figure 7.1.1

- *Potential cost savings.* There is no doubt that competition has resulted in keener prices and business users can often make savings of 10 per cent or more on their annual electricity and gas bills. The actual percentage saving will, of course, depend on individual circumstances and the nature of the agreed contract. It is worth considering a longer-term contract to achieve greater cost benefits over time. If a supplier is able to understand your business and energy needs, it can match the contract to your particular requirements and advise you on how to maximise your energy usage and minimise your costs.
- *Wider range of services.* Business customers can take advantage of a number of additional services, such as electronic billing and profile data, which can highlight electricity and gas usage and demand patterns and act as an aid to more efficient energy management.
- At Eastern we also offer customers the opportunity of using our Business Development Team who can advise on a wide range of energy-management issues, leading to further savings on energy costs. Our service is unique in offering research and development to help customers with new manufacturing techniques and processes to maximise energy usage. Often, the results of this work lead to much improved production processes, which not only save on energy costs but which can help in generally improving an organisation's output.
- *Contract can be tailored to your needs.* When preparing contracts, we are able to tailor these to the specific needs of the individual business. A textile manufacturer is likely to have very different energy needs to those of a hotel, supermarket or office building.
- *A long-term energy partner.* At Eastern we have always been customer-focused and this has allowed us to become energy partners with the businesses that we supply. By getting to know our customers' energy needs over time, we are able to offer valuable advice and guidance on how to get the very best out of all of their energy requirements. This input covers all aspects of the contract in terms of offering maximum efficiency at the best price, a reliable and responsive customer service and, increasingly important, an energy policy that is environmentally sound.

Switching supplier

Switching energy suppliers is a fairly simple process. The first step is to select the companies you wish to quote for your electricity or gas supply. This list could well include your own local supplier, and you will need to give each of these companies copies of your last two or three electricity and/or gas bills. These bills will have your unique 'supply' number on them. The supply number identifies exactly where the customer is situated from a postcode

point of view and also provides the supplier with information that enables it to provide a more accurate quotation.

Once you have decided to switch, the changeover can be very simple. At Eastern we handle all the necessary administration for new customers who join us.

Contracts can be for 12 months, but it is recommended that you sign up for a contract period of at least two years in order to gain maximum benefit from your new arrangement.

It is important also to look at the price structure of your contract over a reasonable period of time – you need to secure a fair price, but it also must be one that allows the supplier, like all businesses, to make a reasonable profit. Otherwise, the supplier might be trying to pitch the contract low in the early period simply to secure the business, and will then be forced to increase prices at a later stage in order to maintain a reasonable margin.

Questions businesses might ask about switching supplier

The gas market is now maturing, but the electricity market is still only partly deregulated. Therefore, there are many questions that potential customers will want to ask. Below I have listed some typical questions that a business might ask before switching electricity supplier.

Do I need to change meters, cabling or other equipment?

No, there will be no need to change the means of physical distribution of your energy. Electricity still comes down the same wires and gas down the same pipes. All that changes is that your bill will probably be cheaper from your new supplier, and your service level should be improved.

If I change supplier, will I become less of a priority to my local distributor?

Not at all. All local distributors are bound to treat you as an equal case in terms of servicing your electrical equipment and supply. The fact that you may not be buying your electricity from them is irrelevant; in those instances they are acting as a local maintenance service provider. In the case of gas, the maintenance and safety of the national supply infrastructure are the responsibility of Transco, a separate company created from the privatisation of British Gas. Your new supplier is acting as a retailer and service provider and purely using the existing gas-supply network to deliver the product.

How much might I save if I switch supplier?

This is very difficult to estimate in general terms, as the savings will depend on a number of factors such as your current usage pattern and demand profile. It is also, of course, affected by the buying and business ability of your new electricity or gas supplier. If it is able to make savings through buying more competitively from the electricity pool or from the gas commodity spot market, these can be passed on to you, the customer.

Will I pay my bill in the same way as before?

Yes, if you wish to. However, one of the key advantages of buying competitively is that you can choose a billing method that is more convenient for your business. You might wish to receive bills at certain times of the month or quarter to coincide with your own financial periods. At Eastern Electricity we also encourage customers to sign on to a direct debit payment method and offer our best prices to those choosing this route. Obviously, this helps reduce our administration costs and we can pass these savings on to customers.

What happens if I need an emergency service and I have switched my contract to a non-local supplier?

When you agree your contract with your new supplier of electricity or gas, you will be issued with details of the emergency number to ring. In the case of electricity, this service will be provided by your local distributor and for gas by Transco – in either case, you are a priority service customer and will be treated as such.

A checklist for switching energy suppliers

If you decide to switch energy supplier then here is a handy checklist of points you may wish to consider:

- *National service* – does the supplier already have customers around the country for which they are already providing a competitive service?
- *Offering a long-term contract* – at Eastern we believe that the best relationships with our customers are long-term ones. It's very easy to offer a quick fix in terms of shaving the price of an existing energy supply price, but if this is just for six months or a year it can defeat the objective of the exercise. The important point is to be competitive over time, rather than just the cheapest for a short period.
- *Additional services* – what services can the supplier offer you as a customer to help you plan your energy costs more effectively and to help you get more from your energy management? Services can range from billing to energy savings advice or help with installing new equipment or

upgrading your site to improve your gas usage. It is important to establish that the new supplier is 'adding value' to the contract.
- *No hidden charges* – check that you are comparing like for like when examining competitive quotes. There are various costs that a supplier may pass on to you as extras, which may not be shown on the original quotation – for example, transmission charges. Make sure that everything is shown and that you are being quoted a complete price.

There is no doubt that the opening up of the energy market to competition can bring benefits to businesses of all sizes. As with all purchases, it is important to have as much information as possible before making your decision. It is hoped that you will find the information in this article of help when you decide to take the competitive route to energising your business.

Thinking about switching?

Both Eastern Electricity and Eastern Natural Gas offer business customers extremely competitive packages, and it's so easy to convert. There are no wires or pipes to relay and no new meters to install. You will receive your gas or electricity via the same method. All that will change is the supplier's name on the bill and, more importantly, the level of service and the price.

Our aim is to work in partnership with you to find the best energy deals for your business. The phased opening of the competitive energy market, which started in September 1998, heralds a new and exciting period in this sector. It's a move that we at Eastern welcome, having prepared for it for some time. Our whole business philosophy is based on being completely customer-focused, so we are looking forward to helping many more businesses to obtain their energy more cost effectively.

7.2

RSL COM – Alternative Telecom Provider

Barry Mowbray
UK Managing Director, RSL COM

Once upon a time, if you required voice services you went to British Telecom (BT). Up to 10 years ago you would have been forgiven for thinking that the telecommunications industry consisted of BT taking the biggest slice of pie, with a few smaller players fighting for the remaining crumbs. But times have changed – technological and legislative changes coupled with improved market conditions have dramatically altered the face of the UK's telecoms industry. As the business world relies more and more on telecommunications to conduct business on a global level, so the telecoms industry has been forced to become more efficient and competitive. Today, the once monopolised industry is opening up into one of the UK's fastest growing marketplaces.

Deregulation opens the market

The Telecommunications Act 1984 effectively changed the face of the telecoms sector for ever. The statute was introduced to ensure that an effective, competitive telecoms infrastructure was in place to meet all reasonable consumer demands. In reality, the Act only succeeded in creating a seven-year duopoly between BT and Mercury, which ended in 1991. Mercury later became part of Cable and Wireless (C&W).

UK telecoms policy received a boost in 1991 when the market was thrown open to full competition in the 'duopoly review' of 1991. In June 1996, the

Department of Trade and Industry effectively ended BT and C&W's international duopoly by issuing 44 full international licences to a number of hungry competitors, including RSL COM. So what has this meant to the business customer?

Corporate telecoms buyers

Over 65 per cent of business users make BT their main supplier, which compares with 73 per cent a year ago (Telecommunications Manager Association survey 1998). The other dominant operator, C&W, has seen its share of the market rise by only 1 per cent. According to the TMA survey, it is the non-traditional, smaller companies which appear to be picking up the significant business. In niche markets, a substantial challenge appears to be developing as new operators build their networks and introduce new services. Call charges have dropped considerably on a national and international level. Few companies now cater specifically for the small and medium business market. However, a lack of knowledge and a deal of suspicion about the telecommunications industry prevail and few look past the now incumbent big two.

Simple to make the change

Recent research by RSL COM has shown that a degree of confusion and naïvety still exists among consumers reluctant to switch from traditional carriers. Many are reluctant to change, as they imagine disruption and upheaval to the office environment and telephone infrastructure. A case of 'better the devil you know' persists. The impetus to change telecoms carriers can be prompted by a number of different reasons, but it is always driven by two dominant factors: price and cost-saving considerations in the first case, followed by reliability and trust in the supplier. With BT as the benchmark, any company offering lower call charges is worth at least a second look, but cost savings must be matched with a guaranteed level of service.

As the telecommunications service is so crucial to the day-to-day running of any business, quality of service is vital. In the TMA 1998 survey, 57 per cent of respondents considered quality of service as the single most important consideration in choosing a supplier. However, only one in five (22 per cent) said that 'overall quality of service' was the strength of their main supplier. Further to this, 82 per cent of communications managers have stated that suppliers often spend little time trying to understand their business needs. Clearly, many business users are concerned about the service provided by their chosen telecoms provider, but what do you look for in an alternative provider? And where do you start looking?

These days everybody's talking cheap.

A confusing mass of offers, discounts and price deals designed to entice you. But consider carefully before you buy.

If you're in business, you'll appreciate that price isn't everything.

What's the point of a low cost telecomms service if it's unreliable? How importantly do you place good customer service on your list of priorities? Is someone, somewhere accountable for the service to your business? And perhaps more importantly, will your telecomms carrier still be around in the years ahead?

Rest assured, RSL COM is here to stay. We're different because we're taking the long term view - not just our business, but also the relationship we have with our customers.

We've invested in our own global, state-of-the-art network - so you can be 100% confident in the quality and reliability of our service.

So when you add it all up, what do you want? Low cost or high value?

To find out more about the unique value we can bring to your business and to open an account, call our Customer Hotline now on:

0800 074 0634

Or visit our website at:

www.rsl-europe.com

RSLCOM

What to look for in an alternative

The first important thing to recognise is that changing carrier should not cause any disruption to the day-to-day running of your business. From the very outset, there should be no cost involved in setting up the new service and there should be no disruption to your business. If your prospective provider cannot guarantee this, you should start looking elsewhere. With some companies offering no monthly charges, the ability to carry ISDN and 0800 number portability – can you afford *not* to change?

Of course, none of the new generation of telecoms companies can say that it has been in business for as long as BT. But is this is a big issue when choosing a new supplier? Without that longevity, you must be reassured that the company is financially secure and you must feel confident that your chosen carrier will be in existence in 18 months' time and still be able to provide an excellent level of service. RSL COM, for example, is one of the world's first truly global, facilities-based telecommunications companies providing international and domestic telephone services to customers throughout the world. From its formation in 1994, to capitalise on the opportunities created by deregulation, it has grown considerably and has recently been valued at more than $1 billion (NASDAQ).

Committed to service

Many telecommunication companies lease lines from major carriers; few of them can boast their own state-of-the-art network. RSL COM's global network is monitored 24 hours a day, seven days a week, to ensure unbroken quality and service. Service failures are detected and repaired before any inconvenience is caused. If a customer reports a problem, it is dealt with by the person who answers the call from beginning to end, without being pushed from one point of contact to another. Clearly, by owning such a network RSL COM is able to control costs and maintain a high-quality service whatever the call destination.

Flexibility to fit your requirements

Today's telecommunications company must be capable of offering customers a broad array of services and be prepared to offer new services to meet business customers' growing requirements.

Business users must be assured that their chosen carrier is not resting on its laurels, but is moving forward, able to add to its portfolio of telephony services as new technology makes new products possible. For its part, RSL COM recently launched Europe's first phone-to-phone Internet telephony service through its subsidiary, Delta Three. By using Internet protocol, RSL

COM is able to offer customers even lower call charges to 16 countries, with more destinations being added all the time. But perhaps the most attractive proposition for telecoms users throughout Europe is the ability of a carrier to provide both fixed-line and mobile telecommunications to their customers. With RSL COM's recent acquisition of Motorola Telco. it can do just that, with both bills coming from the one supplier, which translates into both time and financial savings for the customer.

Top tips – what to look for in your telecoms provider

- *Low call charges* – Are you really getting the best deal on call charges? Many companies now offer much lower national and international call charges than BT with no loss of quality.
- *Customer care* – Do you have a service-level agreement? Look for a provider that can guarantee you that it will listen to your needs and act on it.
- *Seamless transition to new service* – Yes, you can switch telecoms provider with no extra costs, no disruption to service and no disruption to the day-to-day running of your business.
- *Global presence* – Is your provider a truly global entity?
- *Financial stability* – Make sure that your prospective or chosen carrier is still going to be around in 18 months' time and will be able to maintain the level of service you expect.
- *Cutting edge* – Make sure that your phone service is 'future-proof'. You need a company that moves with technology, offering niche services such as Internet telephony, integrated billing etc.
- *Price pledge* – Make sure that the carrier you choose promises to keep you on its latest and lowest tariff.
- *Reliability* – Make sure that your provider monitors its network 24 hours a day.
- *International facilities licence* – Does your provider have one, or is it reselling another company's products?

RSL COM is a global facilities-based telecommunications company with operations in 20 countries across four continents worldwide. As Europe's first commercial provider of phone-to-phone services over the Internet, RSL COM continues to demonstrate its ability to stay ahead of the marketplace and yet remain flexible.

7.3
Maximising the Value of the Facilities Management Provider

Martyn Hayward
Director of Facilities Management Consulting, DTZ Debenham Thorpe

The value of appointing a facilities management provider to a growing business can be measured in a number of ways. The ultimate measure, however, is one of performance.

The basics

Whether internally or externally, there are three principal elements to be balanced by the facilities management provider: costs, business needs and performance. These are illustrated in Figure 7.3.1.

Professional FM providers will recognise that their overall value to a business will be judged on these three elements. In practical terms, the first two mean:

- Costs – meeting the budgets set.
- Business needs – adjusting the levels of service to those appropriate for the business to meet its obligations to its own clients and employees.

But what about performance?

The approach

So far, we have examined what is needed to be conveyed to the provider, but not how this should be done. The most difficult of the three areas to convey is that of performance. Figure 7.3.3 illustrates how this can be achieved.

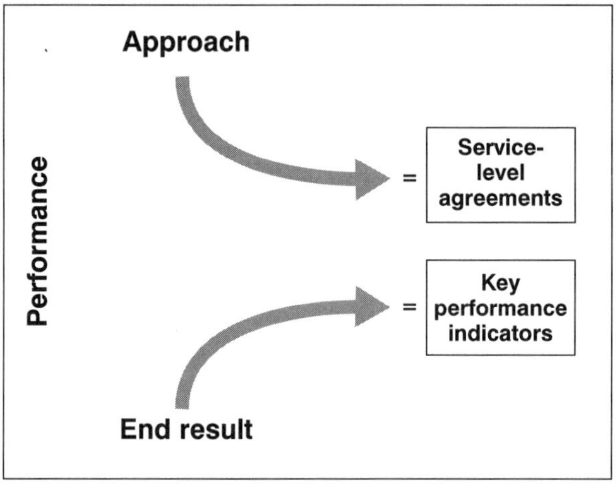

Figure 7.3.3 Conveying the essence of performance

For each of the services to be provided, there are two elements to performance: the approach and the end result. To convey approach, service-level agreements should be used. To measure the end result, key performance indicators should be defined. For both sets of information, a target should be set not only for year 1 but for each subsequent year up to a maximum of five years. This enables continuous improvements to be made and increases in value to the organisation to be gained. Both the service-level agreements and the key performance indicators should not only cover each specific service but also management aspects, such as management reports and customer satisfaction surveys.

The rub

In many organisations, those responsible for FM have little or no understanding, so for them the difficult issue is how to maximise performance without a knowledge base. There are two solutions available. The first is to let the provider define the requirements for you and then adjust their service accordingly. This will take time and may not always provide the required results, as well as being heavily dependent on finding a suitable provider in the first place. The second, that is only now becoming more widely available to organisations, is the use of an independent FM consultancy. These consultants can bring organisations through this stage and sometimes even fulfil an audit role on an annual basis to ensure that maximum value is being obtained from the FM provider. The role of the independent adviser need not be adversarial, but more one of acting on behalf of the organisation by using its specialist knowledge and systems. This can benefit both the providers of the FM service and, more importantly, those receiving the service.

Martyn Hayward is the Director of Facilities Management Consulting for **DTZ Debenham Thorpe**, as well as an external assessor for the postgraduate course in Facilities Management at the College of Estate Management, Reading.

7.4

Making Savings on Advertising?

Alastair Macdonald
Media Audits

For many companies, more money is spent on advertising than on any other item of capital expenditure. Within this, the bulk of the expenditure goes on the purchase of media space. And yet, how much time does the budgetholder spend on media purchasing issues? Unless you employ a dedicated media controller, the answer is probably not very much. On the face of it this seems ludicrous – 5 per cent of someone's time spent on 70 per cent of the expenditure.

Because purchasing media space is a specialised and time-consuming task, companies devolve the responsibility to an outside party – their agency.

Fifteen years ago this would have been the same agency as the one producing the creative work. There has, since, been a growth in media independents and dependents who specialise in the planning and buying of media space, and are not simply a bolt-on to the creative task.

The agency is typically remunerated on a commission basis, taking a percentage of the media spend. In the old days a typical agency commission was 15 per cent. Now, it is not uncommon to find 10 per cent going to the creative agency and 3 per cent to the media buyers, with the client retaining the remainder.

These rates are not set in stone, however, and they should usually be negotiated to ensure that you receive maximum value from your advertising investment.

This negotiation can be perilous for those who are not steeped in the mysteries and jargon of the advertising and media industries, and independent expert advice may be worth considering.

A successful negotiation, however, can lead to significant savings on the expenditure allocated to advertising, and certainly should result in the agency delivering the best value to you. The following checklist should be referred to when examining or negotiating agency contracts.

Agency contract and remuneration checklist

- *Are the creative and media elements separated?* If not, would there be a benefit in introducing flexibility in this area?
- *Is there a different commission rate across countries?* If, say, the UK uses creative work produced in another country, should the commission structure reflect this? In other words, are you paying twice for the same thing?
- *What do you get for your money?* Do you have a contractual guarantee of key, named personnel's time commitment to your business? Are commitments made at a pitch written in as contractual guarantees?
- *Is the level of remuneration performance related?* Such an approach is particularly easy for the media agency's remuneration, as media buying performance is so easily quantified.

The fact is that media buying performance does vary greatly from agency to agency, and even between clients within the same agency. By relating the agency's remuneration to the quality of their performance, you will ensure that you receive the best level of attention and effort, and they will have every incentive to cut the best deals on your behalf.

In drawing up a performance-related scheme, the following issues ought to be addressed:

- The evaluation criteria must be clear, unambiguous and agreed in writing in advance by both parties.
- It is not enough to evaluate purely on the discount that is achieved; parameters to take account of the *quality* of space that you require need also to be included.
- Given that the real advantages in media value are now frequently created from an innovative, well-focused strategy, it is worth considering how to reward the agency for quality work in this area.
- Don't be blinded by seemingly fantastic discounts! Almost all media space is bought at a discount to the negotiating benchmark – you need to establish what level of discount you should achieve.
- Any scheme should be stretching and demanding of the agency, but also realistic and attainable. The best schemes motivate the agency to pull out all the stops on your behalf.

Improvements in the way in which the advertising budget is spent can represent enormous sums of money. Ensuring that your contract with the agency reflects your interests and encourages them to their very best efforts on your behalf can be one of the most effective ways of improving value and/or reducing costs in this area. It can be specialised work, but it is eminently worthwhile, as you are creating a situation where both parties win!

Alastair Macdonald is a board director of Media Audits UK. Having joined the company in 1990 from AGB Television, he has been responsible for many aspects of service development, account handling and general management.

Media Audits is the world's leading advertising consultancy. Founded in London in 1976, the company now works for 200 advertisers around the world, offering peer-group comparisons and diagnostic analysis of agencies' media buying performances, which provide clients with accountability for the media budget and unique insights into how media value can be improved.

Part 8

Site Selection and Management

8.1

The Business Incubator – Driving Tomorrow's Economy

Professor D W Auckland
Director, Campus Ventures Ltd

Starting a business, and particularly a high-technology one, is a difficult and often cruel affair. It is one for which our education system leaves us desperately ill prepared, tending to favour the gifted scholar rather than the gifted entrepreneur. This fact rests uneasily in the emerging economic order in which new high-technological companies led by technologists are seen as prime movers of the results of the latest research quickly to the marketplace in the form of new products and services. The importance of such companies in the regeneration of the industrial base is becoming increasingly apparent, most particularly in the USA where many of today's leading high-technology businesses began as sparkles in the eyes of youthful scientists and engineers. These businesses were, as often as not, the product of a process called business incubation.

Business incubation takes place in business incubators, purpose-prepared premises often located close to universities on which the emerging companies rely for expert help and equipment. They provide a variety of work space, from small single-person rooms to larger premises able to accommodate up to around 15 people. The incubator provides its tenants with a range of services from copying to accountancy. They rarely if ever provide investment advice but a good incubator will run investment clubs bringing technologists and prospective investors together. To ease the early financial burden on its fledgling population, business incubators often operate a soft start to repayment both for rent and for services, ramping up charges in a controlled fashion so that in the final analysis no one misses out.

The process of business incubation began informally in the USA and has evolved over the past 30 years to the point where it is gradually becoming a formally recognised part of the American economy. Because the incubation process, even in the USA, is still evolving, it is difficult to define in great detail. But in so far as it attempts to solve the fundamental problem of how to draw knowledgeable people within the enterprise into the market place as businesspeople, so it embodies some equally fundamental features. Determining these are, first, that the knowledgeable are often short of money, and secondly, they nearly always lack credibility as businesspeople. Thus it is that the incubation of a business is a bootstrapping process in which the newly formed company is moved forward very much on a day-to-day basis under its own steam, earning where it can and developing new products and techniques as money and time allow. This hand-to-mouth existence gives time for owners to develop basic business skills. It also allows them to feel their way in what is probably a niche market, enabling them to fashion their product and service to fit demand and to expand it in the process.

In some incubators, bootstrapping is formalised. In others, it is allowed to progress with relatively little supervision. In the more formal incubators, business development plans are made and targets fixed, with the new companies guided to these using experienced businesspeople as non-executive chairman.

It generally takes two to three years to incubate a company. Having reached the point of so called 'graduation', the company leaves, often taking up premises close to the incubator. With graduation generally comes financial respectability and they are seen as good investment propositions, attracting loan and venture capital in the process.

The one remarkable characteristic of business incubators is the rate at which they generate companies. The author's unit, Campus Ventures Limited, which has adopted a formal approach to incubation, graduates one company per month from within its 25,000 sq ft of operational space. The other remarkable characteristic is that the companies emerging from incubation generally embody high growth and stability. So it is that none of the 35 companies launched by Campus Ventures has gone into liquidation and many are attracting investment on a substantial scale.

These facts and figures are typical of those returned by incubators in the USA. It is this level of performance that has led the incubation process to be viewed as a major economic driver. This understandably fuels the present enthusiasm in the UK for business incubation. But success can only be achieved by being aware of those fundamental factors which underpin its great success in the USA. It is not good enough just to repeat the catchphrases of incubation while doing something else. Instead, we must understand the process and interpret it to fit our system, providing entrepreneurial scientists and engineers with a route to market for their skills and knowledge. Not to do so will seriously damage our economic health.

Professor David Auckland is an engineer by training and was until 1997 head of Electrical Energy Systems Research Group in the University of Manchester's School of Engineering, when he was appointed Campus Ventures Professor of Science Based Business Creation.

Campus Ventures incubates high-technology companies owned and led by scientists and engineers. It is located in the heart of the University of Manchester, whose resources are available to the emerging companies. It has created a total of 35 companies during its two and half years of operation, covering areas of business from software to biotechnology.

8.2

Office Accommodation and Location Strategy – the Key Issues

Jonathan Turner
Director, Property Consulting, DTZ Debenham Thorpe

For most businesses, large or small, locating offices can be a complex process, whether it is the relocation of an existing facility or the establishment of a new operation. It will encompass a wide range of issues, focusing on the operations of the business, human resources, finance and property. The process can therefore be both risky and costly, consequently requiring a well-considered plan, the implementation of which needs to be managed carefully and effectively. This places considerable strain on a company, particularly in terms of management time, and can be further exacerbated if there is uncertainty among the staff, particularly where relocation may be involved. The key issues in such decision-making can usefully be summarised in Figure 8.2.1.

Each business will attach its own weighting to the various different issues outlined above and the influence of one factor relative to another in the formulation of the appropriate accommodation plan and location strategy. Consequently, the locational drivers will vary from company to company.

From a human resource perspective, the location of virtually all major call centre/customer service operations has been driven by the availability of qualified staff. This is not purely because of direct costs (and cost savings),

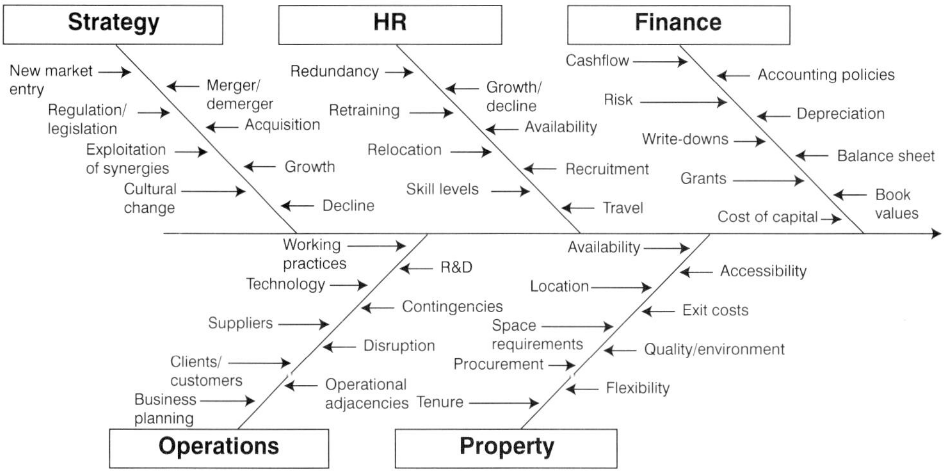

Figure 8.2.1 Key issues in decision-making

but also the impact of the high costs associated with staff turnover and retention. On average, most operators will remain in the job for 18 months, and current overall staff turnover is running at 30 per cent per annum.

In terms of operations, Ford Motor Company demands that its key suppliers all have a presence on supplier parks adjacent to the relevant facility, notably Dagenham and Halewood. This is to reduce the risk associated with just-in-time delivery techniques. Similar trends are evident at Rover, BMW, Mercedes and Honda.

Property is the most important supply-side consideration and availability of suitable premises can be a key factor in either attracting companies to an area or forcing a relocation through lack of supply. Property can also be influential where businesses have existing accommodation that needs to be utilised effectively, both financially and operationally. For instance, in the rationalisation of its UK portfolio, insurance company Guardian Royal Exchange pegs locational decisions on the location of existing freehold offices.

Financial issues are often associated with cost-reduction strategies, including the numerous examples of moves to assisted areas because of the financial incentives available (largely aimed at foreign inward investment). Some businesses are also now focusing on reducing their average occupancy costs per head which, for the office occupier, is of greater significance than the traditional emphasis on rent per sq ft/per annum and incorporates an analysis of all relevant costs and efficient space utilisation. Examples include the financial and business services sectors.

The second strand to finance issues is in minimising property risk. This is linked with outsourcing and is illustrated primarily by the government in

Benefits of best practice and good neighbouring

Sir Neville Purvis KCB

Director General, British Safety Council

Many senior managers still see safety management as a costly legal requirement with no real business benefits, but the facts do not bear this out. By aiming for best practice rather than the legal minimum firms can make improvements in all areas of business, not just accident rates.

It is estimated that accidents and ill health cost UK companies ten per cent of their annual profits. However, by establishing good safety management systems firms can make savings with lower accident costs and insurance premiums, fewer lost working days, reduced sick pay bills and less money spent on training replacement staff.

Many companies can already testify to the benefits of best practice. The Baker Group, a meat packing firm based in Northamptonshire, has seen its insurance premiums fall by £250,000 in just three years. One department at Norwich City Council saves £60,000 a year through reduced accident rates and Unipart Group of Companies in Oxfordshire has saved more than £300,000 since 1996 by achieving best practice.

This kind of success does not happen overnight. To reap the benefits of best practice a positive culture needs to be established in which companies see health and safety management as equal to other business goals. This is achieved through active commitment from senior management, communicating the safety message to staff until health and safety becomes a fundamental part of the overall management agenda.

With at least 80 per cent of accidents caused by management failure, the only really effective way to reduce them is through effective management control. A no-blame culture should be established in which staff are able to report accidents without fear of reprisal. Accident reports should include near misses, which are the best indicators of potentially dangerous situations. All accidents, whatever the outcome, should be investigated to highlight any trends rather than to apportion blame.

Once an effective reporting system has been established management should look at ways to improve the situation. It may be possible to change a process to make it less hazardous. For example, Sanyo Electric Manufacturing was seeing a lot of cut hands at its County Durham site. Many were caused by workers stripping the plastic coating off steel. The process was changed so the steel could be pressed without stripping off the plastic.

Hazardous substances can be replaced with less hazardous materials and, as a last resort, workers can be given personal protective equipment (PPE). Staff should undergo health and safety training to increase their awareness of potential hazards and regular inspections and audits should be carried out.

There is an assumption among some managers that they can not afford to set up safety systems. While it is clear that, on the whole, companies can not afford to avoid establishing a safety culture, it is true to say this may prove comparatively more expensive for small firms. That is why large companies which have good relationships with contractors and suppliers are the key to improving safety in smaller organisations.

The British Safety Council is encouraging good neighbouring as the way forward for smaller firms. Good neighbouring is a system in which larger organisations share their safety knowledge and experience with smaller contractors and suppliers, helping them to improve their health and safety standards by working closely to achieve best practice. This theme will play a key role in European Week for Safety and Health in October 1998.

Larger companies see the mutual benefits of working in this way with smaller companies. Establishing such relationships does not come cheap because of the cost of auditing potential suppliers and contractors, so businesses want to see a good return on their investment. If a supplier's safety record does not come up to scratch it may not get another try and the larger organisation may have to start the audit process all over again.

Big companies with good safety records do not want them tarnished by unsafe contractors. It is in their interests to share their safety expertise with contractors and suppliers to protect their own reputations. Small companies also benefit. They need contracts if they want to continue to operate, but reputable companies will not engage the services of unsafe firms.

The British Safety Council believes good neighbour schemes can help small firms achieve best practice and ultimately achieve all the business benefits this brings for both sides.

terms of the Private Finance Initiative. Other examples include third-party distributors where ownership of the warehouse is retained by major retailers, or call centres which are leased to third-party operators on behalf of the end user, such as Manpower on behalf of IBM.

The minimising of property risk is also evident in the growth of serviced offices. These have typically been occupied either by small, start-up companies wishing to benefit from the established support services and minimal set-up costs of serviced offices, or by large, established companies which need temporary space, such as for project teams or pending a move to permanent offices. In the latter context, Pfizer UK Ltd recently leased serviced offices in Central London while premises for its public affairs office were being fitted out.

Serviced offices can act as a premises incubator for a business, which can take on more space in line with its own growth. Powderject, a biotechnology company which floated on the London Stock Exchange in June 1997, started with 220 sq ft of serviced offices in the Magdalen Centre at the Oxford Science Park, expanding into 2000 sq ft. As a consequence of its growth, the company has now taken a self-contained building on the Science Park of 10,500 sq ft on a more conventional, longer-term lease. There are numerous similar examples across the country, such as in Leeds, where Berisford Blake Thomas (recruitment consultants) and Zeda (IT specialists) which started with 350 sq ft and 250 sq ft respectively within serviced offices, moved to significantly larger, permanent offices of 2200 sq ft and 3000 sq ft. The concept of serviced offices is now well established and serves the needs of businesses in industry sectors.

The issues identified above are not generally taken in isolation in terms of the accommodation and location strategy of a business, but rather it is the combination of key drivers that will determine decision-making on location. These can be further influenced by wider issues such as regulation and legislation. Overall, location decisions will generally represent a compromise across a number of issues, but with emphasis on those most critical to the business.

The approach to formulating and implementing an office accommodation and location strategy is akin to a funnel, moving from the 'general' to the 'specific' through a logical set of steps, as illustrated in Figure 8.2.2.

Step 1 – establish requirements

The first task is to clarify the underlying objectives of the company, setting out the rationale of the operation to be accommodated.

From a property perspective, a space audit would assist in creating a firm and concise project brief, determining the size of accommodation required

HR	Finance	Business operations	Property

⇓

Identify objectives, rationale and benefits

⇓

Establish criteria and formulate strategy

⇓

Prepare and evaluate 'long list' of options

⇓

Select shortlist and review original criteria

⇓

Detailed evaluation of shortlist

⇓

Recommendations for preferred option

⇓

Finalise negotiations and legal documentation

⇓

Undertake physical works to building

⇓

Manage the move

⇓

Post-project evaluation and possible further action

Figure 8.2.2 Accommodation and Location Strategy

(taking into account desired ways of working and forecast staff growth) and identifying a building profile (eg shape, uses and specification, having regard to IT requirements). In addition, the company should consider its preferences towards acquiring the property on a freehold or leasehold basis, or a site to construct its own building, or to negotiate a design and build package with a developer. At DTZ Debenham Thorpe, we have developed a financial model with which we can analyse the costs of purchasing relative to leasing in a given situation to aid such decision making.

A detailed list of criteria should be established, including such aspects as employment (eg availability and cost of labour, including skill levels); particular locational drivers (eg proximity to customers, suppliers and transport links such as airports, seaports or the Channel Tunnel); the environment and availability of amenities (eg leisure, entertainment, recreational facilities, hotels); housing (eg availability and costs – to rent or buy); education (eg international schools); cultural centres (eg strength of local community).

The intended timescale will have a significant influence both on the accommodation plan and what is achievable – is it realistic? Will there be cost implications?

Step 2 – evaluate

The evaluation stages focus on the competitiveness of locations and, subsequently, individual properties/sites. This is achieved by means of constructive qualitative and quantitative analysis by reference to the previously identified criteria, weighted according to their relative importance to the business. Consideration should be given to financial assistance which may be available for new projects, comprising a complex system of grants, loans and other support. These are often specifically aimed at inward investment and can contribute to mitigating costs, particularly at the outset. However, the availability of grants should not be seen as an end in itself, but as a trade-off with other issues.

Financial modelling should be tailored to the specific needs of each project and will probably include the property costs (eg rent and rates), ongoing facilities management/running costs, operating costs (incorporating labour costs/productivity, benefits of synergies, new working practices and new workforce) and one-off costs (eg redundancy, relocation, fit-out, retraining and parallel running), together with assessing the impact on the financial statements. This analysis assists in identifying the negotiation strategy and preferred deal structure to maximise the benefit to the business. It also provides an opportunity to reevaluate the preferred option relative to the original objectives of the accommodation plan.

Implement

Once the preferred option is identified, negotiations can be finalised, the legal documentation agreed and the programme prepared for the occupation of the building and managing the move. Internal layouts for fitting out need to be fully designed, enabling an immediate start on site once the legal documentation is completed, thus avoiding unnecessary delays.

The physical move needs to be carefully programmed and managed, minimising disruption and maximising benefit from the new premises, with IT and facilities support personnel on hand, if appropriate.

Additional issues

Communication

This is a key factor, both internally with staff and externally with customers, suppliers and relevant advisors.

Resourcing

To be successful, the formulation and implementation of an accommodation and location strategy require the commitment of appropriate resources, both internally and externally. The strategic planning stage is crucial, but can take considerable time. A clear decision-making process is required, with continual reference to business plans and the strategic drivers. This is best achieved by having an internal project manager (preferably at a senior level) coordinating the implementation of the project (by reference to the key objectives and budget), often working with an external property consultant.

Summary

- Allow sufficient planning time and management input.
- Ensure that the key criteria are analysed at the outset, including the nature of the property required.
- Know what can be compromised, whether locational, financial or building specific.
- Reevaluate and secure board support at each stage.
- Communicate effectively, both internally with staff and externally with your property consultants.
- Have appropriate resources in place, able to commit time to the project and facilitate efficient decision-making.

Jonathan Turner is a director within Property Consulting at **DTZ Debenham Thorpe**, which specialises in providing solutions to property problems and giving independent property advice to corporate occupiers.

8.3

An Ideal Place To Grow A Business

Simon Freeman

It was at Stanford University in California, USA, in the late 1950s that the first progressive ideas germinated about the synergy that could be achieved between academic institutions and industry. These initial ideas resulted in the establishment of the world's first science park at Stanford.

It was in this creative and commercially stimulating environment that Professor Sir Frederick Crawford taught and undertook research at the university for over 20 years. When he returned to the UK to take over the post of Vice-chancellor at Aston University, he quickly recognised the potential of transferring the science park concept across the Atlantic.

Aston, a leading technological university and business school, was keen to pioneer the concept, together with Birmingham City Council, which recognised a unique opportunity to generate wealth and jobs. The third partner in the launch of Aston Science Park was Lloyds Bank plc.

Combining the facilities of a modern academic establishment with a purpose-built industrial complex gives immediate advantages to both parties involved. In recent years industry has changed, with more and more businesses being technology based. This, combined with the growth in small business start-ups, has produced a need for reasonably priced, flexible starter units that have access to modern facilities.

By locating science parks adjacent to universities, occupants of the business units have immediate access to all of the facilities available on campus. These can typically include library and research facilities, printing services, leisure facilities, shops, banks, postal facilities, conference rooms, computer facilities and even short-term living accommodation.

The advantage for graduates wishing to turn their academic achievements into profitable companies is that most science parks provide accommodation on short-term leases, designed to allow entrepreneurs to grow their businesses without having to worry about being tied into expensive property deals. Starter units are normally fully serviced, with reception, secretarial facilities, meeting rooms, photocopying and so on all available as part of the package. Having this basic office infrastructure on tap gives the occupants more time to concentrate on making their businesses work.

Aston Science Park is built on a 22-acre site adjacent to the university and its operating company, Birmingham Technology Ltd, manages the park and provides support services to the knowledge-based fledgling companies that start up there.

The Business and Innovation Centre was opened in 1983 by HRH the Duke of Edinburgh and provides over 52,000 sq ft of space for growing business start-ups. Within 12 months of its opening, there were 15 companies on site and this had risen to over 40 by 1986. At the same time, with the Business and Innovation Centre acting as an incubator, some of the early companies were already expanding into larger, purpose-built venture units.

By the early 1990s the fourth phase of the park's development was complete and it then housed over 60 companies, a quarter of which had been created by former graduates or academics of the university.

Today, Aston Science Park houses over 100 companies which employ over 1300 people, with more jobs to come. The UK Science Park Association has its headquarters there and no less than half of the space on the park is taken by companies which started within the original Business and Innovation Centre.

The latest phase of development, Priestley Wharf, provides the ideal headquarters for a company whose growth has been aided by the facilities available at Aston Science Park. Callscan Ltd, which started in the Business and Innovation Centre in 1985 employing only four people, now occupies 22,700 sq ft of the new building. The company employs over 90 people and has a group turnover of over £14.4 million. It is a world leader in computer telephony integration and offers a perfect example of how the park can be an ideal location to grow a business.

When asked about his company's continuing success, Tony Scragg, Callscan's managing director, said: 'Being on Aston Science Park has given us the flexibility to grow. We have used all the facilities provided by the Business and Innovation Centre and have also had access to the expertise provided by Aston University. This has given us credibility and the right image – particularly with major international companies.'

The success of companies like Callscan provides continuing proof that the vision of the founders is as right today as it was over 15 years ago. Aston Science Park is continuously developing to meet the growing needs of existing companies and new ventures from the UK and, more recently, from overseas. To quote Derek Harris, BTL's chief executive, 'It is our task to create an environment that will stimulate and support the enterprise and initiatives of companies that may well have the potential of being the world beaters of tomorrow. We have no small companies – just large companies starting out small! '

Simon Freeman is BTL's Business Development Executive. His role is proactively to seek business opportunities, not only for **Birmingham Technology Ltd**, but for all the companies located on **Aston Science Park.**

He was previously with West Midlands Export Link and has a great deal of experience of the overseas trade services offered by both the DTI and the Foreign Office. Simon has lived in Hong Kong, where he worked for the United Nations High Commission for Refugees, and has travelled extensively in the Far East.

8.4

Groundwork – Sustainable Solutions to Brownfield Development

Malcolm Barton
Groundwork

In 1994, the University of Manchester produced a report on the state of brownfield land in the UK and found that the rate at which such land was being created was nearly the same as the rate at which it was being remediated. The difference is in fact so small that it will take some 200 years to remove the blight. Clearly, the problem is too large for any one interest group to be able to provide a solution. New social alliances, working in partnership, are desperately needed. New and growing businesses will be an essential component of such partnerships.

The problem arises from the simple premise that the first industrial revolution is over. This phenomenon, that some claimed started in rural Shropshire before spreading in ripples across the face of the globe, did not originate in the steep-sided valley of Ironbridge by accident. The essential conditions for the inception of this socially shattering event could be found in the immediate vicinity of this rural vale in the form of coal, limestone and iron ore.

Ultimately, other better and more abundant sources of these basic materials were found in places with easier access to markets and the metamorphosis of society from an agricultural to an industrial base rapidly accelerated. These primary industries had one thing in common. They demanded the use of large tracts of land. In South Wales, valleys covered in ancient woodland were sequestered to provide dumping grounds for the detritus of the coalmines and in the industrial heartland of the Midlands industry grew and spread. These industries required a further resource in order to prosper – labour. As these primary industries declined some 200 or so years later, they left behind a legacy of blighted land and abandoned, disaffected communities. The degree of damage varies from the highly toxic to areas that are simply unwanted. The term 'brownfield' was coined to describe this post-industrial land, presumably in an attempt to reinforce the obvious contrast with 'greenfield' sites which have not been subjected to industrial development.

The symbiosis between labour and the old industries has left modern society with a complex challenge. How can we best deal with the large amount of brownfield land that sits cheek by jowl with communities that have, like the land, been abandoned by traditional industries? Brownfield land often represents a double abuse to communities. First, there is the loss of jobs; but secondly, there is the visual and social abuse that derelict land heaps on the communities that have been left behind like flotsam on a beach when the tide has turned. Unsightly land is a magnet for a wide array of unsociable activities, from fly tipping to crime. It reduces a community's self-esteem by being a constant reminder that they are no longer needed. It can be unsafe, but at the same time a lure for children desperately seeking a landscape within which to play. It can be the source of pollution that slowly poisons the environment.

Often, the old industries that used the land and prospered have, in their decline, not made proper provision for the remediation of that land. These industries pre-dated the kind of town and country planning legislation that today imposes an obligation on industry to mitigate the effects of the use of land. The critical question, therefore, is how society is to deal with this problem and, in particular, the role that businesses can play in helping to provide sustainable solutions.

As was stated earlier, new social alliances are needed. Increasingly, traditional vertical organisations that try to deal with single issues such as housing and education are seen as being of limited use. A more holistic approach is required and the business community has a vital part to play.

Modern business increasingly understands that it owes a duty to the concept of long-term sustainability if the problems of the first industrial revolution are to be avoided. Business should be aware that developing new opportunities within brownfield sites can be an excellent way to satisfy this aspiration. But the approach to holism can only be achieved through vibrant, meaningful partnerships if tokenism is to be avoided. This means creating a proper dialogue with communities and this is where an organisation such as Groundwork is ideally placed to assist. Groundwork has, for nearly two decades, worked closely with communities, local and central government and businesses to create partnerships delivering environmental benefits.

Groundwork's main tenets are that any development should be both community led and ecologically informed. Such a philosophy, together with delivery through partnerships, provides a potent solution to the problem of brownfield land.

Groundwork can provide assistance to businesses in developing a dialogue with communities that helps to remove the cynicism towards development found in many places. Through its expertise in providing environmental business services to industry, it can ensure that intended brownfield development achieves optimum sustainability. With a large staff of expert landscape designers, Groundwork can devise the most ecologically beneficial solutions for the physical environment. Carefully considered landscapes have the added benefit of providing an amenable working environment for workers within the development as well as enhancing local nature conservation.

Developing brownfield sites can be costly, but Groundwork, through local authority partners and with links to UK and Europe-based government organisations, can often assist in assembling the necessary funding packages. This holistic approach can be further enhanced by utilising Groundwork's vast community-based expertise, which has been gained from working with many communities in the fields of youth, education, the arts and special needs.

All these operations can, through partnership with businesses, be woven into the solutions for brownfield sites, with exciting and enriching results for all participants. In this light, new businesses can be seen to be actively engaged in the provision of valuable solutions; not, like some of their industrial predecessors, the originators of social problems.

Established in 1981, **Groundwork** is the leading environmental partnership organisation in the UK. Its approach is to develop programmes which link environmental, social and economic regeneration and contribute to sustainable development. These programmes concentrate on three key areas:

- Bringing about physical environmental improvements.
- Integrating the economy and the environment.
- Educating and involving the community.

Groundwork receives core funding from central and local government, but is also able to promote its work through donations from corporate sponsors, charitable trusts, European and UK-based social funds and the various bodies distributing National Lottery funds.

Malcolm Barton is a chartered builder with experience in the construction industry. He has been involved in the reclamation of derelict land and minerals development in the UK, Europe and the USA. His work with Groundwork is mainly concentrated on the development of large-scale, ecologically informed programmes of land regeneration.

Part 9

Using Technology to Manage

9.1

Fast, Faster, Fastest

Mike Maunder
Marketing Director
UK & Ireland, EMC

Size is no longer the most telling factor in company performance. Speed is where it's at. Flexible, agile, responsive ... these words keep cropping up to describe some of the fastest-growing and most successful companies in the UK today. These are the prerequisites for performance at the top of each industry sector.

But how can you ensure that your systems and structures are more flexible than those of your competitors? How can you transform your company into an agile, flexible and nimble competitor in the worldwide trading arena?

- By becoming a learning organisation.
- By becoming intimate with your customers.
- By cutting time to market.
- By leading with courage and conviction.

Over the next five years, technology will be helping to drive the way many organisations do business and will be central to delivering on the corporate aspirations above. Senior managers will have to live with the fact that information is something to be managed dynamically and not just stored passively in some IT black hole. In turn, that means binding together the disparate data that has built up over the years. This will be fundamental to business success.

In addition, as we hurtle towards the Internet age, organisations will find themselves operating in an environment where commercial success is as much about clever and relevant application of information technologies as it is about

business acumen. Organisations will need fast access to information 24 hours a day, seven days a week, as e-commerce creates truly global markets.

The traditional computing model is about to be turned on its head, emphasising shared storage information systems as its key resource, while delegating mainframes and other servers as specialist, bolt-on devices. Indeed, the successful organisations of tomorrow are beginning to realise that investments made today in a consolidated storage infrastructure, at the heart of the enterprise, will reap great commercial benefits tomorrow and beyond.

In short, for organisations to fully embrace twenty-first century commerce with IT at the heart of the enterprise, some radical changes are going to take place. Those who emerge as winners in this challenging business environment will be those who have well-organised IT infrastructures and can adapt and act quickly. And the most vulnerable will be organisations that are shackled by outdated and inflexible information systems.

While knowledge exploitation and information sharing may be having its place in the sun at the moment, the idea in itself is not new. What is new is the power of technology to exploit it, and businesses must exploit the technology quickly to stay ahead of the pack.

Speed is the new buzzword

> *Speed – in delivery, product development, adaptation to new market conditions – is the new competitive battle. We can only win by doing everything faster.* Tom Peters

> *Time is the scariest resource, and unless it is managed, nothing else can be managed.*
> Peter Drucker

> *Time is the cutting edge of competitive advantage. The ways leading companies manage time are the most powerful new sources of competitive advantage.*
> Stalk and Hought

Mike Maunder is the marketing director of EMC, responsible for the United Kingdom and Ireland, and his current responsibilities include developing EMC's strategic business model, sales and marketing strategy and implementing field and marketing programmes for both direct and indirect business.

EMC Corporation, based in Hopkinton, Massachusetts, is the world's leading supplier of intelligent enterprise storage systems and software for mainframe and open systems environments. The company has offices worldwide, trades on the New York Stock Exchange under the symbol EMC and is a component of the S&P 500 Index.

9.2
The Age of E-Commerce

Paul Mountford
Managing Director, Cisco Systems

Electronic commerce takes much of the complexity out of everyday business interactions. It reduces lead times, saves money and enhances productivity, giving new meaning to the 'faster, better, cheaper' model that forms the underlying principle at the foundation of today's global business arena. A wide range of applications is emerging in the virtual marketplace, including the ability to initiate and consummate transactions, check the status of orders, gain access to online service and support capabilities, search and use documentation, and gain access to valuable training.

Cisco Systems and electronic commerce

Cisco Systems is setting the standard for Internet commerce as the world-wide leader in networking for the Internet. Cisco's volume of product orders taken electronically now averages more than $20 million a day. Its goal is to receive at least 80 per cent of all orders over the Internet by the end of 1999.

By taking its orders online, Cisco has not only saved money but has improved productivity, shortened delivery times and virtually eliminated errors. In 1997, it fielded over 240,000 customer service queries on its Website (two thirds of all support activities), saving the company from adding 1000 employees to its payroll. This single activity accounted for £75 million ($125 million) in savings that year.

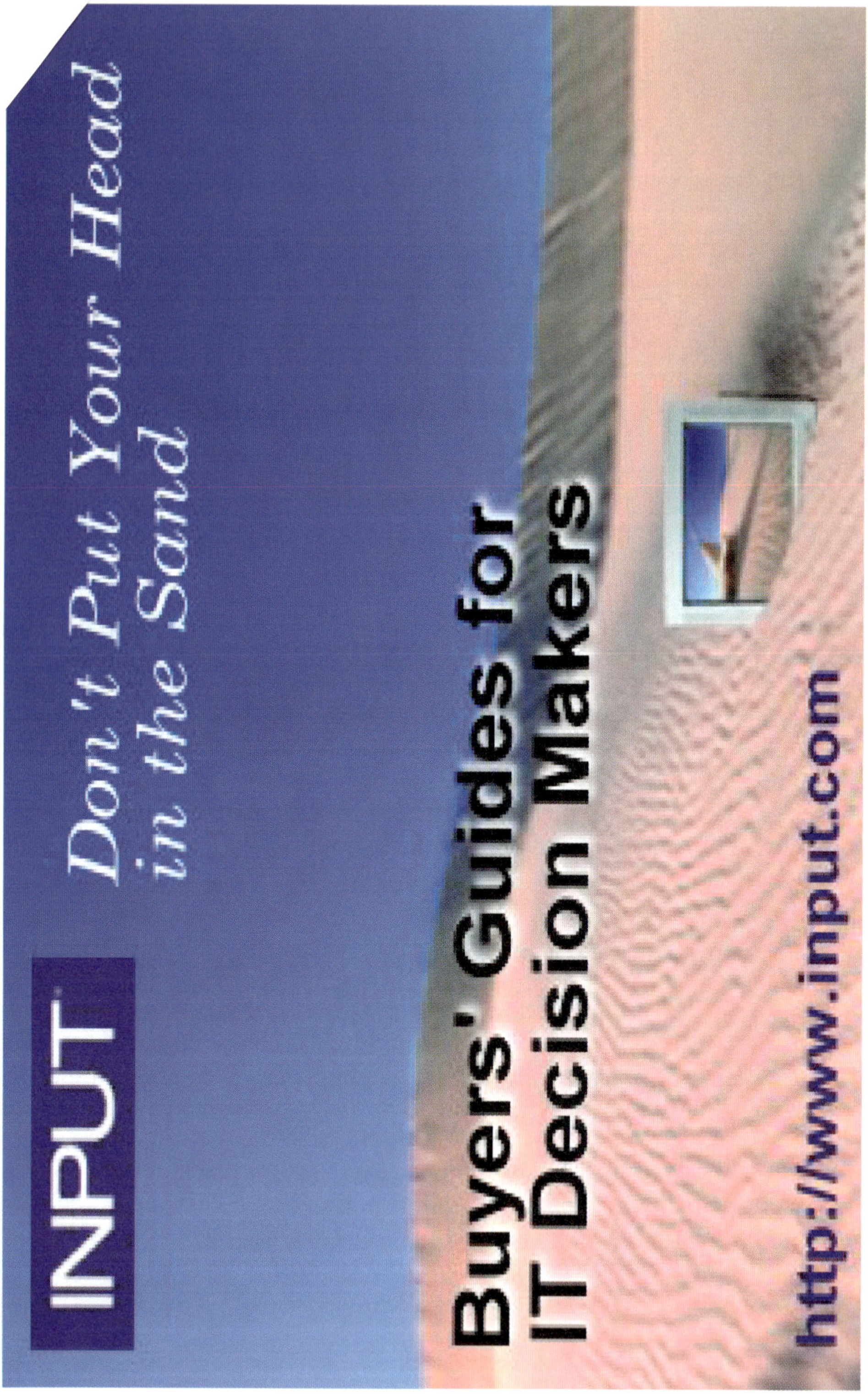
INPUT
Don't Put Your Head in the Sand
Buyers' Guides for IT Decision Makers
http://www.input.com

IT Outsourcing: Caveat Emptor!

by Paul Connolly, Vice President, INPUT

At the turn of the 20th century, it was the norm for companies to have their own electricity generators. The very idea now seems ludicrous. Today, electricity is a commodity supplied on tap by a faceless third party, and thatís the way we like it.

The information revolution has long usurped the industrial revolution, yet it is tempting to question whether Information Technology may go the same way as electricity. With sophisticated IT solutions increasingly available on a plug-in basis, perhaps it is not so fanciful to imagine a time early in the 21st century when in-house IT is a thing of the past, and the term CIO has the same ring about it as wheelwright or blacksmith.

If that sounds heretical, them Iím glad I have your attention. However, to adopt a more pragmatic stance, it is reasonable to assert that outsourced IT is definitely here to stay. The reasons are clear. Organisations are increasingly realising that ìDIYî IT is both costly and non-core to their business. Furthermore, IT is more complex than ever. Pity the poor IT managers who have been at the mercy of the technologists for years, forced into a seemingly endless cycle of change, with ever more sophisticated software running on ever more powerful chip technology.

Add to that the rapid growth in networks, the various standards wars that have been waged, and the endless variety and sophistication of products and tools that have become available, and what has emerged over recent years is an extremely difficult environment to manage. No wonder that IT groups have increasingly sought outside help in supporting and managing complex technologies which barely stay stable long enough to be able to conduct an audit.

The consequence is that IT outsourcing has become big business and, like any big business, one that is open to abuse by unscrupulous practitioners. Hence, a word of warning. Caveat emptor!

So, what qualities should one look for in a prospective IT supplier?

A good place to start is to check whether a supplier is a member of a professional body such as the Computer Software & Services Association. The CSSA is the UKís leading representative body for the IT industry, and its members agree to adhere to a code of conduct, which includes undertakings to (amongst other things):

- Only offer a service where competent to do so
- Ensure all written representation is clear, concise and as free from ambiguity as possible
- Clearly state the charges, exclusions and the terms of payment
- Clearly define in the contract the services to be provided and the method of performance measurement and reporting (a Service Level Agreement)
- Review with the client at agreed intervals all aspects of the services, including any changes that may be required by the client
- Provide adequate cover for the liability accepted in the contract for the provision of the services
- Be prepared to co-operate with other related service providers in the interest of the client.

CSSA membership can confer a good degree of credibility upon a supplier, but thatís just for starters. For proof of capability, organisations looking to outsource should check suppliersí track record by taking up references; the more successful case studies you can find the better.

Beyond that, there is a whole host of soft factors which will give you clues to the genuine capabilities of prospective suppliers. In a recent INPUT survey of IT Directors in the UK, we asked what were the most sought after qualities in an IT supplier. Top of the list was specialist knowledge. As one respondent put it ìwe are looking not just to outsource a problem, but to harness the expertise of the service supplier, and in particular where it applies specifically to our industryî. INPUTís research shows that the ìjack of all tradesî approach is losing its appeal in favour of demonstrable technical and professional expertise within a given sector.

Other much sought after qualities are reliability, flexibility, proactivity and value. The first of these needs little elaboration, but the others are worth pondering on for a moment.

Lack of flexibility in a supplier relationship can prove to be a major problem. Many of the organisations surveyed by INPUT were part-way through a long-term outsourcing deal, typically for the management of a datacentre or multi-user desktop environment. A common complaint, and a source of considerable dissatisfaction, was that the supplier had so far failed to deliver on promises of refreshing the technology when significant advances were made; in most cases, the supplier was content to continue managing increasingly out-of-date technology, leaving the client with an inevitable problem downstream.

This ties in with the parallel claim that many suppliers are passive in their service management approach. Lack of proactivity crops up time and again as a major bug bear amongst IT Directors, many of whom might stay loyal to their suppliers forever if only they were capable of demonstrating proactivity in implementing new technologies, anticipating the clientís changing service needs, and working to improve operational efficiency and cost control.

Which brings me finally to cost itself. Interestingly, low cost is no longer top of the list of requirements when it comes to selecting a service supplier. Surveys reveal that IT buyers are increasingly looking for value rather than low cost, which means the right balance of service quality and price. Rarely will the lowest price equate to the highest quality.

To reflect on my opening paragraph, the role of CIO is most unlikely to disappear for a while yet. However, the nature of the role will increasingly involve balancing and optimising resources in an attempt to meet corporate objectives. CIOs are having to justify their investments in IT more closely than ever, and are becoming highly sensitised to issues such as cost of IT ownership and return on investment.

Over time, the relationships between IT buyers and suppliers will necessarily mature into more equitable partnerships, where both parties are keen to achieve a win-win situation. Most suppliers are beginning to at least pay lip service to partnership and will talk enthusiastically about delivering business value through IT. However, until such time as lip service translates into customer service, caveat emptor will continue to be a wise piece of advice.

Paul Connolly is Vice President of INPUT, an international provider of marketing and information services to IT decision makers. Mr. Connolly has 17 years experience in the IT industry and specialises in providing market research and communications services to IT marketing professionals.

You can contact INPUT at Cornwall House,
55-77 High Street, Slough, Berks. SL1 1DZ. Tel. 01753-530444.

T Developments and Management Structure

Whilst technology has undoubtedly become a business driver, its effective deployment can g major challenges as well as extensive efits. One of the greatest challenges facing iness today is simply that of keeping pace its ever-increasing rate of change.

For most organisations, it is not a realistic on to employ all of the skills required to uate and implement best-of-breed solutions. s is where a technology partner, that is capable dvising over a broad range of requirements, really add value. Given that many of the nologies used within an organisation are rrelated and interdependent, it is important partners are prepared to invest sufficient time nderstand, in detail, their customer's business cesses, objectives and challenges.

There are junctures in an organisation's life e, which frequently prompt a review of their stment in technology - an acquisition or ger, a period of growth, rationalisation, etc. vever, it is just as important to constantly ew its deployment, in the light of new elopments. A partner that is familiar not only current solutions but, also ongoing trends directions, should be able to take a pro-active roach in its advice and guidance, to help d dead ends and achieve real business efits.

The availability of information is probably the le greatest benefit that the technology age provided. Unfortunately, utilising that rmation often remains an elusive goal for y organisations. Instead, they are presented an endless supply of data. The change in inology from 'Data Processing' to rmation Technology' hasn't always lead to a nge in approach. However, in recent years, a ber of technology developments have rded the opportunity to more easily transform into meaningful information. The most ous of these is the Internet.

The Internet has evolved to become a universal way of distributing information not only within an organisation but also amongst customers, suppliers and partners. Of course, the Internet in itself doesn't instantly transform data into information but it does have the ability to make data available in a way that, through its accessibility, can turn it into useful information.

Other developments in technology, such as 'groupware' and 'knowledge management', are contributing to improved levels of information, both in terms of quality and dissemination. This, in turn, creates organisational challenges. In order to ensure an organisation benefits from improved levels of information, it needs to structure itself accordingly. For example, groupware applications such as Lotus Notes can allow flatter management structures, through improved dissemination and accessibility of information. Conventional hierarchical approaches can be revised to facilitate teamworking and more of a project approach. This can be extended to create a remote working environment - teleworking, for example, or hot-desking - where employees benefit from greater flexibility and where the business can benefit from increased productivity.

Managing the change towards an 'information model' requires a willingness to adapt to new working patterns and the continual deployment of best-of-breed technologies. The right technology partner will be able to play an intrinsic role in achieving this.

Supporting facts

- Cisco takes orders over the Internet worth $15.6 million every day.
- Cisco uses its Website to hire staff, saving $8 million a year in recruitment costs.
- Software downloads from the site save $250 million a year in production and distribution costs.
- $40 million is saved on print and production of literature.
- Cisco has 40,000 registered users of its Website (including commercial agents on its Internet World Product Centre), generating 510,000 transactions every month, and customer satisfaction levels are up.
- 63 per cent of Cisco's European sales are made on the WWW; the error rate for orders has dropped from 20 per cent to 2 per cent since going online.
- 70 per cent of technical enquiries, previously handled over the phone, are now answered electronically.
- Cisco's revenues in fiscal year 1997 were $6.4 billion – it expects over $5.6 billion of its revenues in 1998 to be taken online.
- Cisco's market capitalisation is $90 billion.

But where is Europe with regard to e-commerce?

Organisations in Europe are losing out on millions of pounds each year as they continue to contemplate using the Internet as a channel for conducting business. European companies are currently far behind the USA, accounting for only £600 million ($1 billion) of the worldwide Internet commerce, as compared to £4.8 billion ($8 billion) in the USA.

However, Europe's enthusiasm for online business is set to multiply some 25 times by 2001 as its companies begin to realise that the Internet is the only way to trade globally with greater efficiency.

Some of the arguments as to why Europe is yet to adopt electronic commerce include the European telecoms marketplace, multilingual challenges and currency problems.

European telecoms marketplace

It has been argued that monopolies such as Minitel in France are inhibiting the growth of the Internet in Europe. Infrastructure and bandwidth are noted as inhibitors for growth, since they vary widely in their development across European countries. Also, governments are too preoccupied with the impact of the EU and unemployment to commit themselves to electronic commerce.

Cisco believes that for European companies to embrace the internet revolution, starting at the lowest common denominator (in terms of infrastructure) is par for the course, but this does not imply that the uptake of electronic commerce in Europe will be hindered indefinitely. The impact of telecoms deregulation will have a positive effect on electronic commerce as prices will lower and consumer choice will widen.

In addition, competitive realities will make the uptake of electronic commerce a necessity. The internet revolution will influence the competitive position of individuals, companies and countries and nobody in any of those categories can ignore its impact without affecting their future. Moreover, people/companies/countries may soon demand that high-speed Internet access be available, giving regulators and service providers no choice.

Coping with the multilanguage challenge

In order to maximise the potential for doing business over the Internet, European countries need to do business outside their local geographies. This has a multilingual implication that affects set-up costs, maintenance rates and overcoming the cultural barriers with countries that prefer to do business in their 'mother tongue'.

Cisco believes that while working within a multilanguage community presents its challenges, it is feasible for many countries to 'leapfrog' their competitors by responding to market characteristics more quickly than their competitors. This could mean that countries such as those in Eastern Europe could gain a serious competitive advantage by investing in their infrastructure now.

A recent report from Forrester Research, 'Europe's Internet Growth', also highlighted that larger companies will use the Internet to get even bigger and that Europe's early growth period in electronic commerce will 'favour deep pockets, leading brands and readily summoned resources'.

Currency issues

While Europe continues to debate the euro, European countries had to cope with multiple currencies and exchange rates which in turn increased costs for doing business over the Internet.

Cisco believes that increased border commerce will flourish with the introduction of the euro, which will compel countries to trade electronically. The response to language and currency differences is the same:

- Linguistic and cultural differences exist no matter what form of interaction takes place, be it personal or commercial, electronic or paper.
- Electronic tools can lessen the barriers that these differences present through such techniques as automatic translation, user-defined Web pages, push technology, automatic currency conversion, instantaneous transactions etc.

- The Internet is by its very nature a universal communication medium, so it offers the best chance of any medium to overcome these language/currency differences, recognising that such differences will always exist.

Nonetheless, Cisco is adamant that the barriers to electronic commerce in Europe will be overcome because:

- The EU is backing the Internet.
- Forrester's report maintains that despite a host of issues that impede the Internet's growth in Europe – such as telecoms deregulation, conservative attitudes towards technology and inadequate infrastructure – these issues will diminish over the next three years.

The tip of the iceberg

Electronic commerce is becoming more widely accepted, but we have barely scratched the surface of its potential. Electronic commerce reduces lead times, saves money and enhances productivity for all users by removing barriers for both business-to-business and consumer relationships. Inevitably, electronic commerce will soon cease to be a competitive advantage; it will be a competitive necessity.

As the world leader in internetworking technology, products and services, Cisco Systems understands that being competitive is the key to being successful. It developed CCO in order to meet the present and future needs of its partners and customers. CCO is the most innovative online business application in the industry and will remain at the forefront of developments as we enter the twenty-first century.

Paul Mountford has 14 years in the IT industry and prior to joining Cisco ran an independent channel business advising UK companies on international channel and distribution strategy, as well as setting up US technology companies' European channel operations.

Cisco Systems is the worldwide leader in networking for the internet. A 1995 study by the Yankee Group, a Boston consultancy, reported that more than 80 per cent of the routers that form the backbone of the global internet are from Cisco.

9.3

Using Technology to Manage Global Infrastructures

Ray Geoghegan
Director of Alliance Partnerships and Product Management, Unisys

In today's business environment, information technology has undergone a major transition from playing a purely functional role to often being the key to creating business value.

Furthermore, in many markets today it is not the processes or physical assets of a business that differentiate it from its competitors, but its knowledge. Information assets – often the most valuable assets an organisation owns – therefore need protecting, and IT must provide the services to facilitate fast and effective communication and knowledge sharing – wherever people work.

Most importantly, IT infrastructure now provides the means to extend the reach of the organisation to more customers than was ever possible before – and for an increasing number of new businesses, IT provides the primary customer-contact medium.

Now that IT has moved out of the back office to a new position underpinning competitive advantage, getting the infrastructure right to provide an adequate foundation for an expanding business is more important than ever before. IT can no longer be considered a passive service that you rent or buy like other utilities.

Improved communications, including the Internet, and other fundamental changes to the business scene today, such as EMU and the introduction of the euro, have turned the world into a global marketplace. Growing companies that take the global perspective and understand what global IT infrastructures can do to make them competitive in local, regional and global markets will develop advantages over companies that treat IT as a local resource.

Ten things to consider

1. Intranets

To capitalise on an organisation's precious information assets requires efficient communication, and accessibility and sharing of information and knowledge. Companies are rapidly adopting intranets, alongside tools for collaborative working and knowledge sharing, as their benefits become widely appreciated.

2. Extranets

Essential to doing business effectively today are improved communications outside the organisation – with customers, business partners and the whole supply chain. Using such techniques as virtual private networks (VPNs), sometimes running over the Internet, intranets are being extended outside the immediate confines of the organisation into 'extranets', and used to improve communications and trade with external organisations.

3. Flexible working

With the advent of changing working patterns, mobile workforces, remote and home users and the virtual company, the IT infrastructure has an increasingly important role to play within the organisation. Indeed, for some companies, the IT infrastructure has virtually become the organisation. To support remote and mobile users and branch offices, communications facilities – often over the Internet, using secure communications – can be made available to allow unhampered work to continue regardless of location.

4. Help on hand

With IT playing such an important role, users need to be happy users – and that means offering effective help. An efficient helpdesk also improves productivity by reducing downtime – the time that users can't spend working while their problem is sorted out. With remote offices and home workers, an

effective helpdesk facility needs to be available round the clock, a requirement that often moves companies to outsourcing this vital facility to experts.

5. Future expansion

As the business grows and changes and IT plays an increasingly important role, the infrastructure, and especially the bandwidth – the amount of traffic that the network links can carry – will be called on to do more and more. But any infrastructure has a finite, limited capacity, and IT is no exception. So when implementing an infrastructure, it can often make more sense to rent than buy. And when buying, it's essential to choose equipment that is designed to be extendable, to allow the infrastructure to be upgraded swiftly and painlessly when the business outgrows it.

6. Protection of assets

Protecting vital information assets is essential. Security breaches will happen, but their frequency and their impact can be minimised with proper planning – and traceability can reveal exactly who did what and when. An effective security policy will also protect the organisation from suffering expensive downtime due to malicious attacks.

7. Standardisation

With a growing and global organisation, consistency, reliability and intercommunicability are absolutely vital. A policy of standardisation for IT is key to achieving these aims – permitting local choices for equipment such as PC operating environments, servers or networks does not add business value, but does create problems. Systems and services should be designed so that they don't inhibit the flexibility of the business to respond to local markets.

8. Single sourcing

Buying a global infrastructure from a hotchpotch of local suppliers is unlikely to provide an easy ride in areas such as inter-operability. Furthermore, dealing with large numbers of suppliers is an expensive management burden – and assigning responsibility for a total solution isn't easy. Dealing with one source of supply and support, not only geographically but across the range of products, cuts costs and ensures accountability for success.

9. Managing the network

Effective communication is now an expected part of doing business, both internally and externally to the organisation, so any failure can be very expensive. Unfortunately, IT infrastructure isn't a case of 'fit and forget', but needs continuous management in order to minimise downtime due to causes such as equipment failure, software failure or unexpected high demand. To avoid the burden of acquiring and maintaining an expensive internal resource to manage the network, one option increasingly opted for by businesses today is to outsource network management to an expert organisation.

10. Independence

For maximum flexibility, infrastructure should be built on accepted industry standards that are technologically *agnostic*, ie that do not rely on specific, proprietary solutions. Wherever possible, systems must be built to be independent of applications and hardware. Fortunately, the widespread adoption of Internet standards such as IP (Internet protocol) on the internal network means that achieving independence can now become a reality.

9.4

Making the Most of IT Solutions

Simon Hallam
Supply Chain Infrastructure Manager, JBA Software Co

It is debatable whether the technology at our disposal helps or hinders us. At best, it seems to record what is going on, reports where we got it right and where we could do better.

But is that really enough? Surely it can serve us better? Shouldn't it help us do the right things more easily and aid us when things go wrong? Or even give us the opportunity to prevent things going wrong in the first place?

Successful IT implementations are underpinned by a good understanding of what is required from any change in the business. However, it is advisable not to embark on a huge business process re-engineering (BPR) exercise. Today's thinking points towards business process *improvement*, where the processes that are key to the achievement of firm, measured business objectives, are scrutinised for the opportunity to improve them.

And one of the best ways to commence that exercise is to base it around what the world's best companies are doing. Not from a guru's book, but from a model of the supply chain built by those companies themselves, encapsulating their views of best operational practice and software requirements to support those practices.

The Supply Chain Council (SCC) is an independent, non-profit corporation, originated in 1996 by Advanced Manufacturing Research (AMR) and Pittiglio Rabin Todd & McGrath (PRTM), which initially included 69 voluntary member companies.

SCC's objective is to develop a standard supply chain process reference model enabling companies to:

- communicate supply chain issues;
- benchmark themselves;
- influence future supply chain management (SCM) software.

It has grown rapidly and has become the *de facto* organisation to which top tier enterprises must belong, and towards whose operational standards of excellence other businesses aspire.

Council membership is now open to all those interested in applying and advancing state-of-the-art supply chain management systems and practices.

The SCC has developed and endorsed the Supply Chain Operations Reference Model (SCOR) as the cross-industry standard for supply chain management. This contains:

- standard descriptions of management processes;
- a framework for relationships among the standard processes;
- standard metrics to measure process performance;
- management practices that produce best-in-class performance;
- identification of software features and functions that enable best practices.

Using the SCOR model as a basis, it is simple to configure and describe via process modelling *what* your business is to do, selecting the global best practices you wish to adopt and recording current and target values against the process benchmarks that the model suggests. It allows you to take active control of the plan for your business in an easily-understood and communicable way.

The approach gives all employees and supply chain partners a clear, unambiguous definition of the future operation of your supply chain.

Once a clear vision has been documented, then you can turn your attention to *how* that business will operate – who will carry out the activities, what they will do and how they will use IT and other systems to help them.

In today's customer-driven markets, enterprises cannot afford to sit back and wait. Only an active approach can provide any assurance of success, or even survival.

Picture these two scenarios.

Scenario 1 – A letter from Universal Supplies reads: 'Your credit limit has been exceeded. We have stopped your account and will charge interest on the balance outstanding until the whole amount is paid.'

Scenario 2 – A phone call from Allied Supplies: 'You are approaching a point where your credit limit may be exceeded. Your buying pattern indicates that you will place another order within the next seven days. Would you like a temporary increase in your limit to allow you to place that order while you arrange to settle your account? I can do that now on the computer, and we can then review your line of credit requirements.'

Which supplier would you prefer?

Sceptics might point out that if Allied Supplies continues in this way they will run the risk of carrying too much debt. But then again, it may gain new customers from Universal.

So how can we become more like Allied Supplies? Following some form of process modelling to describe and thoroughly understand what we are trying to achieve, we should be able to apply technology to help us carry out those processes most effectively and responsively. It is time that IT systems caught up with today's business needs.

We can do this through workflow techniques, using the infrastructure wrapped around our IT systems to cut out unnecessary delays and push necessary activities on to the desktops of the appropriate users. We can route the process according to the information carried with each individual order, material requisition, schedule call-off or invoice. We can provide individuals with details of potential problems before they arise, and at the same time give them the system tools to enable them to be solved. And, of course, those individuals who can prevent the problems occurring may well reside with one of our partners, suppliers or customers – truly the active enterprise at work.

This vision is not a pipe dream. Nor is it only for multinationals with vast resources at their disposal. This way of working is available to us all, if we have the determination to define what we want our businesses to achieve and the wherewithal to make our IT systems serve us, not rule us.

9.5

The Changing Face of Manufacturing in the Supply Chain

Mark Donkersley
Baan Business Systems UK

Global competition is now inescapable throughout the manufacturing industry. Small- and medium-sized enterprises (SMEs) in particular are exposed to these pressures. Most SMEs are suppliers to larger companies, and most major manufacturing corporations are global or international in their operations. They have the ability to source their supplies of goods and services internationally and to develop supply chain strategies that effectively pass on a large proportion of their own market pressures to their suppliers. Suppliers may simultaneously find major new opportunities in serving multinationals, and face threats as new suppliers appear in what used to be domestic markets. In either case, the competitive pressures are the same: price, speed, quality and a constant need for innovative thinking in design, production and business methods. As a company that started small, we know what it feels like.

Gone are the days of long lead times and predictable product mixes. That scenario has been replaced by customers who increasingly demand product customisation and just-in-time delivery, and markets where rapid response to changing demands and economic conditions are crucial for survival. Successful manufacturers have reacted with a whole raft of new managerial and organisational methods: increased focus and specialisation; concurrent engineering for product quality and speed of development; lean manufacturing to minimise costs; agile manufacturing for flexibility and quick response. All these are dependent on highly effective information management. Therefore, the quality of a company's information systems is central to any successful competitive strategy.

The common factors in any successful response to competition and market pressures are speed and efficiency – the continually increasing ability to do more, faster and with fewer resources, whether of energy, people, finance, material, equipment, transport or assets. The job of manufacturing management has always been to deliver quality goods, on schedule, while continually optimising the use of engineering and manufacturing resources. Now optimisation has to be far more complete, with less time in which to do it and severe penalties on those who get it wrong. The key to resource optimisation is effective deployment of integrated business systems to ensure that information is immediately available in the right form to the right people at the right time, making the company's operations an efficient, responsive integrated business empire.

The IT challenge

In responding to market pressures, companies have found themselves limited by inflexible information systems based on outdated technology. Speed is of the essence, throughout the organisation. If companies are to respond to change, quickly and efficiently, their supporting IT systems must be capable of integration, adaptation and extension, quickly and without excessive cost. SMEs in particular need to be assured of a quick payback.

Baan Business Systems' (BBS) Enterprise Resource Planning software technology developed over the past two decades is purpose designed to deliver those attributes.

It is important not to think of the term Enterprise Resource Planning (ERP) as limiting the technical and business applications included within its scope. The ultimate goal for any company must be to integrate all of its business process applications software within one, unifying IT framework. The goal for BBS is to deliver the integrating framework and all the required business applications — either from its own applications portfolio or from its software partners which have embraced the same framework.

Integration is not a goal for its own sake, it is the only way to achieve ultimate efficiency in the operations of your business. The challenge for SMEs, and for their systems supplier, is to achieve the required integration, flexibility and performance of their IT systems at an affordable cost, in both money and effort.

Large corporations are now universally aware that flexible business process integration is a critical requirement. They are installing the relevant

ERP technology at an accelerating pace. Most SMEs are equally aware of the potential benefits, but they have quite different requirements. Whereas large companies are able to support major implementation projects, SMEs tend to require customised systems at 'ready to run' software prices. They cannot afford lengthy implementations or major business process reengineering exercises, but at the same time, SMEs are demanding software technology and systems architectures just as advanced as those enjoyed by larger companies, but within more affordable computing infrastructures.

BBS has taken up the challenge of meeting that demand.

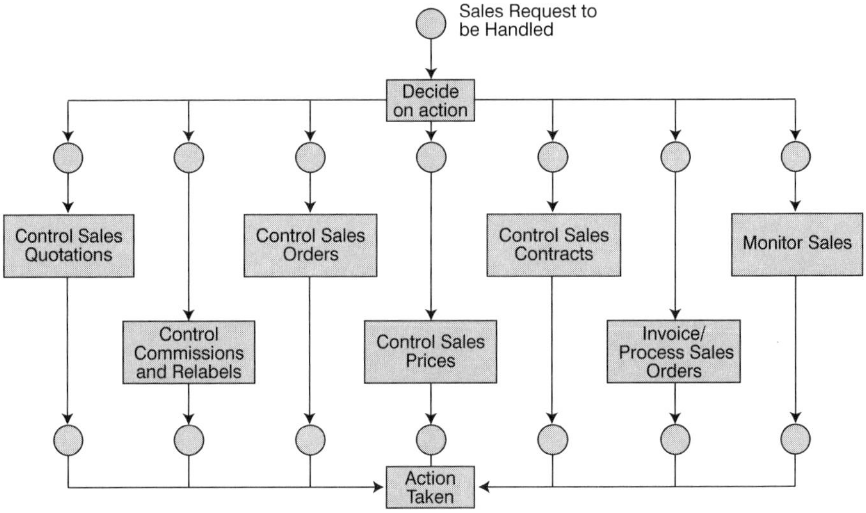

Total SME focus

To be assured of delivering on that promise, BBS has created a strongly focused business strategy closely tailored to the special priorities of the SME sector. To ensure that we continue to deliver on it, we aim to become the world's leading business systems solution provider for SMEs by the year 2001. We believe that no other organisation is dedicating its business so completely to SMEs.

Here's a summary of how we do it.

Our business model, service and support structures and solution delivery methods are all designed to meet the specific needs, economics and dynamics of the SME market. SMEs vary in size by an order of magnitude. They may be autonomous companies, or part of larger corporations. They may operate locally or globally. The hallmark of our business model is adaptability to a wide range of circumstances. We are the global provider with a local face.

Recognising the special needs of SMEs for rapid implementation times and minimal implementation costs, BBS has developed the industry solutions strategy. Based on DEM technology, industry solutions are predesigned business process models that correspond to the characteristic profiles of companies in particular industries and vertical markets, such as mechanical engineering and electronics. By starting with such a model, the solution provider can configure a ready-to-run system for an individual client at little additional cost, reducing implementation times to weeks rather than months. Such predesigned industry solutions greatly reduce the implementation effort involved.

Dynamic Enterprise Modelling (DEM) is a set of tools and methods which have been well proven to reduce the time taken to model a manufacturing company's business processes and configure the appropriate business systems. DEM has been used to build a growing library of generic Enterprise Reference Models that can be used to assemble a company-specific set of process models and so greatly reduce the modelling effort required. Compared with competitive products, DEM is unique due to its direct link to the application. This enables the user to alter processes dynamically at run time, producing significant benefits in terms of time saving and flexibility.

Baan Business Systems provides manufacturing companies in the SME market with industry-specific business software that is cost effective, fast to implement and gives a quick return on investment. There are BBS offices in 22 countries worldwide with over 1200 employees. The company is unique in the SME marketplace. BBS aims to be the numer one provider of business solutions software to manufacturing companies in the SME marketplace by the year 2001.

Mark Donkersley has worked in the UK SME marketplace for 14 years. After working with Baan products for five years, he was asked by Paul Baan, Vendenburg Venture (previously Baan Investment), to set up Baan Business Systems in the UK in September 1997.

9.6

Java Technology™ – the New Fuel for Business Growth

Jon Tutcher
Head of Public Affairs,
Sun Microsystems Ltd

Increasingly in today's rapidly changing business environment, the organisations that grow fastest are those that can respond quickest to the opportunities that a market presents, are closest to their customers in satisfying needs and exceeding expectations, and are able to demonstrate visionary strategies that lead to competitive advantage for their customers.

Information technology, once confined to the role of supporting business processes, is now seen as a company's secret weapon – its spearhead for achieving market leadership, increased profits and global presence.

Information technology executives have a seat at the top table, no longer reporting through the finance director but recognised as key contributors to the business; they enjoy the rewards (and pressures) that being central to business success brings.

Critical to the initial and ongoing success of any organisation are four key issues:

- minimisation of operating costs;
- flexibility to respond rapidly to market changes and opportunities;
- access to enterprise-critical information;

- ability to add value through transparency between a customer and its suppliers – so-called 'supply chain integration'.

The utility model of computing

Computers may have changed the world, but the world has not changed the computing model very much in the past 15 years. Despite incremental enhancements, today's PC-dominated computing architecture largely remains the same as it was in the early 1980s. It is characterised by proprietary hardware that runs a limited range of applications and doesn't share information easily with other computers; productivity gains have been minimal.

The limitations of this model are becoming painfully obvious:

- *For users,* hardware and software incompatibilities are a constant frustration.
- *For system administrators,* the need to upgrade each user's software and keep track of multiple versions is a tedious, time-consuming and costly task.
- *For businesses,* the total cost of ownership for these desktop 'islands of information' is enormous and growing rapidly.
- *For end-users,* although computers are becoming faster and more flexible, they really aren't becoming any simpler to use.

From an IT perspective, there are a number of requirements for fuelling company growth:

- Users need to focus their energies on using systems as productive tools, not on managing them.
- Systems may need to be rapidly updated/upgraded to supply new capabilities and features as soon as they become available in order to optimise a market opportunity, something which can typically only be achieved by a single, central change.
- Existing capabilities may need to be extended to new users, within acquired companies or new suppliers for example, where similar, compatible systems may not necessarily be deployed currently.
- Management needs the assurance that the systems deployed are agile enough to alter with changing business needs, but stable enough to exceed their projected return on investment.
- Systems need to be robust and scalable to overcome unexpected growth.

These growth enablers are critical to any flourishing business and today can be achieved through the deployment of a new computing infrastructure – Java Technology™ – created by Sun Microsystems Inc.

The network is central in the Java Technology™-enabled Internet computing model, characterised by TCP/IP networks and HTML formats, with networked applications developed using Sun Microsystems' Java Technology™. Applications and processing power are distributed among many different types of computers (servers) in many different locations, and the network controls the flow of information among authorised users (clients). User applications are written in Sun's™ Java™ language, enabling them to be run by, and transmitted among, virtually all types of computers.

It is helpful to think of this model as an 'information utility'. In the same way that power and water are stored centrally and distributed locally to 'thin clients' such as outlets and taps, Java Technology™ makes computing network based and accessible via easy-to-use, ubiquitous, low-cost devices. The advent of ubiquitous computing – 'access anywhere, anytime, by anyone, on anything'– is really here.

Java Computing™ is an innovative yet safe way to extend the reach of technology to all manner of new devices – Internet phones, PDAs, embedded processors – with the complexity managed in the network, where it is most cost effective. The core benefits are as follows:

Lower costs

Java Technology™ allows organisations to simplify their information systems and cut costs by managing IT resources centrally. Since Java Technology™ is not a replacement for, but an extension of, their current environments, companies can spend less on their information systems and get more out of them.

Reduced time to market

The platform independence of Java Technology™ eliminates the need to translate software to multiple platforms, and makes programmers two to three times more productive. That means that businesses can deploy applications and get to market more quickly.

Secure extension of the enterprise

Java Technology™ makes it simpler, more secure and more cost effective to extend the enterprise intranet to key partners, suppliers and customers, opening the door to innovative new services and marketing techniques that increase revenue.

Improving customer service

Java Technology™ enables companies to develop and deploy new customer

WHO INVENTED JAVA?

Java is the biggest thing to hit the computer world since electricity. It's a new world language. It's the backbone of the Internet. It's a unique solution that enables diverse devices to talk effortlessly cross-platform to diverse devices. It's the platform of choice for 85% of Internet Service Providers. It's now the language used to develop most new applications. And Sun invented it. For 82 other things you didn't know about Sun visit www.sun.co.uk. THE NETWORK IS THE COMPUTER

JAVA™

Sun microsystems

THAT'S SOMETHING ELSE YOU DIDN'T KNOW ABOUT SUN.

service applications quickly, extend services to new markets with ease and simplify training of customer service representatives.

The traditional model of PC-based, all-purpose device computing is no longer enough in today's increasingly 'wired' climate. The Java Technology™ model offers a way forward by providing safe, secure, anytime/anywhere access to information and services using any simple network device.

This new way of computing – Java Computing™ – has the potential to enable breakaway business strategies for forward-thinking organisations. It is these strategies that will provide market growth and these organisations that will become the new market forces to be reckoned with.

Since its inception in 1982, a singular vision, 'The Network is the Computer™', has propelled **Sun Microsystems Inc** (NASDAQ 'SUNW') to its position as a leading provider of high-quality hardware, software and services for establishing enterprise-wide intranets and expanding the power of the Internet.

With more than $9 billion in annual revenues, Sun can be found in more than 150 countries and on the World Wide Web.

Sun, the Sun logo, Sun Microsystems, 'The Network is the Computer' are trademarks or registered trademarks of Sun Microsystems Inc in the USA and other countries.

9.7

Information on Tap at Adnams Brewery

Information Builders

UK brewers Adnams and Company plc have demonstrated how tradition and innovation can work in tandem, with the successful completion of a management information system pilot project by Information Builders, providers of powerful information management software. This project has enabled them to optimise customer profitability and service.

Described in the Campaign for Real Ale newsletter as 'one of the legendary names of real ale', award-winning Adnams is one of the few remaining British brewers still making horse-drawn deliveries in its local area of Suffolk.

Its continuing success as a traditional family-owned brewery has seen the company increase in turnover to £36 million, which means that in order to be competitive and profitable Adnams has to adopt the most up-to-date business practices at its four sites in London, Cambridge, Norwich and Southwold.

The brewery, one of Britain's longest established producers of real ale, ran a three-month customer profitability exercise with Information Builders, the international software vendors and consultants.

'We have an enormous wealth of data and we have to make it accessible,' explained Adnams IT Manager John Riches. 'We needed a supplier with both the ability and the resources to look at our needs and work with us, both as software providers and consultants, to develop a way to use the information.'

The pilot project was based on customer profitability, using Information Builders' Focus Six software to automate the reporting and analysis of their many customer accounts.

Focus Six can draw on all relevant sources of data across an organisation, such as specific client requirements, accounts and logistics, and is able to present the information in a clear and concise form to suit the user's needs.

'We have a large demand internally and each department has different needs from the same data. We are using Focus Six to extract timely and pertinent information and present it to users in an appropriate form, either on paper or via a screen,' explained Riches.

'The first project that we have been working on is a crossover between sales and logistics – an exercise on customer profitability. During the pilot, we went through a proof of concept process that produced a smaller version of the project on one PC to prove that the front-end delivery was what we wanted.

'Now that this has been successful, we will be moving on to the next one. Basically we are trying to integrate network-based worksharing with our traditional applications which will include intranets and internets. Through Information Builders, we have been able to find a way to get information from our computer systems and use it appropriately.'

Andy Wood, Logistics Manager at Adnams, explained: 'The project kicked off as a logistics initiative. We looked at identifying "cost to serve" for different customers and this led to a customer profitability exercise.

'If an element within the cost of serving a customer changes, then it will affect our profitability. We have to be able to use this information intelligently within the business so that we can drill down to individual customer level and look at the costs that will be incurred when serving that customer and how we can alter the return.

'This is an enterprise-wide initiative, not just a financial one. It is important for the financial team to be able to present figures, but this information also has to be accessed and used by sales and logistics managers, who can then make a decision about cost.

'The role of logistics includes the procurement of stock, order capture storage, delivery and account management, therefore information flow is very much within our remit. We are also client-facing in part – both with the internal and external customer.

'There was a level of flexibility from Information Builders and they were able to deliver precisely what we needed at that moment. They have brought added expertise and have an understanding of both our business and the products that we require. Flexibility is also the strength of their information management and reporting tools'.

In its annual report, Adnams makes a pledge to its shareholders to 'create an organisation which could respond effectively to the ever-changing market place.' Peter Harding, Management Accountant at Adnams, emphasised that the brewery trade is more volatile than most industries, with as many as one third of the Adnams customers in London alone changing suppliers in any one year and the same number of new customers coming on board.

Harding explained that this meant that the company's management information systems had to be capable of monitoring large volumes of frequently changing data efficiently and accurately.

'We can now provide dynamic live data which can be used at board level or frontline. Our salesforce can make use of the product to see how they can better serve the customer and gain more profit for the company,' said Harding.

'Originally we had most of our systems on management reporting divided into areas within the organisation, and spreadsheets and information were not always readily available. We have now built up our management information system as a basis for customer profitability, which enables us to send down costs to each level. We have taken our selling and billing systems and drilled it all down into gross profit into which we can input discount scenarios and different customer requirements. Focus Six is a great reporting tool which offers a real business solution. It also offers the ability to present the information at various levels, which is very important to our department.'

Harding is very positive about how the relationship had developed between themselves and Information Builders. 'Information Builders have been fantastic on the pilot scheme,' he commented. 'They spent many hours with me when I was working to a tight deadline to prepare my first presentation using Focus Six. In that particular case we used PowerPoint as the presentation tool, but the product delivers information through virtually any application depending on your requirements.

'Focus Six will ultimately make money for us as a business solution and the potential for the use of management information systems at Adnams is huge.'

Clive Parminter, UK vice-president at Information Builders, commented: 'Adnams is an excellent example of how our products can be used to benefit businesses. They have a highly unique customer base with constantly changing individual customer requirements and they have recognised at board level that their information systems have to meet these demands.

'Our team has enjoyed working with Adnams on the pilot project and we are delighted that it has been such a success. We always try and look beyond the immediate needs of our clients and identify their overall business considerations and objectives.'

Information Builders, established in 1975, has a global turnover of $287 million. Within the UK, its customers include most of the Times Top 100 companies, including BG, BT and British Airways, as well as smaller companies. Its software is used to deliver business-critical information at the time it is needed, and can be used on virtually any computing environment. Underlying the software products is broad data access including packages such as SAP, J D Edwards, Oracle, and Microsoft SQLServer.

9.8

The Internet – a Driving Force for Change

Alex Fry
Technical Director, JKD

It is already apparent that the Internet presents vast opportunities to businesses, whether it is used for promotions, developing new revenue streams or gaining entrance to new markets. But the Internet offers the forward-thinking business far more than a way to target new and existing customers – it has potentially enormous positive implications throughout the entire supply chain.

With careful planning, it is now possible to use the power of the Internet to improve systems, individual departments, relationships and levels of information to such an extent that significant competitive advantages can be derived from a successful Internet strategy. Indeed, for most companies, a Website is only the first step along the road towards enormous cost savings and increased profitability.

This was the intended goal of EDI (electronic data interchange), a standards-based approach to conducting business electronically. But its inherent inflexibility, and the high cost of implementation, meant that the process was really only practical for large corporations. However, the rising popularity of the Internet has introduced open, flexible standards that can be used by everyone – from multinational conglomerates to sole traders. Most businesses find that they begin benefiting from it the moment they connect.

The most obvious beneficiaries of a well-focused Internet strategy are existing customers. With well-publicised opportunities available in electronic commerce (e-commerce), niche marketing, market research and improved customer services, the important question is how these targets can best be achieved.

The key to developing an effective, client-facing site comes from answering the age-old question: what do your customers want from you? One thing is certain, they will want to know that you are listening to them. The most basic and important aspect of any business site is providing the opportunity to receive and respond to feedback. Responsibility must be apportioned for handling these communications as quickly as possible, and with the Internet response times can be cut from days to hours.

These feedback channels can be developed into extremely cost-effective market research programmes, and the services provided through the site tailored appropriately. It is this emphasis on customer service that will help distinguish your company from its competitors in the new global market.

The ability to tailor content and services to specific groups and individuals makes Internet marketing the most potent new business tool since the invention of the postal service. For example, products can be promoted to an entire database of relevant customers automatically and at very low cost, where before a resource-intensive mailing or telesales campaign was required. By speeding up the sales process, improving the analysis of marketing campaigns and reducing costs, any business can exploit these new opportunities with a far greater degree of flexibility.

For those who have watched the Internet develop into a force for change in business, the publicity surrounding e-commerce comes as no surprise. If there is just one reason for believing that a single European currency is inevitable, it is the rising popularity of e-commerce with businesses and consumers alike, and the increasing sophistication of (and thus consumer confidence in) the technology behind it. The nature of e-commerce and the vast range of services encompassed by the term means that there are very few factors that will prevent any company from conducting some form of business over the Internet – from simple order processing to full credit card transactions.

But the impact of the Internet does not end with the consumer. The relationships that a company has with its suppliers can be significantly improved via the use of Internet technology.

The clearest benefits are derived from the speed with which information can be accessed and exchanged. In basic terms, it is possible to automate standard processes such as the posting of product availability lists, keeping delivery times up to date with the latest information and processing orders. In fact, almost any process that is regularly completed can be automated to the benefit of both parties via a public or private Website.

The automation of these systems will lead to a greater quantity of pertinent management information being instantly available. This, in turn, can facilitate improved decision-making processes, leading to improved relationships throughout the supply chain. Within a business, areas that might benefit directly include product development, procurement and customer services.

If all of a company's suppliers can be persuaded to send this information to a Website, it is a simple matter to compare price lists and availability of similar products and then to choose the most appropriate supplier at each juncture. It is the use and availability of information such as this, provided by the Internet, that will provide you with significant competitive advantages in the medium to long term.

Clearly, the Internet is facilitating the development of a truly global market, with low barriers of entry because there is no longer a need for a physical presence in any country where you conduct business.

Owing to the proliferation of corporate Websites worldwide, it is highly probable that a great deal of the information that your company needs to make informed decisions and strategic alliances and to respond quickly to changes in particular markets is available somewhere on the Internet.

The sheer volume of the information available means that advanced filtering and search techniques are needed to locate certain pieces of information. This clearly requires the education and training of employees, but this additional empowerment will reap enormous long-term benefits throughout the decision-making chain. Although many people are concerned that full access to the Internet may reduce employee efficiency, case studies have shown that the advantages far outweigh any possible dangers.

Unlike traditional IT projects, incorporating the Internet throughout each level of your company need not require huge investment. Tangible business benefits can be achieved relatively quickly and cheaply, if use of the Internet is developed as part of an overall business strategy.

To exploit this new environment fully, experience has already shown us that the implementation of the Internet throughout a company should only be considered after the careful evaluation of existing and intended business practice – usually in partnership with a professional consultant.

Future benefits – whether medium or long term – will come from learning how best to develop your business in conjunction with this new technology. There is no doubt that using the Internet will be a necessity for any successful company in the twenty-first century – and the sooner you consider how best to incorporate it into your business practices, the greater the advantage you will enjoy over your competitors.

Alex Fry is an Internet & multimedia consultant and Technical Director of **JKD**.

JKD is a full service multimedia agency, offering companies of all sizes the skills and expertise necessary to brand, design and develop their corporate identity – whatever the chosen medium.

From the initial consultancy required to establish the most effective media, through to development of the recommended solution, JKD can carry a project through from conception to completion.

The key personnel in each department have years of specialist experience in their respective fields. Together with this experience comes the expertise necessary to apply this knowledge to finding the most appropriate solution for each individual client.

By utilising these attributes, members of the JKD team have worked on projects for such varied clients as BT, Image Bank, Guinness PLC, John Lewis Partnership, British Tourist Authority and Case Technology.

The combined strengths of the company have allowed JKD to establish relationships with companies of various types; from providing technical consultancy and production services to design agencies, to design support for IT departments and technology-based companies. For other companies, such as Stannah Lifts, the John Lewis Partnership and Waitrose, meanwhile, we offer a complete service. The range of consultancy and production services offered by the company broadly cover the three areas of design, technology and editorial content.

Part 10
Rewards and Benefits

10.1

Growth – What a Challenge

Timothy Galpin
Practice Leader, Worldwide Human Resources Strategy Team, Watson Wyatt Worldwide

Growth has always presented challenges for organisations. Timothy Galpin, practice leader for our worldwide human resources strategy team, looks at just how challenging and intimidating today's growth can be.

Given double- and even triple-digit yearly growth rates for many companies over the past four or five years, we would assume that management is getting better at managing growth-related changes. Yet the truth is that most are frustrated or even frightened by the seemingly endless list of issues that come with rapid expansion.

While many of the headaches of company growth are related to operational issues, our experience shows that most problems are created by people factors. In fact, one of our clients who was overwhelmed by the complexities of her company's fast growth rate commented, 'On paper, our growth has looked great to analysts and shareholders, but it has presented people challenges like none I have ever seen. Growth like we have had in the past few years has really raised the bar for our whole management team.'

Why is growth so intimidating?

Growth today is unlike that of the 'good old days' when planning and implementation activities spanned several years and were, in the main, sequential. Major expansions – a push into a new market, the establishment of overseas locations, entirely new manufacturing and so on – were planned for months, phased in over time and often done in isolation from other initiatives.

Today, growth initiatives overlap. For example, an acquisition will overlap with expansion into foreign markets, new product launches and technology implementations. There is no time for either management or employees to catch their breath between initiatives.

When a company grows into foreign markets, even simple communication becomes a challenge, facing language and timezone obstacles. Differences in culture can derail even the most well-intentioned activities, and skill sets can vary widely from region to region.

Fast growth creates huge challenges in creating and maintaining organisational competencies. Skilled workers with key attributes for growth – technology, communication, language, management and leadership skills – are becoming harder to come by as demand for them increases.

The growth challenge

There are many common change dynamics that come into play during rapid growth – shortened timescales, increased uncertainty, intensified scrutiny from analysts and shareholders, strained competency levels, politics and positioning and cultural shifts. Often these are overlooked as growth begins and further ignored as expansion accelerates.

So, what's the best way to avoid the risks associated with these change dynamics? In addition to planning for growth intelligently, ensure that sound change management principles, tools and techniques are applied during the planning and execution of expansion plans. Below are some of the lessons learnt by expanding companies when ensuring successful growth.

Change fast

Fast growth requires fast change. Fast change requires strong decisions and promises that they be made quickly. Productivity, morale and performance almost always fall off during times of change (see Figure 10.1.1) and growth is no different. Early on, people at all organisational levels consider the impact on themselves. Will my boss change? Do I have the knowledge and skills needed? How will I learn them if I don't? Will this change the way I work? Will my workload increase? Moving quickly – but not recklessly – into

are people looking for answers to their personal questions, they also want to know about how operations will work in the future. When they don't hear recurrent messages from management about the growth strategy, initiatives to achieve desired growth, how implementation will unfold and what the timeframe is, people perceive a lack of leadership, direction and control of the company.

Clear, consistent and frequent (weekly) communications – even when no answers, only updates on progress, are available – go a long way towards gaining the commitment of both management and employees. As with any change, the most disconcerting message is that of silence – a message that should be avoided.

Fast growth often overloads the company. When growth heats up, systems, processes and people can easily become overwhelmed. Particularly vulnerable areas are contact points with the customer – sales and service. Many companies experience problems with their salesforce and increased complaints about customer service during periods of expansion. For those employees who interface directly with customers, it is often difficult for them to avoid using the pace of growth as an excuse for problems. Customers often hear comments such as: 'I'm sorry, but we are just putting in a new system,' or 'We have just hired a lot of new people and they are still learning.'

Mechanisms to protect sales and service can include short-term incentives, communication meetings with employees to set expectation levels, information for customer service personnel at helpdesks and call centres, and special advertising aimed at communicating to customers the continued commitment to service.

Manage resistance

Although many of these change-management concepts serve the purpose of helping to reduce resistance, it is important to recognise that resistance is not necessarily an indication that something is going wrong.

Instead, resistance is simply a sign that change is happening. People need knowledge, skills, willingness and belief to accept change. Communication satisfies the need for knowledge. Skills can be enhanced through training and education. Performance management helps remove a lack of willingness. Solid leadership builds a belief in the changes that are occurring.

What does the future hold?

All indications are that expansion will be the norm for many companies into the future. Although growth looks good on paper, the real challenge comes from the people and change-management issues created by it. Applying an effective change management perspective to company growth significantly increases the chances for success. The investment and business risks associated with growth are simply too high to do otherwise.

10.2

Strategic Reward – a Gateway to Improved Business Success

Kevin Spring
Partner in charge of Watson Wyatt's strategic reward team.

Most organisations spend a great deal of time and effort formulating strategic business plans, which include clear objectives for each area of operation. However, many have difficulty implementing these plans because management fails to take full account of the human factor. As the corporate vision unfolds, new strategies are rarely explained effectively outside the boardroom and employees are asked to embrace new objectives without a proper understanding of them. Little wonder that many change initiatives fail.

One of the problems is that some organisations still regard their employees as a cost of doing business rather than a dynamic resource. While they can see that clearly defined business strategies are necessary to direct the organisation, they fail to acknowledge that an informed, engaged and performance-driven workforce powers it. They will accept that employees have abilities, but fail to appreciate that it is ability coupled with motivation that produces optimum output.

Ensuring correct alignment

If employees are not aligned with business strategy, the long-term success of the business will be threatened. It is not possible to achieve this alignment without an effective reward strategy, but unfortunately many organisations have reward strategies that reinforce the wrong behaviours and attitudes, or reflect what the organisation used to be, rather than what it needs to become.

So how does an organisation develop an effective reward strategy? The first step is to translate the business strategy into an HR strategy that will identify the skills, behaviours and attitudes that are crucial to the success of the business. The next step is to consider the kind of reward strategy that will support the HR strategy and ensure a successful outcome. This is a major challenge that provides the HR function with an opportunity to show how it can add value to the business. When the reward strategy is clear, attention can be given to the design of its component parts, including the overall balance between direct pay (cash) and indirect pay (benefits) and issues such as work content, career and status. Too many organisations consider design before the reward strategy has been agreed.

The following model illustrates the process.

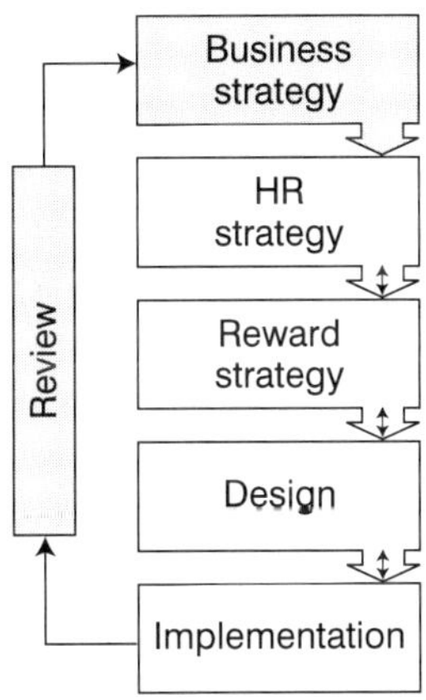

Figure 10.2.1 Reward Strategy Process

Ensuring the right mix

Reward is not the only issue that needs to be addressed when seeking to encourage positive behaviours and attitudes within an organisation. Others include management style, training, job design, communications and a supportive work environment. However, it must be recognised that each element of the reward package delivers a particular message to employees. For example, a well-designed bonus plan will deliver a strong motivational message, whereas a pension plan will deliver a softer message of reinforcement and security. The art is to get the right balance and for messages to support each other and work together.

When an organisation's reward strategy is reviewed, it is often found that mixed messages are being given to employees. It may be that they are being asked to play their part in a challenging environment, with an emphasis on achievement, while the messages that they are receiving through their reward package are more about feeling warm, safe and secure. These are perhaps messages that reflect a bygone era and that may now be the cause of employee confusion about the organisation's future needs.

It is therefore necessary, when assessing the current and potential elements of a reward package, to acknowledge the three main categories that rewards need to address: compensation, security and performance.

When the right balance is achieved in these areas, the reward strategy will become more aligned with business strategy and appropriate and consistent messages will be given to employees about expected behaviour.

In the area of performance, it is important to ensure that the amount of reward available to employees is in line with expectations. These must be managed, but if employees deliver the earth, they may expect (and deserve) to receive the moon. Many incentive plans have failed because employees do not consider the reward to be adequate for the additional effort involved. It then becomes harder to encourage them to go the extra mile. Where sales staff are concerned, it is necessary to ensure that incentives are designed in the light of business objectives and the direction in which the organisation needs to be driven. If an organisation wishes to break into new markets, but sales staff can meet their targets by selling conventional products, it should not come as a surprise if this particular business objective is not met.

A more flexible approach

Employee benefits play an increasingly important role within a total reward package and many European organisations, particularly in the UK, have adopted the concept of 'flexible benefits'. This has been in recognition of the fact that employee needs and preferences are considerably influenced by such factors as age, family commitments, job function, locality and so on. If benefits are provided on a totally prescriptive basis, it is difficult to develop the right kind of 'psychological contract' between employer and employee. For this contract to work effectively, it must respond to the expectations and requirements of both parties and accept that these will not be the same in all circumstances.

Increasingly, flexible programmes are being used to support culture change and the development of a reward strategy that seeks to restructure the way in which employees are remunerated. They can certainly help ease the effects of organisational change and restructuring in a cost-effective way. This is particularly so in circumstances such as a merger or acquisition.

A flexible benefits programme can be a key feature of a reward strategy,

10.3

Pensions: the Flexibility of Defined Contribution

Andrew Cheseldine
Senior Consultant for Watson Wyatt, Financial Services Group, London Office

For a human resources (HR) manager, pension schemes are not an end in themselves, they are merely a means to an end. Ignoring, for the moment, issues of company culture and paternalism, the underlying purposes of a pension scheme are recruitment and retention of the right quality of staff. In this chapter we have made the assumption that, as a small and growing business, you are neither in a position to offer, nor would be willing to provide, defined benefit pension benefits to your employees. The problem with defined benefit (DB) schemes is that they offer guaranteed, fixed (in real terms) future benefits. Thus, the employer effectively writes a blank cheque that can be presented at any time in the future, to cover the additional cost of providing these benefits if the future costs or investment returns do not meet expectations.

Within defined contribution (DC) pension schemes, it is the employees who run the investment risks. The employer defines a level of contribution that it is prepared to make towards a pension scheme on behalf of its employees and that is the extent of its liability. The contribution may be defined in many ways, including a fixed amount in sterling terms, or as a percentage of salary (either including or excluding bonuses and other fluctuating payments). The contribution may also be fixed or variable in relation to:

- the seniority of the employee;
- the age of the employee;

- the length of service of the employee;
- the level of contributions made by the employees themselves;
- the profitability (or other financial measure) of the employer;
- a combination of any or all of the above.

The purpose of this chapter is to draw a correlation between pension scheme design and HR issues, showing how varying the scheme design can achieve different objectives for the HR manager. Key HR issues for small- to medium-sized enterprises (SMEs) at the moment include:

- recruitment of staff;
- retention of staff;
- alignment of benefits to business objectives;
- modifying both corporate and individual behaviour;
- external market pressures from both competitors and clients.

There a number of planning models that we can use as tools to allow employers to focus on key issues. For SMEs, these issues can often be encapsulated in the phrase 'value and values':

- common cultural values that you wish to see adopted by your employees;
- benefits that are fully valued by your employees, thus leading to easier recruitment and higher retention of staff;
- value for money of the benefits that you put in place.

Value can mean many different things to different people. The phrase 'value judgment' implies subjectivity, and when commentators discuss 'simple values' they rarely if ever turn out to be simple.

As an HR manager, you may well want your employees to share common cultural values with your business. These may include a desire for individual empowerment, as SMEs often do not have the resources available to implement tight supervision, even if they want to. This is, of course, one of the strengths of SMEs, in that they are not overburdened with bureaucracy. It therefore makes sense for these cultural values to be mirrored by the employer's pension scheme.

For instance, is it appropriate to expect employees to make day-to-day business decisions worth thousands of pounds, but not allow them to decide how to invest their pension fund, at what age they plan to retire or generally plan their retirement?

Offering a DC pension scheme can, because of its potential flexibility (of investment choice, retirement age and contributions) in comparison to DB schemes, help align your benefits strategy with overall HR strategy. Examples of this could be:

- where overhead costs, and especially variability, are key issues, ensuring predictability of cost, in real terms, in regard to pension contributions;
- where there is little willingness or ability to perform this function for pension benefits, minimising administration.

Your HR strategy may well have established a number of quantitative and qualitative targets for a successful workforce. Table 10.3.1 shows a selection of some of the ways in which a DC scheme can be tailored to minimise barriers to your strategy and reinforce positive benefits.

Table 10.3.1 Tailoring a DC pension scheme

HR strategy issue	DC pension scheme design issue
How many of your existing staff you wish to retain over given periods of time	Employer contributions can be varied in line with length of service
Incremental value of experience diminishes after time	Establish a maximum employer contribution after a set period of time
Whether the skill sets you most value are directly related to length of experience/age	Employer contributions can be varied in line with age
How any skills gap that exists is bridgeable – whether it is preferable to build skills internally though training and experience or 'buying-in' staff who have already acquired those skills with previous employers	Employer contributions can be varied in line with qualifications; eligibility criteria can be varied
Whether the corporate behaviour needs to be modified in terms of motivation	Pension schemes are not great motivation tools – you can, however, align them to other benefits, for example by pensioning bonuses on a special percentage basis or introducing a profit-sharing element.

It is also important to show value for money, both from the employer's and the employees' perspectives. You can obtain excellent terms from some pension providers, but to obtain the best all-round value for contributions you should review the:

- financial issues;
- charging structures;
- investment performance;
- administration; and
- attitude

of a number of providers, selecting the one that best fits your business's culture as well as financial needs.

MARCUS -Changing the Rules of Contract Hire and Leasing

DON'T LET THE THOUGHT OF EARLY-TERMINATION CHARGES PUT YOU OFF THIS SUPERB WAY OF OPERATING VEHICLES.

If you're in business you probably run cars, and if you run cars there's a good chance that at least some of them are on a contract hire or leasing arrangement with one of the hundreds of suppliers in the UK.

So how do you decide which provider to choose? After all they really are all much of a muchness - or are they?

Carlisle based Eden Vehicle Rentals Ltd (EVR) tell us that they are a bit different - and judging by their approach to early termination charges they are very different indeed!

Industry surveys constantly show that termination charges are held by users to be the biggest down side of contract hire - and by non-users as the main reason that they are non-users. And with some justification.

As anyone who has been there knows, getting out of a three year contract mid term can be a very expensive experience - even a work-a-day Ford or Vauxhall could set you back £2000 or more. But those are the rules and nothing much can be done - or can it?

Austen Davies, EVR's Sales Director, disagrees: "Establishing and running a business is quite demanding enough these days and plans and projections are all part of the process it's true. But they are just that - plans and projections - and they change! I have never met anyone who has claimed to be in exactly the position they predicted they would be three years ago, even long established businesses - so what chance do those in the early stages of development have?

Managing Director, Paul Gilligan (right) pictured with Austen Davies, Sales Director.

It's hardly a surprise therefore when business people reject all the advantages of contract hire because of its one big disadvantage - the big bill if they want to send a car back early.

If this is a scenario you can relate to, you could do a lot worse than get acquainted with EVR's pet contract hire and leasing product

M.A.R.C.U.S

EVR supplies cars and commercials nationwide

MARCUS first saw the light of day as a VAT efficient, nearly-new car offering in the summer of 1995. Because the vehicles weren't actually new, and because the big depreciation hit had already been taken, the scheme had something missing - no early termination charges!

Davies again: "We recognised that a "Penalty free" contact hire product might find favour with anyone who had been bitten already - as well as with those who had previously been put off by the size of the teeth!

So EVR launched "soft termination" onto an unsuspecting fleet world.

The soft termination option means that having paid three rentals in advance on a three year contract, the hirer can, if he needs, return the vehicle at any time with nothing to pay other than any rentals that have actually fallen due plus any excess mileage/damage charges. It really is that simple!

MARCUS's appeal was such that EVR soon found that the quantity and quality of nearly new vehicles was insufficient to meet demand, so using their huge negotiating power, (the Company's "fleet" consisted of around 14,000 units at the end of 1998) selected brand-new models were brought onto the programme - all with the benefit of the soft termination option - and users may chose from several hundred vehicles - cars and vans- available at any one time.

You might expect there to be a "cost" associated with the soft termination benefit - but not a bit of it! The rentals on MARCUS cars are highly competitive in a competitive market and the maintenance package is second to none, including all routine servicing and mechanical repairs plus unlimited tyres, batteries, exhausts, etc. Valuable additions such as accident and fuel management elevate the service to rarely experienced levels.

"Our customers aren't reticent about telling what they like and dislike", Davies continued, "and a lot of them are cynical about so called "open disclosure" policies that intimate much and deliver little - an all inclusive package with no frills and no stings in the tail, that's what they want - so we give it to them".

EVR has several hundred vehicles available at any one time.

Another MARCUS vehicle freshly prepared and ready for a new home.

MARCUS vehicles also come with RAC Cover (including recovery and roadside assistance) and GAP Insurance - all at no extra charge - and you don't get that as a rule.

"Rules? If we at EVR don't like the rules, we change them!" says Davies.

They certainly do.

Eden Vehicle Rentals Ltd was established in 1962 and since 1989 has been part of the Yorkshire Bank Group, itself a subsidiary of the world-wide National Australia Bank Group - one of biggest banking corporations on Earth.

Based in Carlisle, Cumbria, EVR has offices in London, Birmingham, Manchester, Bradford and Glasgow.

You can find out more about EVR and MARCUS by calling 01228 511107 - or by sending a copy of this article together with your business card to:

Eden Vehicle Rentals Ltd
Marketing Dept, Kingstown Broadway
Carlisle CA3 0HA
Tel: 01228 511107 Fax: 01228 515827

Having designed a scheme, selected a provider and ensured smooth administration of the scheme, you have one further, very important project to undertake.

Communication is fundamental to DC pension schemes. The communication exercise need not, necessarily, be very involved. However, it is important that you obtain full benefit from your incurred costs (contributions and expenses). Clear, understandable pensions communication will increase take-up rates and the perceived value of your scheme to employees.

The trend in member communication towards financial education in the widest sense has become necessary as there has been a shift of responsibility:

- from the state to individuals;
- from employer to employees by the move from DB to DC pension schemes and especially to group personal pensions (GPP).

Equally, benefits communication programmes are increasingly seen by employers as an opportunity to address corporate and individual behavioural issues. Messages conveyed therefore need to be coherent with the employer's HR strategy.

With all communications, there are certain basics that need to be addressed:

- *Objective(s)* – the most common objectives encompass:
  - helping employees understand financial arrangements so as to make well-informed decisions;
  - setting employer-sponsored benefits in context and providing unbiased advice;
  - properly targeted support and guidance.
- *Audience* – who are you addressing, how much do they know already, what do you expect their attitude to be?
- *Content* – what must, should and could be covered.
- *Delivery media* – what format(s) are most appropriate to the audience and the message:
  - formal or informal;
  - written, audio/visual, electronic or face-to-face presentations (on group or individual bases);
  - bespoke design or 'off the peg', perhaps using the provider's standard literature.

The most important consideration is, what will *work*? A multimedia programme may be suitable for IT companies or banks, but is unlikely to be effective for shopfloor workers. Equally, different media may well be appropriate for the launch of a new scheme compared with updates for existing members. A combination of approaches is often the most effective.

The flexibility that defined contribution pension schemes offer can be a tremendous help in aligning benefit strategy with business objectives. It is, however, only one of the factors to take into account and, as ever, pensions must be viewed in context – the business objectives should drive the HR strategy, which itself determines benefit design.

10.4

Trouble Free Pension: a Case Study

Julia Ward
Senior Consultant for Watson Wyatt, Financial Services Group, Reigate Office

With business plans to draw up, budgets to prepare, suppliers and clients to keep happy and bringing in a profit, the last thing on your mind might be pensions. Considerations such as 'too expensive' or 'too complicated and troublesome' are common excuses, but this need not be the case. Providing a pension plan for employees can be easier than you think. This chapter concentrates on this by way of a case study, highlighting the main decisions facing an employer which wants to set up a cost-effective, 'trouble-free' pension arrangement.

First, why have a pension scheme at all? From our experience, for most employers it seems to be the desire to be competitive (the 'everyone else seems to provide one' approach) and, therefore, to recruit and retain the right people for the job. There is also the opportunity to save National Insurance by paying a pension contribution rather than additional salary. Some employers take a more paternalistic view, however, believing that they have a duty to help employees provide for their retirement, realising that the state will not provide a sufficient level of post-retirement income. At the very least, they can act as facilitators, ensuring good value for money for employees' contributions by engaging advisers to research the market and by economies of scale.

Company A, a small publishing firm with around 125 employees (approximately 25 per cent of whom are part-time), asked for assistance in designing and setting up a pension scheme for its staff. The first step was to establish their objectives, both from an HR and financial viewpoint, while at the same time considering what the employees' expectations might reasonably be.

Company A wanted to provide benefits which:

- resulted in clearly defined, affordable and stable future costs;
- made a positive contribution to staff retention;
- were flexible enough to satisfy the needs of a varied workforce;
- were easy to communicate to employees, allowing them to understand and predict the pension benefits they would receive;
- would keep internal administration to a minimum.

In addition, it was important that any pension arrangement introduced was durable, as the company did not want to have to make significant changes to it in the foreseeable future.

We suggested that feedback should also be obtained from the employees to find out what they wanted from a pension, the results of which were varied:

- To provide good value for money.
- To be flexible enough to meet with job changes, career breaks and varying contributions.
- To provide a good, guaranteed income at retirement.

With the above in mind, a comparison of the different types of pension arrangements, from defined benefits to personal pensions, was presented, with a group personal pension (GPP) finally being recommended. A GPP fitted neatly with the company's objectives and also, to a large extent, the articulated needs of the employees.

Next on the agenda was to agree on the overall structure of the scheme and then to consider the nuts and bolts of actual design.

Most GPP providers offer a complete package which includes administration and fund management, commonly referred to as 'bundled' products. This means that once a provider has been chosen, contributions can only be invested in the funds that they offer, which obviously restricts choice.

Alternatively, a more flexible structure is possible, whereby the administrative and investment functions are carried out by different specialist organisations (the 'unbundled' approach). The beauty of the 'unbundled' approach is that it offers employers the opportunity to design a scheme that suits the needs of a particular company and its employees. It also means that if a manager does not perform to expectations, he or she can easily be replaced, without the employer needing to worry about who would deal with the administration and without employees' pensions suffering the penalties that are still commonly applied to most personal pensions when money is transferred elsewhere. But such flexibility comes at a price. The 'unbundled' approach tends to be more expensive, with the employer usually picking up the separate administration costs.

Bearing in mind that the company's main priority was cost control, it was suggested that the GPP would be established through a 'bundled' product. But there was still the issue of value for money to be considered. In the past, it has been commonplace for an adviser to be remunerated by way of commission. This meant that the pension provider paid over part of the contributions to the adviser to pay for his or her costs. Typically, up to 60 per cent of the first year's contributions could disappear in this way. The result of this approach is that not only is a smaller proportion of the contributions actually invested, but also a 'penalty' would usually be applied if contributions stopped, or the member tried to transfer the funds to another provider. For Company A, this option was not viewed as offering value for money to its employees.

The company decided to pay a separate fee for the advice it had received and for any advice its employees might need, rather than follow the commission route. This allowed for any potential commission earned to be reinvested in the GPP for the benefit of members (in the form of higher allocation rates and/or the removal of a per member monthly policy fee). Not only did this mean better value for money for the members, but such 'clean' contract terms were also easier for the employees to understand.

As for the particular design of the GPP, the following issues had to be addressed:

- eligibility;
- definition of pensionable salary;
- contribution structure.

Although all of these were important, we shall concentrate on the issue of contribution levels (see Figure 10.4.1). The choice of how contributions are structured is varied, from providing a flat rate (regardless of status) to rewarding long-standing employees for their loyalty. It is also possible to tier the rates according to age, as it is generally accepted that pensions are more expensive the older a person is. Some employers offer a flat rate of contributions, but with an agreed top-up if certain financial targets are met. This involves all of the employees in the prosperity of the firm, which may, in turn, lead to increased productivity.

Company A wanted to set a contribution structure that was seen as competitive for a business of its size and also among companies which it saw as its competitors. Recent research showed that the average employer contribution to a GPP (for companies employing fewer than 250 people) was around 5 per cent of basic salary. Bearing this in mind, together with the

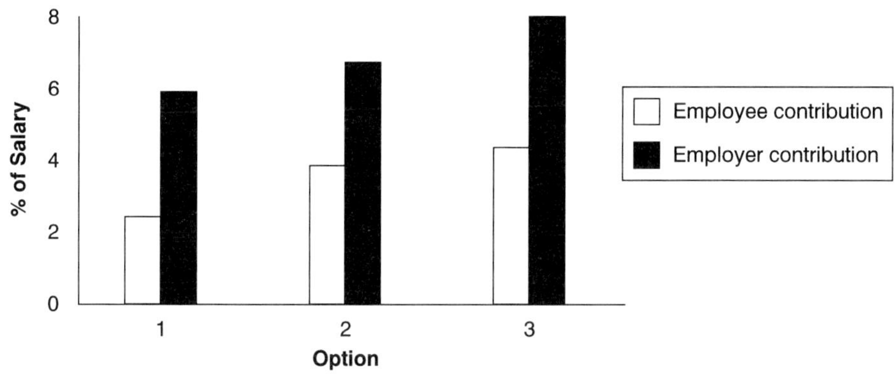

Figure 10.4.1 GPP contribution structure

demands for cost constraint, an employer's contribution of 6 per cent of salary was recommended. While offering this, Company A was also keen that its employees took some responsibility for saving for their retirement and so decided to introduce a compulsory employee contribution of 3 per cent of salary. In order to encourage staff further, it agreed to increase its contribution in line with every additional 1 per cent made by the employee, but capped at a maximum aggregate employer contribution of 8 per cent.

It was stressed to Company A that one of the most important factors when setting up a GPP was recognising that the responsibility of pension planning rested with employees. They must decide how much they pay, into which fund(s) the contributions are invested and what level and type of benefit they choose at their selected retirement date. Therefore, Company A was responsible for ensuring that its employees received the right amount of information to help them understand these decisions and guide them to making the right choices, based on their own personal circumstances. This meant running a clear, structured programme of financial education. The objective of such education was to increase understanding and appreciation of the benefits offered and to motivate employees to take control of their overall financial affairs.

Once established, Company A had very little involvement with the GPP, as the provider dealt direct with members. Innovations such as Internet links, electronic application forms and telephone helplines all minimised the ongoing costs of the GPP.

Company A, knowing that setting up a pension scheme was a big decision, dedicated time and effort in the initial stages to ensure that it had an affordable and manageable scheme that would take them into the millennium and beyond. More than 90 per cent of the eligible employees (including part-timers) joined, and two years on there has been a sufficient reduction in staff turnover for Company A to declare the project a success.

Our experience shows that key indicators for a successful personal pension are:

- the employer's commitment to offering a valuable, and valued, pension package;
- building a clear understanding of both the employer's and employees' objectives;
- comprehensive forward planning;
- general understandability of the pension and its benefits;
- a programme of financial education.

If you bear these points in mind, you can create a pension plan that helps your business to grow, rather than one that becomes an administrative burden, holding back your progress.

Watson Wyatt Worldwide is a leading management consulting firm with more than 5000 associates in 90 offices. Providing advice on employee benefits, retirement schemes and the full range of human resource issues, we work with organisations of all types and sizes.

Appendix: Contact Addresses

3i plc
91 Waterloo Road
London SE1 8XP
Tel: 0171 928 3131
Fax: 0171 928 0058
Web site: www.3ics.co.uk

Accounting Centre Ltd
Tel: 0500 130813

Allied Domecq
Web site: www.allieddomecq.plc

Aston Science Parks
c/o Vector Marketing
Tel: 0121 522 4194
Contact: Mike Skerrett

Baan Business Systems UK
Unit 8
Centre 27 Business Park
Birkstall
West Yorkshire WF17 9TB
Tel: 01924 420900
Fax: 01924 420999
E-mail: jredgrave@baan.nl

The Bank Relationship Consultancy
17 St Helens Place
London EC3A 6DE
Tel: 0171 256 5657

Baylis Generators Ltd
Haven Studio
Eel Pie Island
Twickenham
Middlesex TW1 3DY
Tel: 0181 892 1850
Fax: 0181 891 0673

Brintons Carpets
PO Box 16
Exchange Street
Kidderminster
Worcestershire DY10 1AG
Tel: 01562 820000
Fax: 01562 515597
Contact: Sylvia Herbert

Campus Ventures Ltd
Tel: 0161 273 5110 (University of Manchester)
Contact: Prof D W Auckland

The Caudwell Group
c/o Stuart Laurence Group
Tel: 0161 832 5574
Contact: Iain Macauley or John Bodic

CBI
Centrepoint
103 New Oxford Street
London WC1A 1DU
0171 379 7400

Chameleon Training and Consulting
Renaissance House
Foundation Park
Maidenhead
Berkshire SL6 3UD
Tel: 01628 413641
Fax: 01628 413555
Web site: www.chamcon.co.uk

Cisco Systems Ltd
3 The Square
Stockley Park
Uxbridge
Middlesex UB11 1BN
Tel: 0181 756 8000
Fax: 0181 756 8099
E-mail: pmountf@cisco.com
Contact: Paul Mountford

Copyright Promotions Licensing Group plc
Metropolis House
22 Percy Street
London W1P 0DN
Tel: 0171 580 7431
Fax: 0171 631 1147

Delta Air Lines
Reservations & Ticket Sales
Tel: 0800 414767
For further information about the call centre and the company in general, call Delta's Corporate Communications Dept:
Tel: 0171 932 8376
Contact: Olivia Cullis

Design Council
Haymarket House
1 Oxendon Street
London SW1Y 4EE
Tel: 0171 208 2121
Fax: 0171 839 6033
Contact: Sean Blair

DTZ Debenham Thorpe
44 Brook Street
London W1A 4AG
Tel: 0171 408 7520
Fax: 0171 408 7510

Dutton Engineering (Woodside) Ltd
3 Tyne Road
Middlefield Industrial Estate
Sandy
Bedfordshire SG19 1SA
Tel: 01767 683191
Fax: 01767 692258
E-mail: duttoneng@compuserve.com
Contact: Kevin O'Brien (Engineering Enquiries) or Tina Mason (Business Excellence)

Eastern Electricity
Tel: 0845 600 1998
Eastern Natural Gas
Tel: 0181 362 2828

EMC Computer Systems (UK) Ltd
Tel: 0870 608 7777
Web site: www.emc.com

Euro Sales Finance
Halton House
20–23 Holborn
London EC1N 2JD
Tel: 0171 880 5000
Fax: 171 880 5010

Express Engineering
Tel: 0191 487 2021
Fax: 0191 497 7117
Web site: www.express-group.co.uk

Gresham Bell Limited
Newspaper House
8/16 Great New Street
London EC4A 3BN
Tel: 0171 353 3030
E-mail: info@greshambell.com
Contact: Paul Duncanson

Groundwork Ltd
85–87 Cornwall Street
Birmingham B3 3BY
Tel: 0121 236 8565
Fax: 0121 236 7356
E-mail: info@groundwork.org.uk
Web site: www.groundwork.org.uk

Hewlett Packard Education
Registration and Enquiries
Tel: 01344 763311
Web site: www.hp.com/uk/education

Independent Insurance Ltd
Gordon Henry House
Station Road
Edenbridge
Kent TN8 5LY
Tel: 01732 865211
Contact: Marketing Dept

Information Builders
Marketing Dept
Wembley Point
Harrow Road
Wembley
Middlesex HA9 6DE
Tel: 0181 982 4780
Fax: 0181 982 4764

Isis Innovation Ltd
2 Southpark Road
Oxford OX1 3UB
Tel: 01865 272411
Fax: 01865 272412

JBA Software Co
Tel: 01527 49644
Contact: Kate Scott
Web site: www.jbaworld.com

Jim Shedden
41 Earlbank Avenue
Glasgow G14 9HE
E-mail: JIM@reeveltd.demon.co.uk

JKD
Tel: 0171 793 9399
Fax: 0171 793 9299
Contact: Alex Fry

KPMG
Tel: 0116 256 6000
Contact: John Eggleston

Larpent Newton
24–26 Baltic Street West
London EC1 0UR
Tel: 0171 250 9111
Fax: 0171 251 2609
Contact: Charles Breese

Livingstone Guarantee
Acre House
11–15 William Road
London NW1 3ER
Tel: 0171 388 4242
Fax: 0171 383 3389
E-mail: livgntee.demon.co.uk

Lloyds Development Capital
50 Grosvenor Street
London W1X 9FH
Tel: 0171 499 1500
Web site: www.ldc.co.uk
E-mail: info@ldc.co.uk
Contact: Patrick Sellars

Lombard Business Finance
Lombard House
3 Princess Way
Redhill
Surrey RH1 1NP
Tel: 01737 774111
Fax: 01737 776977

LTE Scientific Ltd
Greenbridge
Oldham
Cheshire OL3 7EN
Tel: 01457 876221
Fax: 01457 870131

Media Audits Ltd
16 Dufours Place
London W1V 1FE
Tel: 0171 734 4080
Fax: 0171 439 2455

Mitel Telecom Ltd
Mitel Business Park
Portskewett
Monmouthshire NP6 4YR
Tel: 0870 909 3030

Norman Price
c/o DTI Innovation Unit
Tel: 0171 215 1479

Pal International
Tel: 0116 272 0820

PPP Healthcare
Tel: 01892 508715

RSL COM
Victoria House
London Square
Guildford
Surrey GU1 1UN
Contact: Barry Mowbray

Sanmex International PLC
5–9 Dalmarnock Road
Glasgow G73 1NY
Tel: 0141 647 2244

Sun Microsystems Ltd
Bagshot Manor
Green Lane
Bagshot
Surrey GU19 5NL
Tel: 01276 416853
Fax: 01276 416707
E-mail: jon.tutcher@uk.sun.com

Unipart UGC Ltd
Unipart House
Garsington Road
Cowley
Oxford OX4 2PG
Tel: 01865 383368
Fax: 01865 383047

Unisys Global Customer Services Europe
Baker's Court
Baker's Road
Uxbridge
Middlesex UB8 1RG
Tel: 01895 862233
Fax: 01895 862253
Web site: www.unisys.com

Watson Wyatt Partners
21 Tothill Street
Westminster
London SW1H 9LL
Tel: 0171 222 8033
Fax: 0171 222 0182

Watson Wyatt Partners (Reigate Office)
Watson House
London Road
Reigate
Surrey RH2 9PQ
Tel: 01737 241144
Fax: 01737 241496
Contact: Julia Ward

Yorkshire Pantry
Tel: 0113 237 0777
Fax: 0113 237 0888

Index of Advertisers